"Jim Stempel has given us in *The Enemy Harassed*, a superb and spirited account of the little remembered but pivotal contest for New Jersey in the aftermath of Washington's famous Christmas 1776 Crossing of the Delaware. He is to be applauded for his extensive research and elegant prose. This is a must read for all students of the Revolutionary War."

–Dr. Cole Jones, author of *Captives of Liberty: Prisoners of War and the Politics of Vengeance in the American Revolution.*

"Jim Stempel has given us a spirited and engaging account of a little-known period in our struggle for independence from Great Britain. This is a welcome chronicle of a series of military encounters that helps explain the critical role New Jersey played as the 'Crossroads of the Revolution.' Here is a story that warrants greater attention in the context of the approaching semi-quincentennial of America's birth."

–David Price, author of *John Haslet's World: An Ardent Patriot, the Delaware Blues, and the Spirit of 1777* and *The Road to Assunpink Creek: Liberty's Desperate Hour and the Ten Crucial Days of the American Revolution*

"Spanktown, Ash Swamp, Quibbletown, Bound Brook, Piscataway—all critical, yet essentially forgotten, small actions between the Ten Crucial Days and the Philadelphia campaign. But Jim Stempel's *The Enemy Harassed: Washington's New Jersey Campaign of 1777* brings them back to life in this rousing and historically accurate accounting. Stempel leads us through the reconstruction of the Continental Army as it maneuvers in the Jersey midlands, responding to British thrusts. We meet the key players and visit the strategic locations while the author weaves a dramatic yet scholarly tale. Definitely recommended."

–Bill Welsch, American Revolutionary War Roundtable, Richmond

"As a Historian's Historian, in *The Enemy Harassed: Washington's New Jersey Campaign of 1777*, Jim Stempel once again takes the road less traveled, bringing to life a period of the American Revolution that had been virtually forgotten. Based upon deep research—obtained in part from a wonderful trove of period diaries, journals, and letters—Stempel wields the artist's brush to recreate the kaleidoscope of combat, maneuver, and counter-maneuver that raged across New Jersey during 1777, which ultimately had a profound impact on the war's outcome. Bound to enthrall readers of all backgrounds and interests, *The Enemy Harassed* is very highly recommended.

> –James Holden-Rhodes, Ph.D., retired Marine Corps combat officer and former Director of the Intelligence Studies Program at New Mexico State University. He has lectured at the CIA, NSA, and National Drug Intelligence Center, among other intelligence organizations, and is the author of *Smart and Faithful Force: Henry Clay Cochrane and the United States Marine Corps, 1861 – 1905.*

"Washington's New Jersey campaign of early 1777 is finally receiving the historical attention it has long deserved. *The Enemy Harassed* offers a lucid account of how the rebel commander-in-chief rebuilt his army and, along with the New Jersey militia, fought with stunning effectiveness after the first Morristown winter. Stempel's new book has offered a window into one of the most important but least understood chapters of the War for Independence."

> –Mark Edward Lender, author of *Cabal! The Plot against General Washington*

"Jim Stempel's account of George Washington's 1777 New Jersey Campaign is both readable and important. *The Enemy Harassed* is a colorful nonfiction book based on meticulously footnoted eyewitness accounts taken from the letters, diaries, and journals of soldiers, militiamen, homeowners, 18th Century newspaper reports, and American and British government records. The Appendix includes excellent biographical vignettes."

–Kim Burdick, author of *Revolutionary Delaware* and frequent contributor to the *Journal of the American Revolution.*

"There were numerous turning points in the American Revolution. None have played a more critical role and been studied less than the New Jersey Campaign during the winter of 1777. In *The Enemy Harassed,* Jim Stempel unveils this challenging time with incredible detail and research. This book is very interesting and is surely destined to become required reading for anyone interested in the American Revolution. I would highly recommend this book."

–Jim Griffith, Revolutionary War Rarities

"This is a very well researched, deep dive into a little-known period of the American Revolution, sometimes referred to as the New Jersey Forage Wars, during the long winter of 1777. Jim Stempel's book addresses that shortfall in a highly readable book that brings to light many recently (re)discovered primary source diaries and journals. He weaves these new sources and heretofore unknown stories together with information from some of the period's better known 'Bloggers' like Jaeger Captain Johann Ewald and British Army Officer Archibald Robertson, to provide a complete and well-rounded history of a critical period in our war for independence. This is a must read for both the serious historian and the casual history reader, and I'm sure you will enjoy it as much as I have."

–Brooks Lyles, LTC, US ARMY, Retired—Historian General, The National Society of the Sons of the American Revolution

"Jim Stempel's appropriately titled *Enemy Harassed* takes the reader past the Ten Crucial Days into the New Jersey Campaign and the summer of 1777. Combining detailed descriptions of the nineteen most noteworthy military engagements with explanations of Congress' legislative efforts, Washington's development as a military leader, and Britain's ultimately unsuccessful attempts to pacify New Jersey, Stempel's vivid prose is sure to captivate anyone interested in the all too often forgotten months between Trenton and the Philadelphia Campaign, 'one of the most violent, bloody, and consequential periods of the entire American Revolutionary saga.'"

–Robert A. Selig, PhD, Historical Consultant and project historian for the Washington-Rochambeau Revolutionary Route. As a reward for his work regarding French involvement in the American War of Independence, Dr. Selig was recently nominated a chevalier of the French National Order of Merit by French President, Emmanuel Macron.

"George Washington's famous crossing of the Delaware River would have meant little if not followed up by more than a year of fighting with the British to keep them out of New Jersey. Jim Stempel covers this critical period of the American Revolution, presenting a well-researched and vividly presented account of this conflict."

–Michael J. Troy, Host, American Revolution Podcast.

The ENEMY HARASSED

Washington's New Jersey
Campaign of 1777

JIM STEMPEL

A KNOX PRESS BOOK
An Imprint of Permuted Press
ISBN: 978-1-63758-615-0
ISBN (eBook): 978-1-63758-616-7

The Enemy Harassed:
Washington's New Jersey Campaign of 1777
© 2023 by Jim Stempel
All Rights Reserved

Cover Design by Conroy Accord

Interior Design by Yoni Limor

Cover image from The Battle of Bound Brook, Herb Patullo, 1929-2020 Used with permission, Washington CampGround Association, All Rights Reserved.

Permuted Press, LLC
New York • Nashville
permutedpress.com

Published in the United States of America
2 3 4 5 6 7 8 9 10

For Sandie, With Love

TABLE OF CONTENTS

AUTHOR'S NOTE xi
EDITOR'S NOTE xiii
PROLOGUE 1

CHAPTER ONE. 17
    The Bridge at Stony Brook
CHAPTER TWO. 29
    Pluckemin
CHAPTER THREE. 40
    Morristown
CHAPTER FOUR 53
    Spanktown
CHAPTER FIVE 64
    Quibbletown
CHAPTER SIX. 76
    Drake's Farm
CHAPTER SEVEN 87
    Ash Swamp
CHAPTER EIGHT 99
    Punk Hill
CHAPTER NINE. 110
    Hudson's River
CHAPTER TEN. 121
    Bound Brook

CHAPTER ELEVEN 135
    Danbury

CHAPTER TWELVE 148
    Bonhamtown

CHAPTER THIRTEEN 157
    Piscataway

CHAPTER FOURTEEN 167
    Middlebrook

CHAPTER FIFTEEN 180
    Howe Tries to Ensnare the Fox

CHAPTER SIXTEEN 194
    Samptown

CHAPTER SEVENTEEN 206
    The Short Hills & Westfield

CHAPTER EIGHTEEN 218
    Amboy

CHAPTER NINETEEN 226
    Sandy Hook

POSTSCRIPT 235
APPENDIX 244
    Biographical Vignettes

BIBLIOGRAPHY 253
CHAPTER NOTES 263
ACKNOWLEDGMENTS 289
ABOUT THE AUTHOR 291
INDEX 293

AUTHOR'S NOTE

*W*hen traveling up the New Jersey Turnpike these days, the impression one often has is of a vast labyrinth of toll roads, highways, factories, and housing developments, appearing to stretch on ad infinitum. This urban sprawl makes it all but impossible to imagine the green hills, meadows, and mountains that once dominated the area. Eighteenth-century New Jersey, however, was a land of remarkable plenty. Prior to—and during the American War of Independence—New Jersey was, as historian David McCullough puts it, "The Garden of America its broad, fertile, well-tended farms, abundant supplies of livestock, grain, hay, food put up for winter." Born and raised in New Jersey, I have experienced both its green fields and smog-choked factories, and while growing up, I was generally aware of Revolutionary activity in the state, the extent and significance of that involvement had not been addressed during my formative education there. Then, one day in passing conversation, Roger Williams, owner of Knox Press, mentioned the Forage War. His comment opened a new and fascinating vein of research.

Curiosity aroused, I began to study the era, and the more I looked, the more I found: skirmish after skirmish, battles royal, whole populations in upheaval, large armies in open maneuver and combat, stunning victories, and tragic defeats—in particular, during the year 1777. Suddenly, I could visualize the roads I had traveled as a youth choked with scarlet-clad British regulars, blue-uniformed Hessians, and American militiamen and Continentals, all hastening toward the roar and fury of battle. Then—although now a longtime resident of Maryland—the Revolutionary history of New Jersey grabbed hold of my imagination, and I dove into further research with a sense of excitement.

What I discovered were many seemingly forgotten diaries and journals written by the officers and soldiers who served in the ranks. There was Thomas Rodney of Delaware, James Wilkinson of Maryland, John Greenwood of Boston, and Stephen Kemble of New Brunswick, who served as a Loyalist officer for the British. I encountered the work of American officer William S. Stryker, who laboriously compiled many of the Revolutionary documents dealing with the war in New Jersey, the journal of Hessian officer Johann Ewald, and the diary and sketches of British officer Archibald Robertson. These began to paint a picture of the Revolution in New Jersey from a kaleidoscope of viewpoints rather than a stiff, one-sided interpretation. Layered on top of those came the writings of the major participants—George Washington, John Hancock, John Sullivan, Alexander Hamilton, and many more—which provide the story with an unfiltered, firsthand glimpse of their thoughts. Rounding that out were many contemporary accounts of the war, modern scholarship, which, given time, brought the New Jersey Campaign of 1777 into full view. In the process, I discovered a forgotten landscape I had never known, towns long gone or subsumed today in more modern jurisdictions. There was Samptown, Drake's Farm, Quibbletown, Spanktown, Turkey, and Connecticut Farms, to name but a few; an older New Jersey that looked far different than today's contemporary map.

In the eighteenth century, words were often spelled (or misspelled) in a variety of ways. But unless that spelling created an obvious confusion, I let the original stand and offered corrections [sic] only where I felt it necessary to do so. This provides the reader a ready glance at the style, language, and communications of the era, along with insight into the people who wrote them. In *The Enemy Harassed: Washington's New Jersey Campaign of 1777*, it is my intention to present a coherent, stand-alone version of this important campaign, which previously has gone largely ignored, a tale of violence and fortitude in which Americans from across many states rose in defiance of British rule and repression, forcing General William Howe to virtually flee the state by sea with his British army. We will peel away whole square miles of asphalt and concrete, uncovering that lost countryside in the process, and, through the use of narrative nonfiction, present a story—not of history as it has often been written but of history as it was actually lived—and in so doing, we will come a bit closer to the true origins of the United States of America.

EDITOR'S NOTE

*A*long with being the editor of this volume, I am a public historian, cofounder of TenCrucialDays.org, and, at the time of this writing, the state historian for the New Jersey Society of the Sons of the American Revolution. As a specialist on the actions of Ten Crucial Days of the American Revolution, from December 25, 1776, to January 3, 1777, I became fascinated with what happened next. The subject of this book has been mentioned in articles, letters, papers, and as paragraphs, or perhaps chapters, in other books. I thought it would be a good time for a fresh look at these actions. The largest battles of the revolution—Saratoga, Brandywine, and Monmouth— were yet to come. But this pivotal period between the Ten Crucial Days and the Saratoga and Philadelphia Campaigns was transformative. Having survived the disastrous New York Campaign of 1776, the American insurgents managed to strike back at Trenton, then Princeton and hem the Crown troops into New York, Long Island, and up the Raritan River to (New) Brunswick. The successes of the Ten Crucial Days were apparent as renewed faith in "the Cause" and were rewarded by increased enrollments and determination to deny the British from either forage or the satisfaction of head-to-head battle in open field. Instead, as Washington welcomed fresh units into the new establishment of his army, he would sting the enemy with hit-and-run tactics throughout the spring and summer, convincing General Howe that given the tenacity of the rebel forces, marching the ninety-four miles through New Jersey to Philadelphia would be untenable. He chose to take a much longer, 469-mile sea route, which delayed the Philadelphia Campaign to so late in the year that there would be no manner of support Howe might ever give to Burgoyne's Saratoga Campaign. Most books on military history are written about big battles or campaigns. The New Jersey Campaign of 1777, which had been launched with Washington crossing the Delaware on December 25, 1776, is a collection of dozens of small battles, engagements, and incursions. Collectively, they honed the skills of the fledgling American army, terrorized the local civilians regardless of their loyalties, and bolstered morale toward the realization of a new nation that would bask in the ideals of self-determination.

As there is no one defining battle, we struggled with a title for this book. Our thanks to Michael Troy, producer of the American Revolution Podcast, who suggested we use George Washington's own orders to Major General Stirling on February 4, 1777, from headquarters at Morristown:

> "My Lord, You are to repair to Baskenridge and take upon you the command of the Troops now there, & such as may be sent to your care.1 You are to endeavour, as much as possible, to harrass and annoy the Enemy by keeping Scouting parties constantly (or as frequently as possible) around their Quarters. As you will be in the Neighbourhood of Genls Dickenson and Warner I recommend it to you to keep up a corrispondance with them, and endeavour to regulate your Parties by theirs, so as to have some contantly out. Use every means in your power to obtain Intelligence from the Enemy wch may, possibly, be better effected by engaging some of those People who have obtaind Protections, to go in under pretence of asking advice than by any other means.2 You will also use every means in your power to obtain, & communicate, the earliest accts of the Enemy's Movements, and to Assemble in the speediest manner possible your Troops either for offence or defence. Given at Hd qr the 4th February 1777.

> *"Orders to Major General Stirling, 4 February 1777," Founders Online, National Archives, Original source: The Papers of George Washington, Revolutionary War Series, vol. 8, 6 January 1777–27 March 1777, ed. Frank E. Grizzard, Jr. Charlottesville: University Press of Virginia, 1998, p. 245.*

After the American Civil War, which was fought mostly in the south, societies and states sprang up to protect the lands on which the battles were fought from development. This was not the case with the American Revolution. As one drives through the towns mentioned in this book, there is scant notice that military engagements occurred on the sites of modern shopping centers, housing developments, warehouses, and parking lots. As America's most densely populated state, millions of citizens live within a short drive of the grounds on which the fighting occurred that is described in this book. The ideals of freedom and justice for which future generations would fight were in foreign lands, such as Tripoli, Meuse–Argonne, and Iwo-Jima. Our founding principles were tested within our borders at the legendary battlefields of Antietam and Gettysburg. But our nation was born in the forgotten colonial towns of Pluckemin, Spanktown, and Quibble-town. History happened in the backyards and byways of New Jersey. As we watch the images of autocracy invading Ukraine, let us remember when, at another time and place, Americans, having just declared their freedom, were protecting their fledgling homeland from foreign invasion. Next time you drive past Newark's Liberty International Airport, look to the west. What you are about to read in these pages happened there. Americans protected their homes and fought for freedom in those hills.

Roger S. Williams

"We are like dwarfs sitting on the shoulders of giants. We see more, and things that are more distant, than they did, not because our sight is superior or because we are taller than they, but because they raise us up, and by their giant stature add to ours."

John of Salisbury

PROLOGUE

A light rain had begun to fall out of a pewter grey sky, spattering dirt as the troops slowly made their way toward the river. Each man had been ordered to pack sixty rounds of ammunition and three days' rations, but few knew where they were going. Most of the troops were dressed in rags; few had overcoats, and many were shoeless. The sun was still a half-hour from setting, and already, the treetops were beginning to slap and bend, a sure sign of foul weather on the wind. It was Christmas Day, December 25, 1776, on the western bank of the Delaware River. Among the tattered, freezing troops at McConkey's Ferry late that afternoon was General George Washington, architect of a planned strike against a brigade of Hessian troops, three regiments wintering across the ice-choked river at Trenton, New Jersey. It is said that genius and madness are at times virtually indistinguishable, and, considering the state of the American Revolution at the time, a fair observation when weighing Washington's chances of success, even now, from the distance of 250 years.

The operation was the offspring of pure desperation; a dreadful state of affairs rapidly approaching implosion. Just a month before, the Americans had been defending New York City; an effort that had ended poorly, to say the least. After a string of heartbreaking defeats, Washington's army had been forced back across the Hudson River into New Jersey, its numbers depleted and morale shattered. Washington set his sights on Pennsylvania at the time, hoping to get across the Delaware River before the British could catch his beleaguered forces on the flat roads that stretched south through New Jersey. For some reason, General William Howe, the British commander, had favored Washington with a less-than-aggressive pursuit, however, allowing him to gain the Delaware by early December and cross what remained of his army over to the Pennsylvania side. Howe, now believing the Americans beaten and with winter closing rapidly, decided against additional pursuit and put his army into winter quarters instead, in posts established uniformly across New Jersey, from Staten Island south to Trenton. Howe then returned to New York City, placing the field command in New Jersey in the hands of Major General James Grant, a Scottish-born aristocrat. Lieutenant General Charles Cornwallis, sharing Howe's take on the situation, immediately asked for leave to visit his family in England, a request that was promptly granted.

While the British army had suffered a considerable number of casualties during the New York Campaign, the Continental army was a shadow of its former self as Christmas approached. Due to repeated defeats, failures, and retreats, Continental currency was on the verge of collapse, credit nonexistent, and food hard to come by. The American public, its enthusiasm critical for the war effort, was nearing demoralization. Things were looking decidedly grim. On December 18, Washington had written his brother, Samuel, solemnly admitting that "if every nerve is not Straind to recruit the New Army with all possible Expedition, I fear the game is pretty near up."[1]

Since then, Washington had received reinforcements, bringing his effective strength up to seven thousand, six hundred. But most of those enlistments would expire by month's end; hence the army would be a phantom by early January—if it continued to exist at all. There are moments so grim that what previously seemed like lunacy suddenly makes perfect sense; the wildest option, the only option, still available. In that sense, on December 25, 1776, for General Washington, the discerning finger of logic was pointing directly and emphatically across the river at Trenton. To bring that logic to life, the general had opted for a sophisticated, three-pronged attack, a plan that even in good weather with well-trained troops might prove challenging, much less in difficult winter conditions with men on the brink of starvation. Nevertheless, the plan was for three separate columns to simultaneously converge on Trenton, one of the most difficult things in warfare to accomplish. The main force—two thousand, four hundred men—was to cross over the Delaware at nightfall, be entirely across—artillery, horses, and all—by midnight, then march nine miles south to Trenton. At the village of Birmingham, north of Trenton, the main force would divide: One wing, under General Sullivan, would continue south along River Road directly into town, and the other wing, under General Nathanael Greene, would loop north and enter the village at the same time from the opposite direction.

Additionally, Brigadier General James Ewing was to cross the river directly opposite Trenton with seven hundred men and seize the bridge over Assunpink Creek south of town, preventing a Hessian retreat in that direction. Lastly, a force of one thousand, five hundred men under Colonel John Cadwalader was to cross over farther south at Bristol, at once creating a diversion while simultaneously blocking potential British reinforcements. The main effort on Trenton proper was to step off at first light on December 26. Indicative of the do-or-die nature of the mission, the password was "Victory or Death." On paper, the plan looked splendid, but war plans often look splendid on paper. Unfortunately, due to the brutal winter storm then blowing in and heavy ice flows in the river, neither Ewing nor Cadwalader would fulfill their assignments. Washington would be on his own.

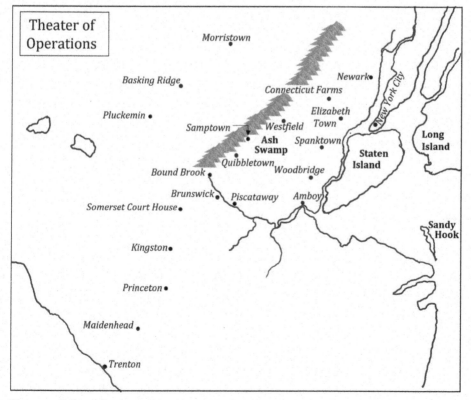

Theater of Operations.

Typically, the crossing got started late. Major James Wilkinson, standing with the troops as they moved toward the boats, provides a glimpse: "Boats were in readiness, and the troops began to cross about sunset but the force of the current, the sharpness of the frost, the darkness of the night, the ice which [was] made during the operation, and a high wind, rendered the passage of the river extremely difficult."[2] The troops were taken over in Durham boats, obtained from the Durham Iron Works, located on the upper Delaware River. Built to transport ore, timber, and grain downriver, they were large, black vessels, sixty feet in length, with an exceedingly shallow draft— perfect for Washington's mission. The troops were poled over, often forty men standing, the artillery and horses on larger ferries. Colonel John Glover's Fourteenth Continental, a regiment of sturdy Marblehead fishermen along with ferrymen, seamen, and longshoremen from Philadelphia supplied the know-how and muscle. Even so, the entire army was not across until three o'clock in the morning; dangerously behind schedule.

John Greenwood, a sixteen-year-old from Boston, was in one of the first groups over and recalled: "We had to wait for the rest and so began to pull down the fences and make fires to warm ourselves, for the storm was increasing rapidly. After a while, it rained, hailed, snowed, and froze, and at the same time blew a perfect hurricane."[3] The conditions grew worse by the minute, horrible for crossing men and animals across any river. Captain Thomas Rodney of Delaware, who would attempt to cross over later that night, recalled the adventure: "When we reached the Jersey shore we were obliged to land on ice, 150 yards from the shore; the River was also very full of floating ice, and the wind was blowing very hard, and the night was very dark and cold, and we had great difficulty in the crossing but the night was favorable to the enterprise." [4]

Through the howling winds and blinding snow of a true nor'easter, the column started toward Trenton, Washington riding the line, tirelessly encouraging his troops forward. As temperatures plummeted, bloody footprints marked the route southward. Two exhausted men staggered from the column and collapsed, only to be discovered later, frozen to death. The going was painfully slow, but somehow, the column finally gained Birmingham, where it divided as planned. Washington rode north with Greene as Sullivan continued along River Road. It was well past sunrise before both columns finally found Trenton. Given the weather, Hessian patrols had scaled back their efforts, and the Americans had not been spotted, the raging storm having provided cover. A rider appeared from General Sullivan, advising Washington that due to the sloppy weather, his men's muskets were inoperable. But retreat, now, was impossible. Fiercely determined, Washington told the courier to return and tell Sullivan: "Use the bayonet. I am resolved to take Trenton." [5]

Around eight o'clock that morning, and just north of Trenton, General Greene advanced with three brigades, Washington leading the center brigade forward himself. Snow was falling so steadily that the enemy's advanced posts could not be spotted ahead. According to Wilkinson, "As he [Washington] approached the village, he inquired of an inhabitant, who was chopping wood by the road side 'Which way is the Hessian picket?'" Frightened, the local man refused to answer. "'I don't know' replied the citizen, waiving an answer. 'You may speak,' said Captain Forest, 'For that is General Washington.' The astonished man raised his hands to heaven, and exclaimed 'God bless and prosper you, Sir!; -- the picket is in that house, and the sentry stands near that tree.'" [6] Heavy snow was still flying as the Hessian sentry spotted the advancing Americans and shouted, "*Der Feind!*" (the Enemy!). [7] Shots rang out as the Hessian fired, then retreated before the weight of the American advance. More Hessian infantry rallied, attempting to repulse the Americans on the north side, momentarily leaving River Road undefended.

Down on River Road, once the rattle of musketry rose clear in the morning air, Sullivan moved forward, Colonel John Stark of New Hampshire leading the vanguard. "It was now broad day, and the storm beat violently in our faces; the attack had commenced on the left, and was immediately answered, Colonel Stark in our front, who forced the enemy's picket and pressed it into the town, our column being close on his heels." [8] Sullivan, after chasing off the Hessian picket-post, advanced into Trenton virtually unopposed, Stark in the lead.

Trenton was then a small town, about one hundred houses—now mostly deserted of inhabitants—built on two central streets, King and Queen. Myth has it the Hessians had been drinking and partying heavily on Christmas, hence sleeping or hungover as Washington's troops attacked, but this is folklore. The Hessian Brigade—three regiments, one thousand, five hundred combined strength—were under the command of Colonel Johann Rall, a veteran commander with a sound, if uninspiring, reputation. They had arrived on December 14 and had eschewed defensive fortifications but had patrolled regularly, on the lookout for raiding parties. The Hessians—fierce warriors with a reputation for barbarity from the German principality of Hesse-Cassel—had a low opinion of both American fighters and leadership; hence, they expected minor, aggravating raids but hardly a major blow. Now, faced with an overwhelming force, confusion ensued.

American artillery quickly unlimbered at both ends of town and began sweeping the streets as Continental troops advanced. Rall formed two of his regiments across King Street, but they were quickly broken under intense artillery fire. Fearing encirclement, the Hessian leader attempted to lead an advance, but this, too, was blown apart. Street fighting ensued, but the Hessian's weapons fouled due to the snow, and many were cut down in the streets and alleyways. Rall eventually led two regiments to an orchard east of town, where he tried to outflank Washington's position. But this effort was spotted and shredded by enfilading musketry and artillery fire. Rall, struck twice by musket fire, fell from the saddle. An officer riding with Washington recalled the Hessian retreat: "They retreated towards a field behind a piece of wood up the creek, from Trenton, which I expected would have brought on a smart engagement from the [American] troops who had formed very near them, but at that instant, as I came in full view of them, from the back of the wood, with his Excellency General Washington, an officer informed him that the party had grounded their arms, and surrendered prisoners."[9] Overwhelmed, some Hessians tried to flee south across Assunpink Creek, but most were eventually surrounded and forced to surrender.

It was all over in less than an hour. Washington's desperate gamble had paid off, and he grasped at once just what he and his men had accomplished. As the Hessians were throwing down their arms, Major Wilkinson, tasked with receiving new orders from the commander in chief, galloped over to where he was sitting his horse. "On my approach," Wilkinson writes, "the commander in chief took me by the hand, and observed '*Major Wilkinson*, this is a glorious day for our country,' his countenance beaming with complacency"—a rare display of satisfaction from a man who, of necessity, had always kept his emotions under strict control.[10]

The Hessians had suffered twenty-two killed (including Rall), eighty-three wounded, and 896 taken prisoner, while the Americans suffered only five wounded and two dead—the two who had frozen to death on the march. Additionally, falling into American hands was over two thousand small arms, barrels of ammunition, six excellent artillery pieces, horses, and the Hessian's entire supply of food, drink, shoes, and clothing.[11] For the weary Americans, it proved an enormous haul.

Amazing as these totals were, they fail to grasp in any meaningful sense the true impact the engagement would soon have on the country. It would not be an overstatement to suggest that news of Washington's victory utterly *electrified* an American public previously benumbed by the war. Of Trenton, author Mercy Otis Warren wrote: "From the state of mind bordering on despair, courage was invigorated, every countenance brightened."[12] Nevertheless, those accolades were still in the future as Washington gauged the extent of his victory, the prospect of advancing still further, and, lastly, the condition of his troops. A conference of officers was held, and opinions naturally varied from pressing on to an immediate withdrawal back across the Delaware. Ultimately, reality prevailed as the weather remained horrendous, the men continued in a state of near exhaustion despite their soaring spirits, and lastly, some of them had gotten into barrels of Hessian rum stored at Trenton, which had rendered them drunk and useless in moments only. So it was agreed to return to Pennsylvania and to fight again another day. James Wilkinson wrote: "The general impulse excited by passion was now approved by reason, and the American community began to feel and act like a nation determined to be free."[13]

They did not have long to wait. Only three days later, in fact, Washington wrote to John Hancock at Congress, explaining his desire to again cross the Delaware in pursuit of what he still fancied a foe in retreat.

> I am just setting out, to attempt a second passage over the Delaware with the Troops that were with me on the morning of the 26th. I am determined to affect it, if possible but know that it will attend with much fatigue & difficulty on account of the Ice, which will neither allow us to cross on Foot or give us an easy passage with Boats...I have taken every precaution in my power for subsisting of the Troops,& shall without loss of time and as soon as circumstance will admit of, pursue the Enemy in

their retreat – try to beat up more of their Quarters and in a word, in every instance, adopt such
measures as the exigency of our affairs requires &
our situation will justifye.[14]

What Washington did not know at the time, however, was that
Howe had gotten news of the debacle at Trenton and, as a result, had
canceled Cornwallis's leave, ordering him back into the field to confront
Washington and rectify the damage as soon as possible. From Jersey,
the commander in chief had received word from New Jersey militia,
now at Burlington, that the British and Hessians had fled the area and
that opportunity appeared to be smiling, therefore, on the American
cause. Another strike appeared opportune. Thus, as Washington was
preparing to cross over the Delaware once again, unknown to him,
Cornwallis was already on the move, marching hard for Princeton.

The second American offensive was set for December 29, this time
crossing over at eight fords rather than one. This proved even more
difficult than the Christmas crossing; the river now far more tumultuous. At one point, the Delaware was frozen hard enough for the men
to cross, but the artillery and wagons crashed through while making
the attempt. Eventually, all made it over, but very soon, another emergency arose. Those enlistments—the very thing that had engendered
the Christmas operation in the first place—were now up, and most of
the men were looking toward home. Word came to Washington that
Thomas Mifflin had had success by offering each man a ten-dollar
bonus for one month of extra service. On December 27, Congress had
fled Philadelphia for Baltimore, fearing the British were headed for
Philadelphia, passing an ordinance that had given General Washington virtually dictatorial powers. In part, it read:

> The Congress having maturely considered the
> present crisis, and having perfect reliance on the
> wisdom, vigour and uprightness of General Wash-
> ington, do hereby resolve, that General Washington
> shall be, and he is hereby vested with full, ample and
> complete powers to raise and collect together, in the
> most speedy and effectual manner, from any or all of
> these United States, sixteen battalions of infantry, in
> addition to those already voted by Congress;[15]

With these powers in hand, Washington rode out before the formed regiments and, in the most favorable manner possible, implored the troops to stay on—but hardly a man was moved. So the general tried again, turning and riding before them once again, explaining in the most evocative terms he could imagine how desperately their country needed them. "My brave fellows," he began, "you have done all I have asked you to do, and more than could be reasonably expected; but your country is at stake, your wives, your houses, and all that you hold dear. You have worn yourselves out with the fatigues and hardships, but we know not how to spare you. If you will consent to stay one month longer, you will render that service to the cause of liberty, and to your country, which you probably can never do under any other circumstances." Slowly, the men stepped forward—at first, a few, then about half. When asked by an officer if the men should be newly enrolled, the commander in chief waved the protocol aside as superfluous. "No," he replied, "men who will volunteer in such a case as this, need no enrollment to keep them to their duty."[16] It was, without question, a profound declaration of respect from the general for his men.

The troop situation had been resolved—at least for the moment. The Continental army, commanded by George Washington, was then deployed amongst the various states, while what was generally referred to as the Grand Army—that is, that fighting force *directly* under the general's command—was to consolidate again at Trenton, where they might fight on ground of their own choosing. During the previous campaign, high ground had been spotted below Assunpink Creek, south of town. The Delaware protected its left; the creek, its front, and there were swamps bordering the right. With their artillery (finally floated across the Delaware), they could turn the position into a fortress, it was thought, and force the British to hurl themselves at it in desperate, frontal assaults, easily savaged by musketry and artillery. It was, to say the least, an *optimistic* plan. Nevertheless, Washington sent word out to his scattered units, and the army began concentrating upon Trenton.

Reports were coming in routinely that British forces were concentrating in great strength at Princeton. But Washington had also received intelligence of a backroad from Trenton to Princeton from Cadwalader, along with information that there were gaps in the British defenses there. While the Crown forces were most certainly marshaling strength for an offensive operation, news of Washington's stunning victory at Trenton also had many of them on edge. For years, they had operated with an attitude of such martial superiority that news of the American's recent victory cracked wide that sense of invincibility. Captain Johann Ewald, a Hessian officer marching with Cornwallis's troops, offers this remarkable psychological insight:

> Thus had times changed! The Americans had constantly run before us. Four weeks ago we expected to end the war with the capture of Philadelphia, and now we had to render Washington the honor of thinking about our defense. Due to the affair at Trenton, such a fright came over the army that if Washington had used this opportunity we would have flown to our ships and let him have all America. Since we had thus far underestimated our enemy from this unhappy day onward we saw everything through a magnifying glass.[17]

Late on the evening of January 1—New Year's Day—Cornwallis arrived at Princeton, where some ten thousand British troops had been collected. The general—hardly reflecting the sudden lack of confidence his troops in the field were apparently feeling—decided to advance straight down Post Road from Princeton to Trenton and overwhelm whatever resistance he found there. At Princeton, Cornwallis had eight thousand British and Hessian troops at his disposal and substantial heavy artillery. Orders were immediately issued to have a fighting force of five thousand, five hundred troops prepared to march at dawn, drawn up and ready, along the road to Trenton. Cornwallis intended to crush the rebels and put an end to this rebellion business once and for all.

Washington soon had information in hand of Cornwallis's strength and intentions. To this, he responded by sending out a strong skirmish force of about one thousand, two hundred riflemen supported by artillery, which took up positions along Post Road from Maidenhead (modern-day Lawrenceville) to Five Mile Run. Cornwallis was on the road by dawn, headed for Trenton, only thirteen miles away. But the roadway, turned heavy mud by a recent thaw, proved problematic. Soon, as well, the British struck the American skirmishers. "Colonel Hand took command of the troops," Major Wilkinson tells us, "and retired leisurely before the enemy, until orders were received from the commander in chief, to dispute every inch of the ground where practicable; Colonel Hand faced about, and advanced to meet the enemy, when a skirmish commenced, that was continued at intervals throughout the day, in which Colonel Hand's riflemen and Captain Forest's artillery were particularly distinguished."[18] The American skirmishers fought furiously, slowing, but having no real ability to stop such a sizable force. By late afternoon, the British had pushed the Americans back through Trenton, where they discovered Washington's army, arrayed for battle on the high ground below the Assunpink.

British Captain Archibald Robertson maintained a diary throughout the war, and he was with Cornwallis's advance. As the Americans faded back through Trenton and the British advanced, he saw the American position looming just ahead. This is what he saw: "their main body was drawn up, about 6 or 7,000, with the Creek and the Bridge in front and a Number of Field pieces. We lost a few men with the Cannonade but durst not attack them." Robertson, an engineer, studied the American position from afar and instantly grasped its strength. "They were exactly in the Position Rall should have taken when He was attack'd from which He might have retreated towards Borden's Town with very little loss."[19]

Cornwallis then began deploying his battalions in line on high ground opposite the Americans. This took time but served as an intimidating experience for Washington's troops, who had never faced such massive force, fully arrayed for battle. To them, the British battalions appeared an enormous red floodtide, soon to break across their defenses and overwhelm them. With an unpassable river at their backs and no avenue of retreat, for many, it seemed a moment of intense crisis. Private John Howland recalled, "On one hour, yes, on forty minutes, commencing at the moment the British troops first saw the bridge and creek before them, depended on the all-important, the all-absorbing question whether we should be independent States or conquered Rebels!"[20] Wilkinson also felt the weight of the moment, writing, "If there ever was a crisis in the affairs of the revolution, this was the moment."[21]

There was now less than an hour of daylight left for maneuver and assault. But if Cornwallis moved swiftly, the result he had come for was still there for the taking, a fact that many on the American side seemed to understand. But the British had endured a difficult march through mud and musketry, and operational daylight was now fading.

A decision had to be made. A number of fierce, probing attacks were launched by the British, but these were broken by concentrated artillery and musket fire. The Redcoats retreated, leaving many dead and wounded behind. The American line held.

Daylight was now almost gone. Cornwallis called for a council of war, and it was generally agreed that the Americans were pinned against the Delaware and would be dispatched with ease come first light. Custom has it that only one British officer objected: Sir William Erskine, who said, "My Lord, if you trust those people tonight, you will see nothing of them come morning"[22]—surely, some of the most prescient military advice ever offered, if true. But, of course, it was rejected. Cornwallis, still flushed with the same overconfidence that had created the Trenton debacle in the first place, elected to await the dawn. That night, a severe cold front blew in from the northwest. The temperature dropped rapidly, freezing the ground and muddy roads that ranged out from Trenton like spokes. The British infantrymen had little choice but to bed down on the frozen ground. Archibald Robertson wrote: "Hard frost and 2 Battalions Light Infantry lay in Trenton without fires by way of Piquets [pickets] to watch the Rebels on the other side of the creek."[23]

But General Washington had no intention of waiting around to have his army pummeled at dawn. Washington held a council of war that night, and the idea was broached that the army could move off to the right on unguarded roads to the east and arrive at Princeton by dawn, delivering an attack to the garrison there, *behind* Cornwallis's troops at Trenton. The plan seemed properly aggressive and was agreed to by all. To cover the movement, large campfires were lit, and a theatrical display of industry performed—preparing and fortifying defensive positions, and so on—as whispered orders passed through the army. Captain Thomas Rodney, of the Delaware militia, recorded in his diary the steps taken next: "At two o'clock this morning the ground having been frozen by a keen N. West wind secret orders were issued to each department and the whole army was at once put in motion, but no one knew what the Gen. meant to do. Some thought that we were going to attack the enemy in the rear; some that were going to Princeton; the latter proved to be correct." The rebels had previously reconnoitered the roads in the area, and local guides knew them well. "We went by a bye road on the right hand which made it about 16 miles; During the march," wrote Rodney, "I

with the Dover Company and the Red Feather Company of Philadelphia Light Infantry, led the van of the army and Capt. Henry with
the other three companies of Philadelphia light Infantry brought
up the rear."[24]

Those muddy roads that had hindered the British all day were now
almost miraculously frozen, providing the Americans with a smooth
exit. Nevertheless, it would be another long, cold, grueling march
through a barren landscape for many men who had yet to recover from
the first long night march to Trenton. Blood from shoeless rebels, just
as with the night march to Trenton, marked the route north. Nevertheless, by first light—around seven o'clock in the morning—the van
had reached the bridge that spanned Stony Brook, south of Princeton.
Having evaded detection by the British at Trenton, their sudden presence south of town represented yet another complete surprise. But
speed and efficient movement remained of the essence if the Americans were to retain the element of surprise.

As the army crossed Stony Brook and closed on the village ahead,
the sun began to rise, disclosing a wintry landscape, remarkably beautiful in the first rays of sunlight. The west wind had settled, the sky
emerged a brilliant blue, and the overnight cold had painted the entire
world, it appeared, with a heavy frost. Wilkinson remembered that "the
morning was bright, serene, and extremely cold, with an hoar frost
which bespangled every object."[25] Before crossing the brook, Washington rearranged his force into two separate columns: one under
Sullivan and one under Greene (much as he had entered Trenton just
ten days before). "When we had proceeded to within a mile and a half
of Princeton," Rodney explains, "and the van had crossed Stony Brook,
Gen. Washington ordered our infantry to file off to one side of the road
and halt. Gen. Sullivan was ordered to wheel to the right and flank
the town on that side, and two Brigades [under Greene] were ordered
to wheel to the left, to make a circuit and surround the town on that
side."[26] General Thomas Mifflin led Greene's wing to the left with
orders to take the bridge that spanned Stony Brook on the Post Road.

Overnight, the British commander at Princeton, Colonel Charles
Mawhood, had received orders from Cornwallis to form two of his
three regiments and have them on the road to Trenton early the
next morning to serve as reinforcements for Cornwallis's anticipated
morning attack. This force also contained about eighty replacements
gathered from various regiments, marching to join their units at
Trenton. Somewhat remarkably, as Mawhood marched out of Prince-

ton and over Stony Brook along Post Road, Greene's column, operating in the fields off to Mawhood's left, was discovered. Mawhood, a fine, experienced soldier, immediately had his column turn back. Then, he led his troops back over the bridge toward Princeton, where, after examining the Americans for a moment or two from afar, he unlimbered his artillery on a nearby rise and led his infantry against Greene.

Mawhood's troops, after several brisk, lethal exchanges of musketry, charged with the bayonet. General Hugh Mercer was leading the American advance on horseback, and Colonel John Haslet was leading Mercer's infantry nearby on foot. The intensity of the British attack initially overwhelmed the Americans. Mercer was unhorsed and bayonetted seven times; the Continentals were forced into a disorderly retreat. Haslet attempted to rally the troops but was shot through the head and fell dead to the ground. Captain Rodney, whose Delaware light infantry was marching with Mercer's advance, recalled the violent collision that took place in an orchard owned by farmer William Clark: "He [Mercer] immediately formed his men, with great courage, and poured a heavy fire in upon the enemy, but they being greatly superior in number returned the fire and charged bayonets, and their onset was so fierce that Gen. Mercer fell mortally wounded and many of his officers were killed, and the brigade being effectually broken, began a disorderly retreat."[27] Mercer, a Scottish-born physician, was one of the rising stars in the Continental army and a favorite of General Washington's. He would suffer for nine days before finally succumbing to his wounds.

Major Wilkinson, who had been riding with Sullivan's wing at the time, had spotted the clash between Mawhood's and Mercer's troops from a distance and observed the initial blasts of musketry. "I well recollect that the smoke from the discharge of the two lines mingled as it rose," he recalled, "and went up in one beautiful cloud. On hearing the fire, General Washington directed the Pennsylvania militia to support General Mercer, and in-person led them on with two pieces of artillery."[28] As Washington approached the fighting, he discovered many of his troops in retreat, overwhelmed by the ferocity of the Mawhood's advance.

At the time, Pennsylvania's local troops (those not in the Continental army) were organized in voluntary associations, hence referred to as "associators." Cadwalader commanded several of these associations, which, when combined, were referred to as the Philadelphia

Brigade—a group of well-drilled but untested recruits. They had recently come up and were desperately trying to hold off the British advance, but victory and defeat now hung in the balance.

Into the vortex Washington rode, heedless of personal safety. Historian David Hackett Fischer captures the scene: "In that critical moment, Washington arrived on the field and took control of the battle. He rode among Cadwalader's Associators and shouted, 'Parade with us, my brave fellows! There are but a handful of the enemy, and we will have them directly.' Washington led his men directly into the center of the battle, within thirty paces of the British line. He was mounted on a white horse, an easy mark for any British soldier, and yet none shot."[29] The associators fought with spirit, staying the British advance, and—now marching to the sound of the guns—more American units began arriving from all across the field. The British fought on with great discipline, but the tide of battle had clearly turned, and soon, they were overwhelmed and forced into retreat. That retreat, pushed by the rising tide of American fighting men, quickly turned into a rout, the Redcoats fleeing down the Post Road toward Trenton as fast as their legs could carry them. Washington, lost in the moment himself, galloped after them, shouting, "It's a fine fox chase, my boys!"[30]

As Washington joined the pursuit up Post Road, Mawhood, accompanied by some tattered British regulars, retreated into Princeton. There, they put up a series of brave but hopeless stands before being driven from the village. As the British fled Princeton, Washington galloped across the snowy fields, still leading the pursuit until aides finally urged him to rein in and return to the army.

The Battle of Princeton was over, another stunning American victory—hard for many to believe and harder still to put into perspective. In ten incredible days, George Washington had somehow managed to breathe life into a movement that had seemed on its last legs, if not already departed. And while the elation over the victories at Trenton and Princeton would continue for weeks, those triumphs were, in fact, just the first volleys of a new chapter in the War for Independence that would involve some of the most constant and violent fighting of the Revolutionary period. Just how that chapter would read and how it would be remembered would be written over the coming months across New Jersey—months of struggle, fighting, hatred, and, yes, valor. It is a remarkable tale, told now through the eyewitness accounts of those who lived, fought, and somehow survived it.

CHAPTER ONE
The Bridge at Stony Brook

*T*here was not a moment to lose. Associators from Pennsylvania's Northumberland County swarmed over the wooden bridge that spanned Stony Brook, just south of Princeton, New Jersey. It was approximately nine o'clock in the morning on January 3, 1777, and every man was mindful of the critical task at hand; not to mention the danger that was rapidly approaching. It was a clear and bitterly cold morning, with the temperature hovering in the low twenties, and the men's breath rose in steamy spouts as they discussed their options. Twenty-three-year-old Major John Kelly walked the span, glancing as he did along Post Road, which crossed the bridge, then disappeared south from Princeton to Trenton, only thirteen miles distant. For weeks, the temperatures had varied between freezes and thaws.[1] Now, from Kelly's height atop the span, he could see that the road—which, just the day before, had been a river of mud due to a recent thaw—had frozen into an icy brown ribbon, snaking across a dazzling landscape of white, frosty fields. In a sense, it was a beautiful, wintry scene. But on this January morning, there would be no time to admire the view.

Kelly's job was to destroy the bridge, an order that had come from Colonel James Potter, handed down directly from His Excellency, General George Washington himself. Washington's small, exhausted army had surprised and overwhelmed the British garrison at Princeton earlier that morning, but the enemy's legions had recently been spotted on Post Road, marching rapidly north toward Princeton, perhaps now only minutes away. Led by General Charles Cornwallis, the main body of the British army easily outmanned and outgunned

Washington's weary lot. And if allowed to cross the bridge and engage
the Continentals before they could safely withdraw, all of Washington's stunning gains of the past few days could easily be reversed. Then,
along the first ridge south, British riflemen appeared, deploying for
action amongst the trees and rocks, recognizable, even from afar. To
effect rapid transit, Cornwallis had left his tents and baggage behind,
rushing forward only with his troops and artillery.

The Northumberland troops were not engineers but resourceful
frontiersmen who knew how to handle a musket and scalping knife as
well as any axe, saw, or plow. One Princeton resident who was watching
recalled that "*Gen*. Washington as *soon* as the *battle* was over Ordered
some of *his* men to be placed near the bridge over Stoney creek on
the main road to hinder the [British] Regulars over and to pull up the
bridge which was scarcely done."[2] With the enemy now at hand, the
destruction of the bridge would have to be done swiftly, under fire,
and by muscle power alone. They would work their way back atop the
bridge, tearing out the deck planks one at a time.

Clifton Thorbahn, writing for the *Lancaster Sunday News* in 1932,
describes Kelly: "He was six feet tall, vigorous and muscular, with a
body so inured to labor as to be almost insensible to fatigue, and with
a mind so accustomed to danger that danger ceased to excite him."[3] If
true, on January 3, 1777, those qualities would serve Kelly well. The men
had only axes, hammers, saws, and their bare hands to work with, but
they dove into the job without a moment's thought. The distinct crack of
axe striking wood reverberated throughout the small valley almost like
the sustained discharge of muskets, announcing to the British riflemen
deploying above the Continental's intent. In response, the Redcoats
loaded their weapons and began creeping carefully toward the bridge.

Spotting the approaching British, Captain Thomas Forrest's
company of Continental artillery—posted nearby earlier to defend
the approaches to the bridge—leaped to life.[4] The cannons thundered
and recoiled, then thundered again, sending their salvos of solid shot
hurtling toward the exposed British skirmishers, who ducked away as
branches toppled and splintered and crashed all around them. The
American artillery, Kelly knew, could hold the British in place, but
only for so long. So the work went on atop the bridge, Kelly and his
men hacking and hammering and ripping the planks up one by one
and heaving them into the icy water below, sweat, despite the frigid
air, beginning to line their faces. The work continued at a fever's pitch.

Responding to Forrest's guns, the British unlimbered several pieces of their own, which took direct aim at Forrest's cannons, along with the bridge itself. Unfazed by the whistling balls flying around them, Kelly's boys continued methodically demolishing the bridge, utterly determined.

Driving his army hurriedly north during the early morning hours on Post Road toward Princeton, British field commander General Charles Cornwallis was in a foul mood. The night before, he had Washington and his Continentals virtually pinned against the banks of the Delaware River, primed for annihilation. But daylight had faded into the inky darkness of a January night before the *coup de main* could be delivered, so he had postponed the final assault until the coming dawn. Unfortunately, when the British awoke and moved forward, they discovered only the smoking remnants of the campfires Washington had left burning behind, and the Continentals were nowhere to be found. British officer Archibald Robertson recorded the shocking moment in his diary: "At Day Break reported that the Rebels were all gone which it was generally thought was toward Borden's Town. Until about 8 o'clock as very Brisk fire of Small Arms and Smart Cannonading was heard in our Rear towards Prince Town, upon which the Guards and Grenadiers British had orders to go back as quick as possible and the Light Infantry and Hessian Grenadiers to follow."[5]

Cornwallis's hesitation had resulted in not just an error, or even a critical error, but a potential catastrophe. Washington's stealthy dash during the night toward Princeton had put the entire British war effort in jeopardy. In December, General Howe had established a string of posts across New Jersey from Staten Island south to Trenton. The Redcoats established their largest base at Brunswick (modern-day New Brunswick), just eleven miles north of Princeton, where a large depot of supplies was located—ammunition, artillery, food, clothes, and a war chest overflowing with seventy thousand pounds sterling. If the Rebels were to spirit off with all, or even most, of those supplies and funds, they might devastate British operational capacity for months; possibly years. Little did Cornwallis realize at the time that that was precisely what George Washington had in mind, for the American general would later write to John Hancock, explaining: "My Original plan when I set out from Trenton was to have pushed on to Brunswic."[6]

The strategic rationale of establishing these small, unsupported British posts across Jersey was already being questioned and not by fools unfamiliar with sensible military protocols. After the debacle at Trenton, for instance, Stephen Kemble, deputy adjutant-general of British forces in North America, had doubted the wisdom. "Why Post so small Detachments as to be in danger of Insult [attack] as happened in Rall's Affair upon the Frontiers of your Line of Communication," he wondered, "or why put Hessians at the advanced Posts, particularly the Man at Trentown, who was Noisy, but not sullen, unacquainted with the Language, and a Drunkdard?"[7]

Should Washington's troops sweep through Brunswick and capture those precious supplies and enormous war chest, Cornwallis had to know that far sooner than later, everyone in Britain—from commoner to Lord—would demand an accounting. As General Charles Cornwallis was in operational command of the king's troops in New Jersey, there was little question that very soon, all those angry fingers would be pointing directly at him, along, of course, with General Howe, demanding some sort of sensible explanation where no sensible explanation existed. Washington had now essentially leapfrogged over Cornwallis's army and was *between* the main British force and Brunswick, much closer to all those resources than was Cornwallis himself. Brunswick was but lightly guarded, only eleven miles northeast of Princeton, and Cornwallis, then pushing his troops up the road to Princeton, had no idea whatsoever just how close to Brunswick, Washington might really be. Thus had speed become an imperative on the British march north.

General Charles Cornwallis.

The Hessian officer, Captain Johann Ewald, had been with Cornwallis since the beginning of the operation and provides our narrative with some insight into British intentions and operations. "On the 30th [of December]," he explains, "reports came in almost hourly of the approach of Washington's army. Since Lord Cornwallis arrived at Princetown, it was planned shortly afterward to give the enemy a beating and thereby repair the damage at Trenton." Thus, as previously described in the prologue, Cornwallis intended to deliver Washington a fatal blow somewhere near Trenton. But failing daylight had sabotaged his plan. Ewald continues: "We intended to renew the battle at daybreak, but Washington spared us the trouble. This clever man... had decamped at nightfall. Since he could not risk returning across the Delaware, he made such a forced march under cover of darkness that he wound up at Princetown, where he overwhelmed the Corps of General Leslie."

Cornwallis, supremely confident of a morning success, awoke to discover that Washington and his army had vanished. In military terms, Washington had stolen the march on the British, and Cornwallis now had a problem on his hands. Ewald continues: "At daybreak of the 3rd, we suddenly learned that Washington had abandoned his position. At the time we heard a heavy cannonade in our rear, which surprised everyone. Instantly we marched back at quick step to Princeton. We found the entire field of action from Maindenhead [modern-day Lawrenceville] on to Princetown and vicinity covered with corpses."[8] This, then, was the tactical situation as Cornwallis approached Princeton on the Post Road, his army rushing forward at the quickstep only to reach the crest of a short rise and discover Major Kelly and his Northumberland Militia directly ahead destroying the bridge that spanned Stony Brook, potentially blocking their path forward.

Cornwallis rode forward personally to assess the situation, and he immediately noticed the narrow valley the road traversed as it passed over the bridge below. Trouble, he reasoned, in the form of ambuscade might well be lurking there. More artillery was subsequently ordered up to lend its weight to the British guns already on hand, but all this would require more precious time—something the British general could scarce afford to lose. As the teams of horses jumped to life, and the artillery carts jostled forward—drivers bouncing atop the carriages on the frozen, rutted road—the distinctive sounds of a bridge being feverishly dismantled filled the frigid valley—axes and hammers ringing, saws slashing; the salty oaths of American militiamen—unmistakable in the distance.

At Stony Bridge, Kelly and his men were well underway with the destruction as, one by one, the decking planks were cut, sawed, or pried loose and tossed over the side into the water. Unfortunately, as the British artillerymen found the range, this work became increasingly hazardous as the lethal, six-pound, solid shots fired at them smashed through the nearby trees, crashed off the rocks, or tore through the bridge planking itself, sending showers of deadly splinters flying every which way. Then, when the additional British guns were finally manhandled into place, the crest above the bridge began to roar with smoking artillery, and the air around the straining Pennsylvanians grew wild with hissing projectiles. Fortunately, they had nearly dismembered the entire deck structure when one of the shots struck a plank Kelly was standing on and launched him like a circus act up over the side of the bridge, then down into the icy water below. Furious but uninjured, he yanked himself out of the freezing water as his clothes froze instantly around him. Unfazed, he later made a British scout his prisoner before returning to his unit—a remarkable performance, if ever there was one.[9]

Meanwhile, Cornwallis, realizing he could not hazard Washington getting too far ahead on the road to Brunswick, ordered his dragoons and some light infantry to locate a ford and wade across Stony Brook, even before repairs to the bridge had begun. As the British advance approached the brook, the Northumberland troops vacated the bridge, their work now complete, the shots from the British artillery increasing in intensity. Peeking out his window, a Princeton resident recalled the moment: "In a little time our men Retreated, and the Regulars [British regulars] were Obliged to Cross the brook at the ford with their artillery almost middle deep in water," [10] a trying task for any army in mid-winter. As Kelly and his men ran for the woods, Forrest limbered up his pieces and likewise departed. The valiant stand at Stony Bridge by Forrest, along with the Northumberland associators' heroic destruction of the span, had momentarily stymied the British, gaining Washington valuable time to put distance between his departing troops and the British vanguard.

Captain Thomas Rodney, who had fought on the field at Princeton that morning with his unit of Delaware infantry, underscores the importance of the rearguard action at the bridge. "As soon as the enemy's main army heard our cannons at Princeton (and not 'til then) they discovered our manoeuvre and pushed after us with all speed and we had not been above an hour in possession of the town before the enemy's light horse and advanced parties attacked our party at the bridge but our people by a very heavy fire kept the pass open until our whole army left the town."[11]

After the British had been shattered and run out of Princeton, the Americans swept into town, a village that had been overwhelmed by the ravages of war and was now largely abandoned. One mile north of the Quaker village of Stony Brook, Princeton had been settled around 1724, and by the outbreak of the Revolutionary War, it was known as a college town, the college having opened in 1746. Silas Deane, a delegate to the Continental Congress from Connecticut, described the pre-war town in a letter to his wife. "Princeton is a new town and, though the best situated to command a good air, has not good farmhouses and settlements. The College is an elegant building of stone, well calculated, and to appearance well provided...The people are neat, and there is elegant entertainment for strangers at the taverns."[12] Captain Rodney, upon entering the village after the battle, seemed somewhat more impressed. "This is a very pretty little town on the York road about 12 miles from Trenton; the houses are of brick and are very elegant especially the College which has 52 rooms in it; but the whole town has been ravaged and ruined by the enemy." [13]

Washington had hoped to rest his men briefly in Princeton before shoving on toward Brunswick, but Cornwallis's arrival on the town's outskirts only an hour after the Americans had entered put a quick end to that. Nevertheless, many of the men made good use of their limited time, searching about for any form of food, clothing, or booty that might be of use. James Wilkinson, in command of an infantry company, wrote later of his experience. "We found in the town some shoes and blankets, which were very opportune, and for my own part, I made a most seasonable acquisition in a break-fast at the provost's house, which had been prepared for a mess of the 40th regiment, who the steward in-formed me were sitting down as the fire [shooting] commenced."[14]

After the guns ceased firing, those inhabitants of the village who had remained behind began crawling out of their cellars, where most had taken shelter during the engagement. Princeton had been a peaceful, tranquil community, and many of the citizens were understandably terrified by what they had just experienced and had good reason to imagine the worst. One citizen recalled that "We Presently went down into the Cellar to Keep out of the Way of the Shot. There was a Neighbour woman down in the Cellar with us that was so Affrighted that she Imagined that the field was covered with Blood, and When we came out of the Cellar She called Earnestly to us to look out and see how all the field was quit red with Blood. When none was to be seen at that Distance." [15]

For many of the civilians, the fury and earth-shaking rumble of battle must have seemed a horror almost beyond imagination. Nevertheless, while their time in town was short, the victorious Americans tended to the wounded of both sides with equal care and consideration. Thomas Olden, a resident, wrote approvingly of the decency displayed by the American soldiers: "Almost as soon as the firing was over our house was filled and surrounded with Gen Washington's Men, and himself on horseback at the door. They brought in with them on their Shoulders two Wounded Regulars [British], one of them was shot in at his hip and the bullet lodged in his groin, and the other was shot through his body Just below his short ribs." The local man recalled vividly the care the British soldiers received. "They was both," he insisted, "Used *very* tenderly by the Rebels (as they *call them*)." [16]

While the Americans were happy to tend to the wounded British soldiers, the exhilaration they all felt, by both surviving the battle and winning another stunning victory, could not be contained. In just ten days, they had flipped the calculus of victory and defeat on its head, for it was the Redcoats who were now confused and on the run, where, just ten days before, the American cause had seemed beyond despair. The joy the Americans now felt beamed from their faces like the rays of a rising sun, and Mr. Olden could not help but take notice. "Immediately after the battle (as I said before)," Olden continues, "Gen Washington's Men came into our house Though they were *both* hungry and thirsty some of them laughing out right, others smiling, and not a man among them but showed Joy in his Countenance." [17] Not an American soldier that morning had to be told what they had accomplished— they knew.

With Cornwallis now in close pursuit, Washington realized he had to quit Princeton as soon as possible and point his weary little army north, Brunswick still very much on his mind. So, as Forrest's guns boomed behind the Americans at the bridge, and Kelly's men ripped the last planks from the decking, the drums began beating the long roll, and the troops slowly, wearily shuffled back into formation. Once formed, General Washington led them out of the village and headed north once again on Post Road toward Brunswick. Behind them, they left the British cannons they had discovered spiked (the Americans had not the means to haul them away); all the sundry supplies and hay they could not drag off, burning, great funnels of smoke rising above the village as they departed. Captain Rodney recalled the triumphant scene: "Just as our army began our march through Princeton with all their prisoners and spoils the van of the British army we had left at Trenton came in sight, and entered the town about an hour after we left it, but made no stay and pushed on towards Brunswick for fear we should get there before him, which was indeed the course our General intended to pursue." [18]

The Americans may have departed Princeton smiling, but for the entering British, it was a far different story. They had now been bested twice in ten days by an army they previously despised as inferior to their own, and the dreadful sight of their regulars lying dead and wounded from Maidenhead to Princeton proved a gloomy, uncomfortable, disorienting experience. The Hessian Ewald was there, and his diary reflects the utter dismay the British felt as they began to grasp just how horrible their defeat at Princeton had been. "In the afternoon the entire army reached Princeton," he wrote, "marching in and around the town like an army that is thoroughly beaten. Everyone was so frightened that it was completely forgotten even to obtain information about where the Americans had gone." [19]

Muskets, packs, hats, and bodies littered the field, firm testimony to what the Americans had accomplished in their victory and what the British had lost. Historian Richard M. Ketchum puts a strong period on the affair. "Whatever the total may have been..[the British].. had been shattered, at a cost to the rebels of 30 enlisted men and 40 officers killed.... It had all happened in the space of about forty-five minutes—with two little armies meeting head on in a field outside an obscure college town—but the effect was to be far beyond the numbers involved." [20] There is little question the British were stunned by what they discovered at Princeton.

The bewildered British shifted their gaze once more toward Post Road, which ran north to Kingston, then on to Brunswick, where the Americans were now thought to be headed. Archibald Robertson, entering Princeton with the main column of Redcoats, gives voice to their concerns: "On our approach and firing a few cannon on the stragglers the Rebels retired precipitately, toward Kingston with the greater Body and some to the Right and left into the woods. As our Rear did not come up until near 4 in the Evening we could not pursue them quickly as it was said they intended the same coup upon Brunswick."[21] Ewald agreed with Robertson's assessment, noting emphatically that "the enemy now had wings, and it was believed that he had flown toward Brunswick to destroy the main depot, which was protected by only one English regiment."[22]

While the British believed the Americans had every intention of attacking Brunswick—as had been the plan from the outset—the fact was, for the Continental army, reality was rapidly setting in. Many of Washington's men had been on their feet for almost two days, marching and fighting with precious little food, drink, or rest. While the adrenaline of combat and the elation of victory can surely animate men, those wondrous tonics will only carry them so far, and as Washington studied his exhausted troops as they stepped off at Princeton, it became increasingly obvious that they were at the limit of their physical and mental endurance. A stunning triumph might still be beckoning just up the road at Brunswick, but with men almost dead on their feet, that stunning triumph began to take on the dark glimmer of a dangerous chimera far more than practical reality. A few miles north of Princeton, the road forked at Kingston. The right fork led straight toward Brunswick, while the left led north along Millstone River toward the small village of Somerset Courthouse (modern-day Somerville). It was there where a final decision would have to be made.

As the Continentals trudged away from Princeton, Cornwallis sent his light infantry and dragoons off to locate and run down Washington's small army, hoping to disrupt the American withdrawal or at least hold them in place. If successful, they would prevent the dreaded attack upon Brunswick, saving Cornwallis's reputation. To discourage just such an attempt, however, Washington had turned to Captain Joseph Moulder, a fifty-three-year-old Pennsylvanian. Moulder subsequently placed his company of guns on a hill overlooking Millstone River, which bordered the route north. Moulder's company had performed brilliantly earlier that day at Princeton, and he was to be severely tested once more that afternoon. Rand Mirante, writing for the *Journal of the American Revolution*, explains: "The artilleryman's mission was to cover the withdrawal by Washington's army and delay the pursuit by a furious, fearful (for his gold supply in Brunswick), and thoroughly flummoxed Lord Cornwallis, coming back up the Post Road from Trenton with the main British column. Moulder's orders were to spike and abandon his guns to save his precious, experienced crews when the enemy closed in." [23]

The guns of Moulder's company began blasting away as the British closed quickly around him, indeed so rapidly that he could not bring up his artillery horses to remove the guns. Rather than spike and abandon his pieces, however—as he had been ordered to do—he fought courageously in the retrograde, firing, then having teams of men pull each artillery piece back several paces before reloading and firing again. Finally, aided by a squad of Philadelphia cavalrymen, Moulder not only drove off the British van but managed to haul his artillery pieces safely away in the process.[24] (Interestingly, Moulder was hauled before a board of inquiry several days later for not having spiked and abandoned his guns as ordered. But when the true and heroic nature of his actions was disclosed, he was promptly exonerated.)

As Moulder was handling the rearguard, George Washington reached the fork in the road at Kingston, three miles northeast of Princeton, just prior to eleven o'clock in the morning. A momentous decision awaited. His generals gathered round as snow began to fall again, covering the marching men and pelting the roads leading north. Here, they debated their alternatives: Should they press on toward Brunswick, despite the depleted condition of the troops, or take the left fork toward Somerset Courthouse, leaving the opportunity to possibly end the war with a quick strike behind, perhaps forever? James Wilkinson recalled the meeting: "Pressed as we were for time, it was the desire of the commander in chief, and the inclination of every officer, to make a stroke at Brunswick, which had been left with a small garrison, in charge of General Mathews but our physical force could not bear us out the men had been under arms eighteen hours, and had suffered much from cold and hunger. The commander and several general officers halted at the forks of the road in Kingston, willist our troops were filing off to Rocky hill, when the exclamation was general, 'O that we had 500 fresh men to beat up their quarters at Brunswick.'" [25]

While a strike at Brunswick remained painfully tempting, in truth, it had become operationally impossible—in fact, an invitation to disaster—should the British horse descend upon Washington's exhausted men on the open road. In the letter to John Hancock mentioned above, Washington explained his reasoning: "The harassed State of our own Troops (many of them having had no rest for two nights & a day) and the danger of loosing [sic, losing] the advantage we had gained by aiming at too much induced me by the advice of my Officers to relinquish the attempt."

So the Continentals took the left-hand fork and continued marching toward Rocky Hill and, farther along, Somerset Courthouse. It was hardly one of George Washington's more aggressive decisions, but it was certainly one of his wisest. For Washington and his men, the question that remained as they labored through the falling snow late that afternoon was what, exactly, had they gained from their ten days of spectacular success? The New Jersey Campaign had begun on December 25, 1776, as Washington crossed his troops over the Delaware River and put them on the road toward Trenton, but where and how would it end? For them, the coming days, weeks, and months of fighting in New Jersey would provide the answer.

For the British, on the other hand, the questions that now loomed seemed a bit more ominous. For an astonishing ten days, after all, the British had been outwitted, outmarched, outfought, and clearly outgeneraled by an enemy previously thought to be vastly inferior and on the cusp of implosion. How had that happened, and what might it portend? How long, for instance, might colonists fight on for their freedom before it dawned on them that they were already free? How many months might pass before the words of their *Declaration of Independence* were no longer conceived as mere words at all but as profound and obvious *truths*? Put differently, might the Americans, by dint of time and endurance alone, emerge from this seemingly interminable conflict as the free-minded people the British and their Hessian auxiliaries were laboring so desperately to prevent? And if so...what then?

CHAPTER TWO
Pluckemin

*L*ate on January 3, through falling snow and dropping temperatures, Washington's Continentals dragged themselves north up the road toward Somerset Courthouse, utter exhaustion now a distinct possibility. On that day alone, they had slipped away from Trenton in the nighttime darkness to march thirteen miles to Princeton. There, they had fought and won a battle, only then to be told an hour later that they were to form and march once more. Now, slogging their way through the cold and snow, they were bound for Somerset Courthouse, a good seventeen miles north of Princeton, hence a total of thirty miles in one day through freezing temperatures with precious little in the way of food, drink, or even clothing, for that matter, to sustain them. Many were without shoes. Over time, cold, exhaustion, and hunger numb not only the body but the mind, and as the weary column trudged along, it eventually moved by reflex alone—one foot after the other, one foot after the other—silent and somber as an army of ghosts, increasingly covered in whiteness, waiting only the command to halt.

Bordering the road, the Millstone River (named years before when a millstone accidentally tumbled into the water) ran slowly north, dropping out of the hills of western Monmouth County. Fed by numerous creeks and snaking tributaries, the river swam some forty miles north before joining the Raritan River near Van Nest's Mill (modern-day Manville). From there, the Raritan ran north to Bound Brook before turning southeast across central New Jersey, then eventually out to the Atlantic. As the American column struggled northward, the river ran beside them, slow and ice-laden, fresh white flakes collecting on the barren branches above.

Back at Kingston—now miles behind the marching column—two roads emerged along the Millstone, one running east along the river's northward course, the other along its western bank. Washington had selected the eastern road, while at Kingston, Cornwallis had divided his army, sending dragoons and his light infantry up the western route to keep an eye on the Americans while at the same time frantically marching the bulk of his army at the double-quick toward Brunswick.

The area Washington's troops were marching through was then sparsely populated; indeed, the entire prewar population of New Jersey had yet to top one hundred and thirty thousand, [1] making the state one of the least populated of the rebelling thirteen. General Washington was leading his men north toward the Watchung Mountains, three parallel ridges that overlooked New York City to their east, rising to heights of no more than five hundred feet but high enough for the Americans' purposes, with narrow passes the British would find uncomfortable to enter. Where exactly General Washington would winter was as yet unclear, but it was hoped the ridges would at least protect his weary men from British attacks, allowing them to rest and recover.

Some two miles north of Kingston, the narrow road wound its way into the small village of Rocky Hill, where a bridge spanned the Millstone, connecting the parallel roads. British horsemen had been dogging the Continental's progress from the opposite bank, but at Rocky Hill, the danger of a sudden and violent collision between the two contingents suddenly became a distinct possibility. A weary Captain Rodney was leading the American column north, and he recalled the moment vividly: "Our Army marched on to Kingston then wheeled to the left and went down the Millstone, keeping that River on our left; the main body of the British army followed, but kept on through Kingston to Brunswick: but an division or a strong body of horse took the road to the left of the Millstone and arrived on the hill, at the bridge on that road just as the van of the American Army arrived on the opposite side." [2]

General Washington had spotted the potential collision of forces ahead and promptly galloped forward to the head of the American column. Rodney continues: "I was again commanding the van of our army, and General Washington seeing the enemy, rode forward and ordered me to halt and take down a number of carpenters which he had ordered forward and break up the bridge, which was done and the enemy were obliged to return." [3] On the open road, mounted dragoons could be enormously effective against infantry when caught by surprise, riding men down with slashing sabers. But in the narrow confines of a river valley—against veteran infantrymen aware of their presence and prepared to resist—a cavalry charge would have been virtually suicidal. So the British dragoons were forced to watch as the Americans destroyed yet another bridge literally beneath their noses, the threat of Continental muskets enough to dampen their enthusiasm. Out of options, the British cavalrymen had little choice but to turn and proceed back down the Millstone from whence they had come.

The reward the Continentals received for their general's heady response was an additional ten-mile slog through snow and cold, but at least now without the threat of mounted assault, for Rodney tells us: "We then marched on to a little village called Stone brook or Summerset Court House about 15 miles from Princeton where we arrived just at dusk." Unfortunately, when they tumbled into Somerset Courthouse, they were greeted, not with warm food, shelter, or even good news, but with the discouraging report that local militia had just allowed a substantial cache of British supplies to slip through their fingers without firing a shot, when, in fact, the prize had been theirs for the taking, underscoring just how disjointed, inept, and ineffective much of the Revolutionary effort actually was. Militias—numerous as stars in the heavens, it seemed at times—dominated the wartime landscape, some professional and useful, others almost useless. The Continentals at Somerset Court House could only shake their heads in disgust. "About an hour before we arrived here," Rodney complained, "150 of the enemy from Princeton and 50 which were stationed in this town went off with 20 wagons laden with Clothing and Linen, and 400 of the Jersey militia who surrounded them were afraid to fire on them and let them go off unmolested and there were no troops in our army fresh enough to pursue them, or the whole might have been taken in a few hours." [4]

Disheartened, the men nevertheless made the best of dreadful conditions, still animated by their recent victories. As Ketcham points out, "By the time the last rebel regiments staggered into town it was eight o'clock at night and freezing cold, and there was no place for them to stay but outdoors." [5] Many of the men's personal baggage—rations, blankets, and the like—had been sent off in the wrong direction, so it was upon the frozen, snow-covered ground where they would have to spend the night—a hard reward for two days' fighting and thirty cold miles on the march. "Our army was now extremely fatigued not having any refreshment since yesterday morning," Rodney wrote in his diary, "and our baggage had all been sent away the morning of the action at Trenton, yet they are in good health and high spirits." [6] Years later, James Wilkinson recalled gazing out over the same snowy scene, where "many of the militia, whose baggage had been sent to Burlington, lay in the open air without blankets."[7]

As the Americans hunkered down for a dismal night on the snow-covered ground with nothing to warm them but their recollections of victory, the British were still hard on the march, rushing toward Brunswick. The potential nightmare of Washington's troops racing off with his money and supplies had induced in General Charles Cornwallis a sense of deep concern, for which his troops were paying the price. Those not sent off to reconnoiter Washington's whereabouts were to spend the entire night on the road, desperately seeking Brunswick before Washington's phantom legions might swoop in and race off with all those supplies and coinage—that, at least, was the fear.

Archibald Robertson relates the British experience during their long night march. "About ½ after 4 we again began our march towards Brunswick and after a most fatiguing forced march all night long in frost and ice we reach'd Brunswick about 6 in the morning of the 4th. Throughout this whole Expedition," Robertson added, "we certainly allways erred in imprudently separating our Small Army of 6,000 men by far two [too] much and must hope it will serve as a lesson in the future never to despise [hold in contempt] any Enemy two much." Despite the exhaustion of the march, Robertson remained upbeat and pleased by his men's attitudes. "Our troops went this very great fatigue with great Spirit," he wrote proudly. "The last march was upwards of 30 miles after having been on the Alert for several nights running."[8]

Johann Ewald and his company of foot Jägers shared the same forced march, noting the almost frenzied nature of the nighttime effort. "Hurriedly the army was issued three days rations of biscuit and brandy," while still at Princeton, "left behind the stores, all the sick, the wounded, and the greater part of the baggage, and moved with such haste toward Brunswick that, although it was only a five-hour march, over one thousand waggoners first reached Brunswick toward evening of the 4th. If the enemy had pursued them with only a hundred horsemen, one after another would have been captured," a clear indication of just how desperate Cornwallis was to return to Brunswick and protect his base. Interestingly, Ewald shared Robertson's analysis of the British failure: a failure grounded in complete overconfidence. "But the enemy was despised," he writes, "and as usual we had to pay for it."[9]

As the sun rose on a cold and dreary January 4, Washington had his troops up and moving toward the village of Bound Brook. Captain Rodney brings the difficult journey to life: "At daylight this morning our army was again in motion and passed on towards Brunswick and crossed the Raritan over a bridge 6 miles above that Town, but the General found the army was too much fatigued to attempt Brunswick as the enemy's main body was so close after us, he therefore changed his course and went on to a place called Pluckemin situated among the mountains of Jersey about 10 miles from the last place."

Pluckemin, raided before by the British in 1776, was a small village on the southwestern rim of the Watchung Mountains established during the early 1700s. The surrounding hills offered protection for the Continental army while it rested. Rodney continues: "Here he [Washington] was obliged to encamp and await the coming up of nearly 1,000 men who were not able through fatigue and hunger to keep up with the main body, for they had not any refreshment for two days past and as all our baggage had been left at Trenton the army in this situation was obliged to encamp on the bleak mountains whose tops were covered with snow, with-out even blankets to cover them. Most of this army were militia and they bore all this with a spirit becoming Free-men and Americans." [10]

Charles Willson Peale, who was then a noted American painter and scientist, was with the Pennsylvania associators, and he tells an interesting tale of their night on the mountain. "We then got under weigh," he wrote, "and arrived within a mile of a little village called Pluckemin, where we halted; orders came to pull down a fence that was at our right, at the foot of a small mountain, and march up in companies." Some gunfire was then heard, but it turned out to be nothing more than soldiers in the vanguard trying to light fires with their muskets. Peale continues: "I then went to the town and got a barrel of flour, and put stones in the fire to bake our bread on; and, before night, got some beef, and made sumptuous meals. The men were very industrious, in baking, all the forepart of the evening," Peale wrote in his diary, then described their accommodations for the evening. "The place which fell to our lot was rather steep, and nothing but a heap of stones. I found it to be a very hard lodging place. When one part of my body was hurt by the points of these stones, I would change my position to get relief, and was continually moving the entire night, now and then making the fire better. The wind was rather unfavorable, blowing immediately up the hill." [11]

Washington moved into the John Fenner House, along with several of his generals, while the army encamped nearby. "The wounded were quartered in the village; the prisoners were housed in the Lutheran Church; and the army camped on a hill south of the village. Washington used the Fenner House as his headquarters. It was here that he wrote his official report of the Battle of Princeton. Among the notables with Washington were Dr. Benjamin Rush and Generals Greene, Knox, and Sullivan." [12]

Here, there was time to investigate the British wagons seized during the battle. And as the stragglers slowly came up, these were quickly examined and useful provisions distributed amongst the men. By nightfall, things began looking up. "To-day we continued here," Rodney wrote, "and our troops were pretty well supplied with provisions and in the evening most of those who had lagged behind had come up." Still, the army was worn to the bone, and exhausted men often do careless things. Discharging a musket into a pile of leaves and twigs to start a campfire, for instance, often served as a Revolutionary expedient, but in the hands of men numb from fatigue, a useful expedient can become a deadly mistake. "Here," Rodney tells us, "Sergeant McKnatt was accidentally shot through the arm by one of our own people, who fired off his musket to light a fire and as there was not one surgeon in the whole army I was forced to dress it myself and the next day got one of the prisoners to do it." Seems the surgeons had not been told of the army's movements back at Trenton, and none were now to be found. [13]

The army rested at Pluckemin for an additional day; Washington seeing to the basic needs of his army. It was here where he finally had an opportunity to sit and collect his thoughts and begin notifying Congress, along with his outlying commanders, of his recent successes and evolving strategy. He first wrote to John Hancock, providing a report of the army's recent movements and actions, along with his own thought process throughout the brief campaign. It began:

I have the honor to inform you, that since the date of my last from Trenton I have removed with the Army under my command to this place. The difficulty of crossing the Delaware on account of the ice made our passage over it tedious, and gave the Enemy an opportunity of drawing in their several cantonments and assembling their whole Force at Princeton. Their large Picquets advanced towards Trenton, their great preparations & some intelligence I had received, added to their Knowledge, that the first of January brought on a dissolution of the best part of our Army, gave me the strongest reasons to conclude, that an attack upon us was mediating.

The commander in chief then went on to explain the results of the battle at Trenton, his nighttime movement to Princeton, and the successful American victory there, reiterating the fact that Brunswick, with its war chest and vast stash of supplies, had been his ultimate goal. He then concluded the letter by providing Hancock with the latest intelligence of British movements as he then understood them.

From the best information I have received, Genl Howe has left no men either at Trenton or Princeton. The truth of this I am endeavouring to ascertain that I may regulate my movements accordingly --The Militia are taking spirit and I am told, are coming in fast from this State, but I fear those from Philadelphia will scarcely submit to the hardships of a winter Campaign much longer, especially as they very unluckily sent their Blankets with their Baggage to Burlington – I must do them justice however to add, that they have undergone more fatigue and hardship than I expected Militia (especially Citizens) would have done at this inclement Season. I am moving to Morris town where I shall endeavour to put them under the best cover I can. Hitherto we have been without any and many of our poor Soldiers quite bear foot [sic] & ill clad in other respects.[14]

The engagements at Trenton and Princeton had put everything in motion, and only time would tell how it would all end. From Washington's perspective, it appeared he may have Howe and Cornwallis on the run and, with a push here or there, be able to run them out of Jersey altogether. On the other hand, from the British point of view, they were only correcting the strategic folly—as Stephen Kemble had pointed out—of maintaining posts too distant from one another to be easily supported. From their perspective, then, what Washington was observing was hardly a retreat; merely a redeployment.

Nevertheless, Washington saw opportunity in all this and immediately turned to General William Heath, then commanding a Continental division in the New York Highlands above New York City, for assistance. Through maneuver alone, Washington envisioned drawing the British out of Jersey. New York City, along with its deep-water harbor, was utterly essential to the British war effort, what with its line of supply stretching all the way back across the Atlantic to the British Isles. Hence, any threat to the city would be considered potentially fatal and would be opposed immediately and aggressively. A Continental threat in that direction, therefore—even a feint—might send the British scrambling out of New Jersey to combat it, freeing Jersey from the Redcoats without even firing a shot. It was a clever yet sensible plan, and Washington suggested it to Heath in writing on the 5th.

> It has been determind in Council that you Should move down towards New york [sic] with a Considerable force as if you had a design upon the city – that being an object of great importance, the Enemy will be reduced to the necessity of withdrawing a Considerable part of their force from the Jerseys if not the whole to Secure the City – I shall draw the force on this Side of the North River [Hudson River] together at Morristown – where I shall watch the motions of the Enemy, & avail myself of every Circumstance. [15]

Washington then looked south to where General Israel Putnam had crossed the Delaware to Burlington on January 5 with roughly six hundred troops recently gathered in Philadelphia. There, Putman discovered another five hundred men left behind during Washington's recent campaign. Marshaling these, he moved to Trenton, where the commander in chief's letter eventually found him. In a

portion of that letter, Washington made clear his state of mind and
intentions for the coming days. Notice that he clearly believed he
had the British on the run.

> After the Action we immediately march't for this
> place – I shall remove from hence to Morristown –
> there shall wait a few days and refresh the Troops –
> during which time I shall keep a strict watch upon
> the Enemies motions – They appear to be pannick
> struck and I am in some hopes of driveing [sic] them
> out of the Jerseys – It is thought advisable for you to
> march the Troops under your command to Crosswix
> and keep a strick watch upon the Enemy upon that
> quarter.

Lastly, Washington added this note regarding the necessity of
continuing intelligence efforts, asking Heath to keep out as many
scouts as possible.

> You will keep as many Spies out as You will See
> proper, a number of horsemen in the dress of the
> Country must be Constantly kept going backwards
> & forwards for this purpose, and if you discover any
> motion of the enemy, which you Can depend upon
> and which you think of Consequence – Let me be
> informd thereof as soon as possible by Express.[16]

Meanwhile, the men at the Pluckemin camp went about their
normal routines, trying to find food, clothing, shoes, blankets, or
anything of use. Charles Willson Peale added this note to his journal
for the 5th:

> Some of Capt. Shippen's men [a reference to Marine
> Captain William Shippin, killed in action at Princ-
> eton] joined my company, whom I supplied with
> rations. The weather is very favorable, though rather
> cold; for had it rained or snowed we should have
> been badly off, as many of the men had no blankets.
> We spent this night much better than the last...Many
> of the men, in their hard march on an icy road, were
> entirely barefooted. I got a raw hide to make them

moccasins; but made a bad hand of it, for want of a proper needle or awl. [17]

Unfortunately, the elements of suffering and death were never far removed from the affairs of the Continental army, and January 5 would be no different. On the battlefield at Princeton, General Washington had discovered a youthful British officer who had been severely wounded. The officer turned out to be Captain William Leslie, nephew of Brigadier Alexander Leslie, the officer who had been in command of the brigade the Americans had just attacked and run out of town. William had been seriously wounded during that action. Doctor Benjamin Rush, who was then serving essentially as the surgeon general of the American army, knew the Leslies well and doctored the young officer's wounds as best he could. Leslie was then loaded into a wagon and carried with the Americans to Pluckemin for additional care but soon succumbed to his wounds. Washington responded to the young man's passing with kindness and grace.

Thomas Rodney, well aware of Leslie's death, explains: "This morning the General ordered up 40 of our light Infantry to attend the funeral of Col. [Captain William Leslie] Leslie one of the enemy, to bury him with the honors of war. They readily obeyed in paying due respect to bravery, though in an enemy, but as I had not paid any attention to Military Funeral Ceremonies, I requested Capt. Humphries to conduct it."[18] In 1937, the Historic American Buildings Survey visited Pluckemin, and their report contained this paragraph: "While the army was encamped here Captain William Leslie, son of the Earl of Leven, who had been wounded at Princeton, died and was buried with full military honors in the Lutheran Cemetery. Dr. Rush, who was a friend of his family, attended him and several years later erected a headstone over his grave."[19]

Washington then sent his aide, Colonel John Fitzgerald, off under a flag of truce with a letter notifying General Leslie of the death of his nephew. James Wilkinson remembered the event well, recalling Fitzgerald's trip:

He [Fitzgerald] was courteously received" wrote Wilkinson, "and introduced to most of the general officers, who spoke freely of the trick General Washington had played on them, and the race they had run, as they had made a forced march from Trenton to Brunswick – such was the alarm for the safety of their magazine...The recital of Captain Leslie's death, and the respect with which his body had been treated, affected General Leslie so sensibly, that he retired to a window and shed tears; and when colonel Fitzgerald returned he sent his acknowledgments to General Washington."[20]

Before the British would finally depart New Jersey in the coming summer, many, many more tears would be shed, lives lost, and graves dug across that war-shattered state. In the morning, Washington was prepared to march his army on to Morristown, situated safely within the heart of the mountains. There, he would struggle to keep his dwindling force together, continuing the fight however he could.

CHAPTER THREE
Morristown

During the long night march of January 3–4, the British army raced back to Brunswick, desperate to defend its base, supplies, and war chest from Continental plunder. When the sun rose on January 4, and no rebels had yet miraculously tumbled out of the clouds—as Johann Ewald had sarcastically suggested—General Cornwallis drew a sigh of relief and began planning a new defensive arrangement. The British would now abandon the previous range of far-flung posts and consolidate around Brunswick and Amboy (modern-day Perth Amboy). Brunswick would remain the headquarters, while Amboy—where the Raritan River opened into Raritan Bay—would offer favorable resupply from the Atlantic. In terms of positioning, what had once been a long, extended finger of posts had now rapidly been contracted into a tight fist. British military leaders might still be downplaying Washington's twin victories as if nothing of significance had occurred, but their latest defensive posture suggested a new and unspoken element of fear.

Captain Ewald, a professional soldier, was ever mindful of the army's new defensive posture. He explains the arrangement: "Since this place [Brunswick] lies in a valley surrounded by hills, several redoubts and fleches were erected to cover the approaches from South Amboy, Princetown, and Millstone." Redoubts were outworks, four-sided earthen fortifications with an entrance in the rear and with firing platforms erected inside. Redoubts were usually surrounded by a ditch, abatis, or other defensive obstacles. A fleche was a form of redan, also built of earth, but two-sided and shaped like an arrowhead, also open at the rear.

Units were quartered along the defensive perimeter to prevent easy access for the Continentals and rebel militias while simultaneously facilitating ready support if attacked. Two battalions of infantry were quartered northwest of Brunswick at the Raritan bridge; others at Bonhamtown, Piscataway, and along the road to Quibbletown (modern-day New Market). "I received my post," Ewald tells us, "at a house beyond New Brunswick on the road to Princetown. This house lay isolated on a hill and was constructed of brick, three stories high."[1]

Johann Ewald was then a thirty-two-year-old captain of the Hessian Jägers Corps. Born in March 1744 in the Province of Cassel (modern-day Kassel in Germany), Ewald lost both his mother and father early in life and was raised and educated by his grandmother. At the age of sixteen, he joined the infantry as a cadet and saw considerable action during the Seven Years' War, known as the French and Indian War in the colonies. He remained in the army after the war, studied at the Collegium Carolinum, and was later promoted to the rank of captain.

In 1776, and to bolster its forces in North America, Great Britain turned to the many principalities in what is now modern-day Germany, with whom the royal family had ancestral ties. Indeed, since King George III was also the elector of Hanover, the British government was able to conclude numerous treaties with many German heads of state. Financial arrangements were struck by which the various principalities were lavishly rewarded for the use of their armed forces, called auxiliaries in North America. An enormous number of these troops took part in the American Revolution. "Of the estimated 29,867 German troops sent to America, 16,992 were from Hesse-Cassel, 5,723 from Brunswick, 2,422 from Hesse-Hanau, 2,353 from, Anspach-Bayreuth, 1,225 from Waldeck, and 1,152 from Anhalt-Zerbst. In the rebellious colonies all these German troops were indiscriminately termed 'Hessians.'"[2] At the war's end, many Hessians remained in America to begin new lives.[3]

Ewald departed Cassel on May 9, 1776, in the Second Division of Hessian troops commanded by Lt. General Wilhelm von Knyphausen. They marched to the coast and sailed to England, where they were loaded onto a substantial convoy of British transport vessels bound for America. The journey was both lengthy and trying. Upon reaching New York, Ewald wrote, "only a person who has rediscovered land after a strange sea voyage can imagine the joy we felt on seeing the coast. For twelve weeks we had seen nothing but water, and had lived over twenty-one weeks in a sort of imprisonment upon these floating palaces."

Although only a captain, Ewald held a position of distinction. "The Jägers were the elite of the Hessian troops. As the name Jägers implies, the Jägers or rifle companies first drew their rank and file from among hunters, foresters, and others who were expert at shooting... They were equipped with rifled guns with hexagonal bores and better sights than those of the smoothbore musket...The Jägers wore green coats with carmine collars, cuffs and lapels, with green vests trimmed with gold." As soldiers, the Jägers were expert marksmen, generally utilized as scouts and skirmishers. They were feared by the Americans for their marksmanship and ruthlessness.

Soon after deploying along the road to Princeton, Ewald's company was shifted rearward to what he describes as "White's plantation," an abandoned farm near the Raritan River. Neither the conditions at his new quarters nor the condition of his troops inspired optimism. "After a very exhausting campaign," he wrote, "the quarters, where the soldier could not even get straw for his bedding, were to serve for refreshing the troops. For this whole region had been completely sacked during the army's march in the past autumn, and had been abandoned by all the inhabitants. The entire army had been stripped bare of shoes and stockings by the constant marching during the bad weather. Uniforms were torn and the officers, especially those of the Jägers companies, had almost nothing on their bodies. The winter now began to set in severely, for snow had fallen for several days over a half-man deep." [4] Described by one German noble as "a man of keen intellect, great courage, with an exceedingly honorable, strict military character," Captain Ewald would fight throughout the coming campaign in New Jersey. Known for his intelligence, honesty, and thoughtful commentary, we will return to his writings frequently for a fair-minded evaluation of events as they unfold.

As the "winter now began to set in severely," the American army broke camp at Pluckemin and began the trek toward Morristown, the location in the mountains Washington had selected for winter quarters. The march route twisted through mountains and valleys, in all rising 131 feet from Pluckemin to Morristown, a rocky, uphill climb of twelve miles. "We left Pluckemin this morning and arrived at Morristown just before sunset," Rodney writes. "The order of march, was first a small advance guard, next the officers who were prisoners, next my Light Infantry Regiment, in column of four deep; next the prisoners flanked by the riflemen, next the head of the main column, with the artillery in front." [5] Charles Willson Peale recalled the morning clearly: "I loaded the wagon, and moved on in the rear of the army. The sun was up some time, and, being hungry, I went into a small hut on the roadside and got some bread and milk...Marched on and joined my company. Our march was through a very mountainous country, about twelve miles to Morristown, where, after some time, we got into houses, where I slept on the planks rather coldly." [6]

Originally named New Hanover, Morristown had been settled in 1715 by New York Presbyterians, moving west for open lands and a better life. In 1739, the village was appointed the county seat of newly created Morris County, named for Lewis Morris, then the sitting royal governor of the colony of New Jersey. As a tribute, the village was renamed Morristown. "The town is situated among the mountains of Morris country, about 18 miles from Elizabethtown [modern-day Elizabeth], 26 miles from Brunswick, and 50 from Carroll's [Coryell's] Ferry," which is on the Delaware River. By the mid-eighteenth century, the hamlet boasted approximately two hundred and fifty residents, a few churches, and two taverns, with businesses and homes built around a central village green. It was an industrious area, featuring prosperous mills and farms, thought capable of supporting Washington's army of roughly three thousand during its winter stay.

Morristown's location made strategic sense, what with the American army being significantly smaller and less powerful than their British foe and expecting to increasingly lose even more men over the coming winter months. James Wilkinson explains the strategic benefits the location offered: "This position, little understood at the time, was afterwards discovered to be a most safe one for winter quarters of an army of observation, and such was General Washington's. The approach to it from the sea-board is rendered difficult and dangerous by a chain of sharp hills, which extend from Pluckemin by Bound brook and Springfield to the vicinity of the Passaic river; it is situate in the heart of a country abounding with forage and provisions, and is nearly equidistant from New York and Amboy, and also from Newark and new Brunswick, with defiles in rear to cover a retreat should circumstances render it necessary."[7]

General Washington moved into Jacob Arnold's tavern on the green, while the men were quartered in various homes throughout the village. Thomas Rodney wrote agreeably of his accommodations, pleased that "our whole Light Infantry are quartered in a very large house belonging to Col. Ford [Colonel Jacob Ford Jr.] having 4 Rooms on a floor and Two Stories high."[8] Charles Peale seemed less enthusiastic regarding his quarters, however, writing, "I have mended my boots. Got a hide, and made moccasins for the men. My lodging nothing better than last night."[9] Still, while the new lodgings might have been chilly, they were no doubt an enormous improvement over the freezing, stony mountainside where most had camped just days before.

From his quarters at Arnold's tavern, Washington wrote John Hancock once more, advising him of the army's movements along with the strategic picture, as it appeared to be emerging, confirming—by and large—what Ewald told us earlier. "The Enemy have totally evacuated Trent & Prince towns & are now at Brunswick & several posts on the communications between that & Hudson's River, but chiefly at Brunswick. Their numbers and movements are variously reported, but all agree, their force to be great." Strategy aside, the physical hardships his army had endured, and the men's dire condition, continued to be the commander in chief's principal concern. As a result, his army was literally deteriorating before his eyes, and unless a check could be put upon the flight, Washington realized he would soon have precious few troops to fight with, whatever the strategic situation.

> The Severity of the Season has made our Troops, especially the Militia, extremely impatient, and has reduced the number very considerably. Every day more or less leave us. Their complaints and the great fatigues they had undergone, induced me to come to this place, as the best calculated of any in this quarter, to accommodate and refresh them. The situation is by no means favourable to our views, and as soon as the purposes are answered for which we came, I think to remove, though I confess, I do not know how we shall procure covering for our Men elsewhere.[10]

To better understand the manpower situation, some background information may prove beneficial. During this period, the Continental army was going through a period of transition. The Continental army had come into being in June 1775, when the Continental Congress essentially adopted to its purpose the New England Army of Observation, the force that had gathered at Boston. These troops enlisted for terms that expired at the end of the year, and this force was called the "First Establishment." A "Second Establishment" was later authorized by Congress, with troops generally enlisting for one year, from January 1, 1776, to December 31, 1776. A "Third Establishment" then became necessary, and this was authorized by Congress in September 1776. These new units were to be assigned to the "Main" or Grand Army in January 1777. This process was ongoing as Washington took up headquarters at Morristown. Many of the "Third Establishment" regiments would not appear until later that spring, while many "Second Establishment" ceased to exist and had to be reconstituted under the third establishment. The militia troops, on the other hand, were called to service for short periods of time, often only thirty days; hence they were constantly flowing in and out of camp.

Today, George Washington is regarded as an almost mythical figure, the father of his country, and surely one of the most important of the nation's founding fathers. But in January 1777, that fame was still far in the future for the real George Washington, a man who, at the time, could easily have remained little more than a historical footnote (if that) if the Revolutionary effort had been defeated, or simply fizzled away, as appeared likely more than once before. The man who sat in Arnold's tavern that January may have just won three important victories, but the scope and meaning of those successes were not yet clearly understood. And no matter how glorious, those wins had by no means improved the scores of seemingly intractable problems that haunted the army. Nevertheless, over time, the Revolutionary effort would become virtually synonymous with the name of George Washington. So to understand the Revolutionary War, and the campaign in New Jersey he was about to oversee, it would serve us well to take a brief look at the real George Washington.

George Washington was born on February 11, 1731, in Westmoreland County, Virginia, to Augustine and Mary Ball Washington. He was raised in a family of reasonable means, although hardly considered affluent by the standards of the day. He grew up in the Tidewater region of Virginia but also on a farm along the Rappahannock River near Fredericksburg. As a result of the family's limited means, Washington was schooled only sporadically. He never received the formal education or, most certainly, the college education that other sons of greater means enjoyed as a matter of form. His father died when he was eleven years old, and his half-brother, Lawrence, inherited the family plantation on the Potomac River that would later be named Mount Vernon.

Beyond the cities along the Atlantic coast, the America of Washington's youth was a frontier society, and George possessed the physical size and imposing features that made him a natural in a world where endurance, strength, and innate intelligence meant everything. Historian Joseph J. Ellis crafts a striking image of the youthful Washington, implying, "a very tall young man, at least six feet two inches, which made him a head higher than the average male of his time. He had an athlete's body, well proportioned and trim at about 175 bounds with very strong thighs and legs, which allowed him to grip a horse's flanks tightly and hold his seat in the saddle with uncommon ease. His eyes were grayish blue and widely set. His hair was hazel brown, destined to darken over the years, and usually tied in a cue in the back. He had disproportionately large hands and feet, which contributed to his awkward appearance when stationary, but once in motion on the dance floor or in a foxhunt the natural grace of his movements overwhelmed the initial impression."

Washington was powerful and athletic, Ellis tells us, "the epitome of the man's man: physically strong, mentally enigmatic, emotionally restrained." [11] Although schooled on a limited basis, Washington was tutored in mathematics, surveying, and map-making, and it was as a surveyor where, in 1749, he first made his mark. Then, because of his surveying activity in the wilds of western Virginia, he was appointed adjutant of the Northern District of Virginia, a military position he had actively sought. In turn, this position opened a world of new possibilities. In 1753, Washington was commissioned by Governor Dinwiddie to deliver a letter to the French commander in the Ohio country, far west of the Blue Ridge. The journey took Washington through tedium and travails, and his thrilling account of the trip was later published, giving Washington name recognition in both America and England.

General George Washington.

Despite warnings from British authorities, the French nonetheless continued their incursions into the Ohio country. Dinwiddie then received secret orders from London to send a military force to the Forks of the Ohio to establish a fort to defend British territory, and Washington was again selected to lead the mission. Things went horribly awry, however, when Washington's party surprised a small group of French soldiers along the way. Washington led an attack, which quickly descended into chaos. Most of the Frenchmen were killed, either by the troops under Washington's command or his Iroquois allies. The incident sparked an international crisis between England and France when the allied Indian leader Tanaghrisson, the "half king," murdered Lieutenant Jumonville after his men had surrendered to Washington.

Meanwhile, receiving news of Washington's fatal attack, French troops and their Indian allies advanced against Washington's force, which had taken position in a hastily constructed stockade called "Fort Necessity." There, his command was rapidly surrounded and attacked by the enraged French. Surrendering after a nearly hopeless defense, Washington's life was spared, but he was forced to sign an incriminating document of surrender. This incident temporarily ended Washington's military adventures, but he returned to serve as a volunteer aide to General Edward Braddock in another westward expedition to the Forks of the Ohio in 1755, designed again to drive the French out of the Ohio country.

Braddock was attacked by the French and their Indian allies after sending a portion ahead to cross the Monongahela River. The British were mauled; Braddock mortally wounded. Washington responded coolly, however, managing a skillful retreat under fire, for which he was later highly commended. For these actions, Governor Dinwiddie rewarded Washington with a new commission: colonel of the Virginia Regiment, charged with protecting the colony's frontier. In 1759, he commanded a contingent consisting of the First and Second Virginia Regiments in the Forbes expedition, which took Fort Duquesne, situated at the confluence of the Allegheny and Monongahela rivers (modern-day Pittsburgh). As a result, Washington gained firsthand experience handling and disciplining troops, while his reputation as a capable military officer flourished anew.

In 1759, after returning from the Forbes expedition, Washington retired and married Martha Dandridge Custis, one of the wealthiest widows in Virginia. They moved to Mount Vernon along with Martha's two children, Patsy and Jacky, and it was at Mount Vernon where Washington assumed the lifestyle of a Southern planter. By marriage, Washington had inherited a vast estate, including capital resources, numerous farms, and the slaves that lived on the farmlands. He was soon elected to Virginia's House of Burgesses and, over time, became known as a reasonably adept politician. It was during his Mount Vernon years that Washington became familiar with Enlightenment thought and politics, both of which eventually had a profound influence on his life. That his understanding of Enlightenment theory never extended to his slaves, or the institution of slavery, however, is a fact for which Washington has been justly criticized and which haunts his legacy to this day.

During the early 1770s, Washington strongly sympathized with the colonies in their growing disputes with the English crown, and he was elected to the First Continental Congress as a delegate from Virginia. This Congress urged the organization of independent militia companies, and Washington became colonel of the Fairfax Independent Militia. As war loomed on the horizon, he appeared at the Second Continental Congress dressed in his colonel's uniform, silently but obviously lobbying for command of American forces. In 1775, Congress commissioned him the commander of the American militias, then gathered at Boston in open rebellion against the king's troops. He accepted the commission and, except for the reimbursement of expenses, declined payment for his services.[12] Importantly, the congressional delegates still felt as though some form of reconciliation with the crown could be achieved. Hence, Washington's commission called for the defense of liberty, not independence.

This, then, serves as a brief history of the man who, in January 1777, sat in Jacob Arnold's tavern with the weight of the American Revolution increasingly upon his shoulders alone. Moreover, in July 1776, the Second Continental Congress adopted the Declaration of Independence, turning the war from one maintaining liberty to one defending independence. While it is true that Washington had acquired great wealth through marriage, it is equally true that he had acquired a vast archive of practical know-how through hard-won experiences of success and failure on the American frontier, experiences where often a single misstep spelled the difference between life and death. More than once, he had faced both death and dishonor, only to survive by struggling onward, and the development of that steadfast persistence would continue to serve him well throughout the American Revolution.

As soon as Washington arrived in Morristown, letters again began to fly from his headquarters, covering a wide range of topics. He wrote to Congress about the foundry that had been established near Philadelphia for casting Continental artillery; to General Cornwallis regarding the safe passage of baggage and medicines; to General Benjamin Lincoln in New York concerning his cooperation with General Heath, and again to Heath, reiterating the need for an immediate movement toward New York City, something Washington considered critical at the time. The American commander in chief knew that the British vastly outnumbered his army, but a divided enemy was also a potentially vulnerable enemy:

> I beg you will keep up every Appearance of falling
> down upon New York, as that will be the surest
> Method of obliging them to withdraw their whole
> Force from this side to protect the City, and as I am
> confident they have not proper Magazines estab-
> lished there, they must put to the most extreme want

for provisions. If they throw part of their Force into New York, they will leave themselves in such a Situation, that we may, in all probability fall upon them with Success.[13]

So, as Washington rested his men and tried to discern the evolving strategic situation, for the moment, it appeared things had settled down, at least in terms of fighting outright. But then, he received a rather stunning and encouraging report of an American militia action near Elizabethtown, just miles from New York City, an area the British and their Hessian auxiliaries had controlled with seeming impunity for months. British dragoons, in support of a regiment of Waldeck infantry, had marched from Elizabethtown toward Springfield with the intention of sweeping the region clear of rebel militias. Unfortunately, they were themselves very roughly handled by those same militias, as British officer Stephen Kemble explains in his journal:

> Major Crewe's attempt to cut off a Detachment of the Rebels near Springlfield, which was endeavoured to be put into Execution on the 5th.; but, the Waldeck Detachment not behaving well, he was enabled only to take 4 or 5 Prisoners, and run a great risk of being cut off himself; made his way to New Ark, and got in on the 6th. Lieut. Mesnard, of the 17th., went out with about 12 Light Horse and 50 Waldeckers marched about 4 Miles, came to a Hollow, halted the Waldeckers, and proposed to Return, having observed some appearance of an Enemy, advanced a little himself, and was fired upon; the Waldeckers, in attempting their Retreat up the Hill, found their passage stopped, and retreated from the Rebels to a House, where they sustained some fire, but were in the end all taken Prisoners. Mr. Mesnard, finding his Retreat cut off, with about 10 Light Dragoons marched towards Springfield, thro' which place he went thro' a smart fire, had several of his Men and Horses Wounded, but luckily got off with all but one, a Servant.[14]

Kemble's description of the action is accurate but incomplete. He fails to mention that the British were driven from Elizabethtown and prevented from foraging in the country while having several supply wagons confiscated by the American militia. If Lord Cornwallis fancied this attack a substantial event or a minor nuisance is unclear, but in a letter dated January 8 to Lord Germain in London, he surely appeared unimpressed with its significance, as it goes unmentioned. Indeed, this correspondence smacks of the same contempt for American arms that had led to Washington's ten-day romp over the crown's forces at Trenton and Princeton in the first place, and which had come close to allowing the Americans to abscond with his entire war chest in the bargain. Ewald might have joked that the Americans now had "wings," but if any lessons had been learned by General Cornwallis, they are hard to detect in his letter to Germain. In part, it reads:

> The unlucky affair of Raal's Brigade has given me a winter campaign. Washington is with about 7,000 men in Morristown, our quarters were too much exposed, and it was necessary to assemble our troops; that is now done, and all is safe. He cannot subsist for long where he is, I should imagine that he means to repass the Delaware at Alexandria, the season of the year will make it difficult for us to follow him, but the march alone will destroy his army.[15]

So there you have it. Cornwallis need not lift a finger, for Washington was about to destroy his own army while recrossing the Delaware, thus ending the war while the British rested comfortably in their winter quarters. But Washington had no intention of recrossing the Delaware, and the notion that the American army was soon to be "destroyed" while on the march seems little more than misplaced optimism. After ten days on the run, had Cornwallis really learned nothing?

In those early days of January 1777, the two combatants had become like calculating pugilists, boxers eyeing one another across the ring from their individual corners. One, the British heavyweight, perfectly capable of pulverizing an opponent with a stunning right hook—once close enough to throw it, that is. The other opponent, the Americans, were certainly the lightweights, lacking size and punching power but quick, agile, and maddeningly hard to get a crack at. Neither could afford to make a mistake, yet it appears Cornwallis already had, at least in terms of assumptions. For the Americans were not going to "repass" the Delaware, nor were they going to waste away in the Watchung Mountains near Morristown for lack of provisions. In fact, angry and emboldened by their recent victories, they were about to come out swinging.

CHAPTER FOUR
Spanktown

*I*t was with good reason that Captain Ewald and his Hessian Jägers could quarter in any building within the area they were stationed that January. Indeed, the entire British army could pick and choose their lodgings—from abandoned homes to plundered farms to pillaged mansions—across central New Jersey, for most of the inhabitants had fled the widespread ravages that had occurred as the British marched south the preceding fall, from New York all the way to the Delaware River. While some reports of atrocities were surely overstated propaganda, cooked up to enrage the citizens against the marauding enemy, the most damning reports came from the British themselves, often filed by their own horrified officers.

The outrageous behavior had begun in New York in late 1776, as it became increasingly evident that General Howe had the Continentals on the run. Historically, victorious armies had rarely treated innocent civilians caught in the maelstrom with anything approaching decency, and the British regulars and their Hessian auxiliaries appeared more than happy to live up to that unfortunate standard. British officer Stephen Kemble—a Loyalist who had grown up in New Jersey—while campaigning in New York on Thursday, November 7, noted the troubling, evolving conduct: "Scandalous behavior for British Troops; and the Hessians Outrageously Licentious, and Cruel to such a degree as to threaten with death all such as dare obstruct them in their depredations. Violence to Officers frequently used, and every Degree of Insolence offered. Shudder for Jersey, the Army being thought to move there shortly."[1]

Stephen Kemble may have shuddered for Jersey, but most British officers did not share his concern. For all intents and purposes, Revolutionary New Jersey had appeared to the British regulars and their Hessian auxiliaries as a land of milk and honey. Dotted with prosperous farms and small thriving communities, crossed with abundant rivers that ran east to the Atlantic, all these sourced from crisp flowing tributaries that fed wells, crops, and livestock, the average American farmer lived a lifestyle well beyond what most European peasants could even imagine, and prosperous New Jersey was no different. There were orchards, haystacks, and attractive young maidens, and all this prosperity looked as if it had been—for men generally drawn from the lower rungs of European society—created for pillaging. Historian David McCullough notes, "The plenty of New Jersey, the 'Garden of America,' its broad, fertile, well-tended farms, abundant supplies of livestock, grain, hay, food put up for the winter, barrels of wine and beer for the taking, were all too much to resist...Accounts of houses sacked, of families robbed of all they had, became commonplace."[2] So commonplace, in fact, that on November 24, Stephen Kemble recorded this troubling note: "Am told the Light Horse have proceeded as far as Second River [or Watsessing River, a tributary of the Passaic], but don't know with what certainty, for his Lordship will not be able to restrain the Troops from plundering the Country; Their Excesses in that report carried to a most unjustifiable length."[3]

So apparent were the depredations that Captain Ewald—a man of moral conviction, often dismayed by wanton cruelty and destruction—noticed the barren landscape almost immediately upon leading his troops across the Hudson River from New York. "On this march we looked upon a deplorable sight," he wrote. "The region is well cultivated, with very attractive plantations [farms], but all the occupants had fled and all the houses had been or were being plundered and destroyed."[4]

(For the purpose of clarification, it should be noted that much eighteenth-century correspondence often refers to New Jersey as "the Jerseys." This is because, from 1664 to 1702, there were actually two Jerseys: one West Jersey, the other East Jersey, each with its own governor and capital. The area of New Jersey was first claimed by the Dutch and originally named New Netherlands. Later claimed by the British as the spoils of war, the British renamed the area New Jersey after the island, Jersey, in the English Channel. In 1702, the two Jerseys were united into one political unit. The habit, however, of referring to New Jersey as "the Jerseys" remained a rhetorical tradition for years after the unification.)

In the autumn of 1776, that united New Jersey countryside may have appeared quite idyllic to the European troops then marching and marauding their way south toward Philadelphia, but the human reality suggested a more complex reality. The people of New Jersey, for instance, while generally tranquil and respectful of one another, were nevertheless a potpourri of different nationalities and religions. Swedes, Finns, Dutch, English, and Irish, to name but a few, lived in the colony and worshipped as Catholics, Lutherans, Jews, and Presbyterians. Far more tumultuous than faith or national origins, however, was the ever-escalating disharmony between the rebels (or Whigs) and those loyal (or Tories) to the British crown. It has been estimated that two-thirds of the colonists across the rebelling thirteen colonies actively supported the rebellion, while the other third remained fiercely loyal to the crown. As a result, Rebel vs. Loyalist became a nasty form of civil war in many of the newly self-declared states, and over the course of the Revolution, countless scores were forged and settled on the basis of political loyalties alone.

As a result, in the fall of 1776, as Washington's beleaguered army trudged south across New Jersey, obviously defeated and hopelessly outclassed—abandoning rebel sympathizers to the oncoming British—angry Loyalists suddenly appeared with mischief in mind. Typical is the case of a young Dutch minister in Hackensack named Dirck Romeyn, related by historian William M. Ketcham: "While a crowd of cheering Tories looked on, British and loyalist troops ransacked the house, emptied the barns, drove off the livestock, and left the place a desolate, hollow shell, punctured with broken windows and doors. Fortunately, Romeyn was away at the time and managed to escape with his sick wife and eight-year-old child to New Paltz. That same day the Tories and British descended on the home of William Christie in Schraalenburgh (modern-day Closter), stripped it of everything but the heavy furniture, and carried off his hogs and a horse." [5]

This explosion of sudden hostility, coupled with the collapse of Continental authority, had in New Jersey the effect of driving many rebel sympathizers into the arms of the crown. Adding to this shift was a proclamation issued by Sir William Howe, offering a form of pardon for those who accepted its terms. Posted in New York on November 30, it read:

> **Proclamation by the commissioners for restoring Peace to America**
>
> **Referring to the Declarations of 14th July and 19th September last; and commanding all persons in arms to disband, and all general and provincial congresses, committees, conventions, or other associations to desist and cease from the treasonable acts of levying money, raising troops, fitting out armed Ships and vessels, imprisoning or molesting the Kings subjects, and to relinquish all usurped power and authority. Also offering a free pardon to all treasons and misprisons of treason to any person who within 60 days from the date of Proclamation claims the benefit there of and subscribes a proper declaration testifying his obedience to the laws.[6]**

For those in New Jersey previously sympathetic to the rebel cause—who had watched Washington's demoralized troops limp past their front doors, then disappear down the road, only later to be savaged, ruined, and dislocated by Tories, Hessians, or British troops—the promise of a free pardon began to have the ring of good sense about it. So many flocked to sign the king's pardon, offering up declarations of obedience in the hope that their lives might return to a semblance of normality.

Unfortunately, things did not turn out as they had hoped. The Loyalists still knew who they were and, doubting their sincerity, continued to pillage, destroy, and generally run riot. The Hessians and British, on the other hand, never thought twice about honoring the Proclamation and continued stealing, plundering, and raping at will as if nothing had changed. So much for "obedience to the laws," a term that for many began to sound empty indeed. Thus, for all their groveling and pretense of loyalty, it seemed they had accomplished nothing. Indeed, in some ways, they had actually gone backward, for before, they had at least been thought of as "rebels," whereas now, they had assumed the posture of disloyal, untrustworthy, and cowardly scum, hated by *everyone*.

Over the intervening month or so, the utter unfairness—the brutal injustice of this—began naturally to boil in the hearts of many of those who had flocked to sign the Proclamation. As it became more and more apparent that the British authorities did not care one whit for them or their loyalty but had used them to simply pacify the region, a seething hatred for the British, Hessians, and the Tories began to fester. Governor William Livingston of New Jersey railed: "They [British] have warred upon decrepit age; warred upon defenseless youth; They have committed hostilities against the professors of literature and the ministers of religion; against public records and private monuments; against books of improvement and papers of curiosity; and against the arts and sciences." [7] In short, the British had trampled upon virtually everything that mattered to the people of New Jersey, and, over time, that injustice would be repaid with more than mere contempt.

During the preceding autumn, the British had passed through Jersey largely unobstructed, the population cowed and pacified; George Washington, Congress, and the Continental army seemingly beaten and powerless to stop them. Yet now, Washington and his Continentals had risen triumphant, almost like a phoenix, dazzling the British and the world, for that matter, in a stunning display of martial wizardry. Word of Washington's twin triumphs at Trenton and Princeton had shot through the rebellious states like a bolt of lightning, inspiring rebel hearts while simultaneously discouraging the enemy. As noted by author Richard M. Ketcham: "But as thrilling as the news of Princeton was, for the country, coming so quickly after the triumph at Trenton, it was Trenton that meant the most, Trenton and the night crossing of the Delaware that were rightly seen as a great turning point. With the victory at Trenton came the realization that Americans had bested the enemy, bested the fearsome Hessians, the King's detested hirelings, outsmarted them and outfought them, and so might again." [8]

So the critical question that remained for those previously cowed Jersey rebels was, now that Washington had swept north from Trenton into the mountains of Watchung, would the British be allowed to operate throughout the Jerseys with the same impunity they had before? Or would all that seething hatred burst forth in some defiant-yet-practical form? James Wilkinson provides one answer:

> If the yeomanry of the Jerseys, panic struck by the triumphant march of a victorious army, and seduced by the blandishments and fair promises of the British com-missioners, shrunk from their duty and abandoned the standard of their country, in November and December, 1776, they discovered before January, 1777, that the powers, of the invaders were limited, and the promises of their commissioners perfidious. Stung with remorse by the retrospect of their pusillanimity, and fired with indignation by the outrageous injuries they had suffered, they again resumed their arms, and the old and the young, determined to avenge their wrongs upon the authors of their misery, and the enemies of their country; hence-forward the militia of the Jerseys stood preeminent among the defenders of the public cause.[9]

Put simply, according to Wilkinson, the militia action at Elizabethtown on the 5th was not an aberration at all, but rather the beginning of something violent and escalating.

At that moment, Washington had no idea what the true resentment level of the local population was, but his standing view of militias was that they were fundamentally unprofessional and unreliable, as demonstrated once again by the recent failure of the militia at Somerset Courthouse. He wanted a professional army—properly trained, equipped, and signed on for a substantial commitment—so that he could compete against British regulars with regulars of his own. Washington's own reputation had taken wing as a result of his recent twin victories (indeed Frederick the Great of Prussia, at the time considered Europe's reigning military genius, is said to have remarked that Washington's victories "were the most brilliant of any recorded in the annals of military achievements."[10]), but that admiration had had precious little practical effect on the American army. In fact, in many ways, the American force at Morristown was no better off than they had been on December 25, 1776, the day they had gathered at McConkey's Ferry to launch their attack against the Hessians at Trenton.

General Sir William Howe.

Admiration for their recent victories might prove satisfying, but it was not food, shoes, or clothing. Worse still, the number of men available for operations in New Jersey was dwindling daily and at an alarming rate. The militia units, as previously described, were called out for short periods and hence tended to come and go with some frequency. In a letter to John Hancock, Washington made this deteriorating situation clear: "The fluctuating State of an Army composed Chiefly of Militia, bids fair to reduce us to the Situation in which we were some little time ago, that is, of scarce having any Army at all, except Reinforcements speedly arrive."

This glaring lack of fighting men left the commander in chief in the uncomfortable position of having to fake his numerical strength in hopes of keeping the British at bay, but that expedient simultaneously damaged his ability to recruit—the classic double-edged sword. In fact, it was a game that could not be played forever and already appeared to be unraveling. "For to boast of our superiority in that respect on the one hand," Washington explained to Hancock, "and to call publicly on the people for Assistance on the other, is an impropriety too glaring. Indeed, it has been already noticed in some publications I have seen from New York."[11]

So, Washington was again forced to fight a war without the means of fighting it, a situation that rendered him essentially impotent. Worse still, should the British get wind of the army's true condition, they might decide to risk their luck by running those gaps in the Watchung Mountains with a major force after all and send the American Revolution tumbling back into critical condition once more. For all the praise the recent victories had brought the Americans, for all practical purposes they were back to their dismal, pre-Trenton condition.

While a major offensive was out of the question, still, some creative movements could at least be considered. To better winter the troops, for instance, the decision was made to quarter the divisions at varying locations removed from Morristown but not so far removed that they could not support one another in times of emergency. The divisions were also posted to cover the approaches from Brunswick and Amboy, where the British had now gathered in strength. The individual commanders were given independence of action to constantly annoy the enemy while not bringing on a major engagement, which the Americans, of course, were incapable of winning.

As such, General Philemon Dickinson's troops were posted at Somerset Courthouse, while Israel Putman remained south at Princeton. Nathanael Greene moved his division to Basking Ridge, Nathaniel Warner to Millstone; William Maxwell and Adam Stephen to Metuchen, while John Sullivan covered Scot's Plain (modern-day Scotch Plains) and Chatham. Lastly, General William Alexander (referred to as Lord Stirling by the Americans) was at Quibbletown (modern-day New Market, originally named Quibbletown supposedly due to an ongoing argument between early settlers). This arrangement covered significant ground and offered widespread offensive opportunities, but it naturally left each individual command in danger of annihilation if surprised by a superior force.[12] Hence, constant vigilance would be of the essence.

With supply virtually nonexistent, and manpower dwindling daily, Washington had few offensive options, yet it was becoming increasingly apparent that the requirements of the British army left them vulnerable as well. In a letter to General Heath—who had yet to mount a serious demonstration toward New York City as previously requested—the commander in chief expressed his thoughts: "Forage for the Winter will be one of their greatest Wants, and I highly approve of your Intentions of collecting all you can, not only to put it out of their reach, but as it will be most servicable to us."[13]

Since before the days of Alexander the Great, armies on the march had relied upon animal strength to move their supplies, siege trains, bullion, and booty. While on campaign, horses, mules, and oxen provided the brute strength to haul wagons, battering rams, and ballista across mountain and desert alike. But animals need food, and for grazing animals, that meant fodder—generally wheat, hay, barley, clover, and wild grasses. Thus, feed for the eighteenth-century army was akin to petrol for the modern military, and for the British—with their vast supply train, abundant artillery, and mounted cavalry—this meant tons of food delivered daily. Deprived of fodder for its animals for any length of time, any eighteenth-century army would be rendered as impotent as a modern military without gasoline for its vehicles, and any impotent force soon becomes a vulnerable target. The British, now self-confined to the environs of Brunswick and Amboy, would of necessity be forced to venture out into the local countryside to either purchase or impress this essential commodity or watch their animals wither and die. Hence, from George Washington's point of view in January 1777, denying the British fodder for their animals and forage for their soldier's needs became a prime and utterly sensible strategic objective. If he could not beat them on the field of battle, perhaps he could deny them the ability to reconnoiter, resupply, and maneuver.

Somewhat remarkably—at least from Washington's perspective—he did not have to lift a finger to initiate this strategy, for the people of New Jersey initiated it for him. "The British concentrated all their forces upon Brunswick and Amboy...Sufficient time, however had elapsed while they remained in possession of New Jersey, to make people fully aware of the true character of the enemy that was deluging their soil with the blood of their friends and kindred, and every day the English cause lost ground. 'Sufferers of all parties rose as one man to revenge their personal injuries and particular oppressions,' and whenever attempts were made by the British to forage in the surrounding country, they were obliged to go in large parties, and generally sustained some loss."[14]

W. Woodford Clayton, in his history of the region, explains that "taking advantage of the consternation of the enemy, and the advance of the American Army [toward Morristown], General Maxwell, with the militia under his command, came down from the Short Hills, compelled the British to evacuate Newark, had a brush with them at Springfield, drove them out of Elizabeth Town, and fought them at Spank Town (Rahway) a couple of hours."[15] Just before dawn on Sunday, January 5, about ninety militiamen ambushed roughly twenty men of the British Forty-Sixth Regiment. The clash was over one thousand bushels of salt near a British depot, an essential preservative prior to refrigeration, and the contest became hot. Pinned down, the Loyalists fought back for over two hours while sending off desperate pleas for reinforcements.[16]

Spanktow—or Bridge Town or Rahwack (modern-day Rahway), custom tells us—received one of its numerous early names when a pioneer inappropriately rebuked his fiancée in public, but this is tradition only. Clayton continues: "If Spank Town had never had the name before it was entitled to it from this time certainly on account of the *spanking* rate at which Maxwell came down from the Short Hills [this refers to the area near modern-day Plainfield, not the modern-day town of Short Hills] with his militia and punished the rear of the retreating enemy." Both sides were already on the hunt for forage and supplies, and this clash at Spanktown was one of the earliest in what would become an ongoing pattern. "As to the 'one thousand bushels of salt' which was stored here, it was probably a cargo which had been brought up the Rahway [River], which was navigable by small vessels as far up as the old bridge, which gave to the place at an early time the name of Bridge Town. The principal fort at Elizbeth Town being in possession of the British, this salt and possibly other valuable stores were brought in here to be more secure from the enemy." The fight then raged for two hours "at a place called Spank Town, about five miles from Woodbridge where a party of our men attacked the enemy at that place; they [the Loyalists] sent for a reinforcement to Woodbridge, but the Hessians absolutely refused to march, having heard we were very numerous in that quarter." Eventually, two English regiments marched to the Loyalist's relief, arriving in the nick of time to save their lives but not the shipment of salt, which was spirited away by Maxwell's troops.[17]

The British, who just weeks before had rested confidently in their winter posts dotted across Jersey, were now entirely reconfigured in and about Brunswick and Amboy, and everywhere else on the run.

Their patrols were being attacked and overrun, potential ambush lurking behind every rock, tree, or rail fence. Thus, the order of the day was to safely secure all their troops and provisions behind the outer screen of their new defensive positions. British officer Stephen Kemble's journal note of January 8 speaks volumes as to this complete change in outlook. *"Wednesday, Jan. 8th.* General Vaughan with the Waldeckers and 71st Regiment, Marched to Amboy, about 11 o'Clock, the 7th and 26th, a little before to Elizabeth Point, had all the stores over by half after 11, and the two Regiments by half past 2 o'Clock, very happy that my Rear Guard was not Insulted. About 3 in the Afternoon sent a Flat Boat for some Rum and Provisions that had been carried by mistake to the lower ferry, in the attempt to take which off She was seized by the Rebels, and a Sloop fired upon."[18]

Suddenly, the British could not move in New Jersey without fear of "insult." Shortly thereafter, for instance, *The Pennsylvania Evening Post*—the first daily newspaper in the colonies, and at the time decidedly Whig in its outlook—crowed a bit effusively as follows: "We are informed, from good authority, that many of the inhabitants of Monmouth county in New-Jersey who received written protections, are now determined to return them to his Britannic Majesty's Commissioners in CARTRIDG-ES."[19] Stephen Kemble, apparently sensing this new shift in the winds of war, added this revealing note to his journal on January 10: "Am told the Rebels are much elated with their late success."[20]

CHAPTER FIVE
Quibbletown

*A*s spirits rose for rebel sympathizers that January, and as enlistments bumped upward from the victories at Trenton and Princeton, the situation at Morristown remained far from satisfactory. To John Hancock, Washington complained:

> Reinforcements come up so extremely slow, that I am afraid I shall be left without any Men, before they arrive. The enemy must be ignorant of our Numbers, or they have not Horses to move their Artillery, or they would not suffer us to remain undisturbed. I have repeatedly wrote to all the recruiting Officers to forward on their Men as fast as they could arm and cloath them, but they are so extremely averse to turning out of comfortable Quarters, that I cannot get a Man to come near me, tho' I hear from all parts, that the recruiting Service goes with great Success.[1]

The men's enlistments of the First Establishment were running out, and—weary, ill-fed, ill-clothed, and footsore from months of marching and fighting—few could be talked into staying on. Captain Thomas Rodney, for instance, tells us that on January 14, "this day most all my company set off home though I tried all in my power to prevail upon them to stay until brigade went."[2] Soon, Rodney would follow them down the long road to Delaware. Likewise, it was for Charles Peale, whose unit also voted to depart, having already stayed on for days beyond their enlistments. On the 19th, they all had their bags packed and were on the road before the sun was up. "Rise at 5 o'clock to prepare for our march homeward. I desired the company to get their breakfasts before day, and we got under arms before sunrise. We marched off very fast, and passed through Bristol, and turning to the right of Pluckemin, we got to New Germantown, 21 miles from Morristown, at 3 o'clock, the men exceedingly fatigured."[3]

General Washington was simply caught between the departure of the Second Establishment and the arrival of the Third. Twice he had asked (ordered, actually) General Heath in New York to make a serious diversion toward New York City, with the hope that such a move would force the British either to withdraw from Jersey entirely or shift enough forces to the city that a strike at the British who remained behind at Brunswick would become instantly feasible. But nothing had come of that, and Washington was becoming frustrated. "I have not heard from Genl Heth since the 14th instant," he confided again to Hancock, "which I am amazed at. I am quite in the dark as to his Numbers and what progress he has made."

Problem piled upon problem. Washington was now fighting in New Jersey, a region he was only slightly familiar with. For the smaller force, capable only of swift lightning strikes against the larger foe, then withdrawing rapidly before being trapped, intimate knowledge of the land—the roads, bridges, defiles, creeks, river fords, and so on—was essential for practical planning. Yet beyond the main roads the army had used previously to move north and south, the countryside remained as mysterious as the surface of the moon. The solution to this challenge seemed simple enough—accurate maps!—which Washington had attempted to procure before, all to no avail:

> The want of accurate Maps of the Country which has hitherto been the Scene of War, has been of great dis-advantage to me. I have in vain endeavoured to procure them, and have been obliged to make shift, with such Sketches as I could trace out from my own Observations, and that of Gentlemen around me. I really think if Gentlemen of known Character & probity could be employed in making Maps (from actual Survey) of the Roads – The Rivers and Bridges and Fords over them – the Mountains and passes thro' them, it would be of great Advantage."[4]

The general's desire was, in fact, both practical and visionary. Unfortunately, it was also wildly premature. Good maps of the American countryside did not exist on any scale during the Revolutionary period and would not for quite some time. Both sides attempted to circumvent this deficiency by employing local guides, but most "locals" were just that; hence their knowledge of the road network was extremely limited. Thus, military operations involving trips of more than just a few miles often found themselves lost or hopelessly misdirected. Indeed, even during the American Civil War, generals of both sides still decried the lack of accurate maps. Bedeviled by more than one road with the same name, towns on maps that did not actually exist, inaccurate signs, and bridges or fords often in the wrong place— or nowhere to be found—navigating the American countryside remained an exercise in exasperation until the twentieth century. Not until the automobile was invented and Americans took to the roads did accurate maps of the countryside beyond the major cities become largely available. So maps can be added to the long list of wants that handcuffed General Washington and his staff as they contemplated their meager options early that January.

For the British, on the other hand, despite their recent setbacks— not to mention the rash of sudden attacks on their foraging expeditions—the future still seemed entirely promising. Their long supply line that stretched from the harbor at New York City across the Atlantic remained secure, a fact that assured a steady flow of provisions and manpower. In terms of fighting men, the Redcoats still enjoyed a vast superiority over their rebel foe. On January 8, for instance, Major Stephen Kemble prepared a distribution of British manpower in the colonies, which determined the following: With the commander in chief at Brunswick, 13,799; on New York Island (Manhattan) 3,311; on Staten Island, 856; at Paulus Hook (modern-day Jersey City), three hundred and sixty; at Rhode Island, 2,631, and provincials (Loyalist infantry) at Kings Bridge, north of New York City, two thousand, for a total of 22,957 effective troops, easily swamping anything Washington could put in the field. Indeed, despite their recent misfortunes, British attitudes appeared remarkably upbeat, as Kemble recorded in his journal: "*Jan. 11th to Friday, 17th*. All Quiet. Great preparations making for the Queen's Birth day on to-morrow the 18th. The King's Commissioners gave their first Dinner on this day: a Ball and Fire Works at the General's in the Evening."[5]

For Kemble, things may have seemed "All Quiet," but if so, it was the quiet before the storm. On January 20, Archibald Robertson tells us that "Lieutenant Colonel Abercromby with 500 men went on a foraging party towards Hillsborough."[6] That party, consisting of British and Hessian troops, departed Brunswick bound for Abraham Van Nest's Mill on the Millstone River, where it was reported abundant flour was stored for the taking. The British marched unimpeded to the Millstone, then turned north toward Van Nest's mill (modern-day Manville). But the area between Brunswick and the river was teeming with rebel lookouts. The large column was easily spotted, and the alarm promptly raised.

It can be recalled that General Philemon Dickinson's division was encamped near Somerset Courthouse, only some two to three miles northeast of the mill. Dickinson, born in Maryland in 1739, had been raised in nearby Delaware, where his family moved when he was young. Educated by tutors, he later graduated from the College of Philadelphia (the modern-day University of Pennsylvania) in 1759, then went on to practice law. Promoted to the rank of major general in the New Jersey Militia, he would prove an effective field commander despite the overall ineffectual condition of Jersey's militias. Dickinson, receiving the alarm, responded at once by marshaling two companies of Continentals, four hundred New Jersey militiamen, fifty Pennsylvania riflemen, and one piece of artillery. One militiaman recalled the subsequent engagement in some detail: "Staid here in peace till Monday morning we then received an Alarm and were ordered to march to Boundbrook, we arrived there between 11 and 12, then hearing that the Enemy was plundering Millstone [Van Nest's mill], we immediately marched for that place, being joined by a considerable body at Boundbrook we marched on till we passed Raritan Bridge, hearing several Cannon fired while on the way. After crossing the Bridge, the Battallion I was in was taken off for the left wing, I crossed Millstone, some distance below the Bridge, wading through the water, more than knee deep."[7]

A bridge spanned the Millstone near Van Nest's, and the British had positioned three pieces of artillery on a bluff overlooking the bridge, with the bulk of their troops nearby, to secure their passage back to Brunswick. Dickinson's left wing headed straight for the mill, while the right wing sought to engage the foragers near the bridge. The British had plundered the mill by the time the Americans arrived but had not yet drawn off their booty, which was sitting in a column of wagons in the lane leading to the mill. An eyewitness explains that the British "were posted at a bridge at Millstone river, near Abraham Vannest's mill, which is two miles from Somerset Court House. In order more effectually to prevent our men crossing, the enemy had placed three field pieces on a hill, about 50 yards from the bridge, when our men found it impossible to cross there, they went down the river, broke through the ice, waded across the river up to their middles."

As this was taking place, the left wing surprised the Redcoats guarding the wagons. "We immediately marched towards the road [after fording the river], and fired upon the Baggage Guard, who were retreated that way."[8] Another militiaman led one company in toward the wagons and later recalled the encounter: "They had plundered the mill of grain and flour, and were on their way back to Brunswick, but had not got out of the lane leading from the mill to the great road. We headed [blocked] them in the lane. The team laden with the flour was the first we fell in with; the lane, 100 yards, was filled with 4-horse teams. Davis ordered us to fire, and then we shot part of the 1st team, which stopped the whole drove. The drivers left their teams and run. A guard escorting the teams made their escape."[9] So the plunder had been recovered, but the Redcoats still remained in strength down along the river.

Back at the bridge, the Americans wheeled their artillery piece into position and opened fire as the men of the left wing began a flanking operation. "The main body of the Enemy lay just over south of the Bridge," the militiaman recalled. "Before we crossed the River below, our main Body [right wing] began the Attack at the Bridge with one Field piece and made the Enemy give way. They continued their fire upon the Enemy some time. Our wing, after driving the Baggage Guard, pursued on and flanked the Enemy. After a short engagement, finding ourselves greatly overpowered with numbers, we received General Orders to retreat, having had 1 man killed and 2 wounded, and we had taken 2 of the enemy prisoners. We then retreated back to the River, lest our retreat should be cut off."[10] Dickinson had taken the British by surprise and had thwarted their foraging expedition in midcareer. The result was a superb operation. The haul for the Americans proved considerable, reportedly "43 baggage wagons, 104 horses, 115 head of cattle, and about 60–70 sheep."[11]

Local ambushes against small enemy patrols were one thing; turning back a significant operation of five hundred British and

Hessian regulars, supported by artillery, was quite another, and the Americans had every reason to crow. Washington was elated when he got the news, and he reported as such to Congress a few days later:

> My last to you was on the 20th instant. Since that, I have the pleasure to inform you, that General Dickinson, with about 400 Militia, has defeated a foraging Party of the Enemy of an equal number, and has taken forty Waggons and upwards of an hundred Horses, most of them of the English draft Breed, and a number of Sheep and Cattle which they had collected.
>
> The Enemy retreated with so much precipitation, that General Dickinson had only an opportunity of making nine prisoners, they were observed to carry off a good many dead and wounded in light Waggons.
>
> This action happened near Somerset Court House on Millstone River. General Dickinsons behaviour reflects the highest honour upon him, for tho' his Troops were all raw, he lead them thro' the River, middle deep, and gave the enemy so severe a charge, that, altho' supported by three field pieces, they gave way and left their Convoy."[12]

The British must have been stunned by news of this event, for they immediately doubled the strength of their next foraging expedition, and even this met with some resistance. Archibald Robertson confirms the plight of the first expedition at Van Nest's Mill and the augmented manpower of the subsequent mission: "Part of this Corps [the forage party at Van Nest's]," he wrote, "was attacked by the Rebels, which occasion'd such disorder Amongst the Waggon Drivers that 42 Waggons were left behind. 21st [of January] Sir William Erskine went out the same route with 1,000 men. We return'd with our forage without Molestation. Part of the Guards that went towards Boundbrook had a little Cannonading. They had 2 or 3 men wounded."[13] The British army was far larger and more professionally trained than the Americans. For them to be forced to mount one thousand men simply to go out into the country to forage for feed and provisions provides a good indication of just how violent and steadfast the resistance in New Jersey had become.

If the embarrassment at Van Nest's Mill had been an isolated incident for the British, it might have been easily forgotten. Unfortunately, it was far from isolated. Early in January, for instance, a group of American forces attacked a superior force of the king's troops along the Raritan River, about three miles north of Brunswick. They drove off the Redcoats, taking six hundred head of cattle, fifty wagons, and horses that were so emaciated they could barely walk—a clear indicator of the increasing lack of fodder in the region. Then, on January 16, British General John Vaughan was almost killed on the road near Brunswick when a bushwhacker, hidden behind a fence, took a shot at him. The unknown bushwhacker was immediately dispatched by a dragoon, but the point had been made that no one on the British side was safe, even near Brunswick. The following night, local militias attacked a picket post at Brunswick, losing three men and thirty captured but underscoring the same hostile message.[14]

On January 16, at Bonhamtown, a small village on the Raritan River between Amboy and Brunswick, an American force reportedly three hundred and fifty strong attacked a British unit of seven hundred, killing a colonel and twenty men outright while mortally wounding a lieutenant colonel and thirty to forty infantrymen. Then, at Woodbridge, a hamlet northeast of Bonhamtown, on the 23rd, American forces numbering three hundred assaulted two full British regiments, killing numerous officers and regulars while losing only two of their own, those taken as prisoners. North of Woodbridge on January 15, Colonel Oliver Spencer led his New Jersey militia against some one hundred Hessians at Connecticut Farms (modern-day Union) in an extended skirmish, killing several and taking seventy prisoners. A few days later, New Jersey militiamen attacked a foraging party of Waldeckers near Springfield, killing several while taking the remainder prisoner without suffering a single loss.[15] For the British, it was becoming increasingly evident that their efforts to subdue the population were having the opposite effect.

The British and Hessian troops responded with wanton violence, often cruel and general in nature. Reverend Alexander MacWhorter, a pastor from Newark, had fled the area when the British invaded New Jersey in late 1776, only later to return to discover a scene of desolation.

In a letter later published in the *Pennsylvania Evening Post*, he wrote: "Great have been the ravages committed by the British troops in this part of the country, as to what has been done by them in Trenton, Princeton, &c you have seen. Their footsteps with us are marked with desolation and ruin of every kind."

Not knowing from whom the shots against them were being fired, the British responded viciously against Tory and rebel families alike, making no distinction. Violence only begets violence, and rape often becomes a cruel byproduct. So it had become in New Jersey. MacWhorter continues: "Yea, not only common soldiers, but officers, even British officers, four or five, sometimes more, sometimes in a gang, went about the town by night, entering into houses, and openly inquiring for women...Their plundering is universal, and their robberies so atrocious, that I cannot fully describe their conduct...John Ogden, Esq; an aged man, who had never done much in the controversy one way or another; they carried out of his house everything they thought worth bearing away; they ripped open the feather beds, scattered the feathers in the air, and carried the ticks with them; broke his desk to pieces and tore and destroyed a great number of important papers, deeds, wills &c. belonging to himself and others, and insulted and abused the old gentlemen in the most outrageous manner, threatening to hang him, and sometimes to cut off his head."[16]

Violence quickly became universal. The complaints of rebel sympathizers, such as MacWhorter's, were being echoed in number and volume, just as this article taken from the *New York Gazette and the Weekly Mercury*, a trumpet of the Loyalist cause, points out. "The Ravages of the Rebel Army in and about the Jersies are shocking to Humanity. Several Persons upon the bare Suspicion of being well-affected to legal Government, have had their Property seized, and their Houses and Furniture entirely demolished. They have harassed the poor Farmers in general, that all Agriculture is stopt, and every Prospect is opened to an approaching Famine."[17]

While Reverend MacWhorter's examples of pillaging certainly had the ring of truth about them, there is little doubt that both sides took advantage of the situation to enrich themselves. Unfortunately, many of the New Jersey militia units seemed as actively engaged in plundering their neighbors as they were in contesting the British. This pattern of behavior drove General Washington to distraction, as it ran counter to the entire point of the Revolution and increasingly turned the citizens against the Continental cause. He responded to this in late January with a letter to William Livingston, governor of New Jersey. Written in the most emphatic language imaginable at the time, the correspondence clearly expresses Washington's deep sense of unease and frustration.

> The irregular and disjointed State of the Militia of this province, makes it necessary for me to inform you, that unless a Law is passed by your Legislature to reduce them to some order, and oblige them to turn out in a different Manner from what they have hitherto done, we shall bring very few into the Field, and even those few, will render little or no Service.

> Their Officers are generally of the lowest Class of people, and instead of setting a good Example to their Men, are leading them into every kind of Mischeif, one Species of which is, plundering the Inhabitants under the pretence of their being Tories. A Law should in my Opinion be passed, to put a stop to this kind of lawless Rapine, for unless there is something done to prevent it, the people will throw themselves of choice into the hands of the British Troops.

> But your first object should be a well regulated Militia Law. The people, put under good Officers, would behave in quite another manner, and not only render real Service as Soldiers, but would protect, instead of distressing the inhabitants.[18]

As this violence escalated, the road network around Bound Brook and Quibbletown became a focal point of contention, and Hessian Johann Ewald became hotly involved in the mushrooming bloodshed. The Hessian Jägers, or light troops, were particularly adept at skirmishing, and their sharpshooting skills were promptly put to use. "On the 8th patrols were conducted toward Bound Brook and Quibbletown," he tells us, "places not yet occupied by the enemy. The news arrives that Washington had taken up his headquarters in Morristown, and their entire army had been quartered in and around this area, partly in cantonment and partly in wooden huts. The advanced posts were at Baskin Ridge." Soon, however, the Americans began expanding their operations, and the two sides eventually clashed in the countryside surrounding Quibbletown. Ewald continues: "On the 12th we received information that the enemy was marching toward Quibbletown and Bound Brook, and from this time on we patrolled constantly as far as these areas." Then on the 13th: "The Americans entered Bound Brook and Quibbletown and visited us toward ten o'clock in the evening. Their intention was to surprise my post nearby, but since they were greeted with shots from the sentries, they merely fired several hundred shots in the direction of our picket's fire and withdrew."

Ambush and skirmishing grew in intensity over the coming days as the Americans sought to disrupt British movements and, in particular, their foraging attempts. Thus, a fatal bullet might be fired at any time from behind any tree, stone fence, or barn door. "The Jägers post duty now became quite serious," Ewald wrote, "since Bound brook and Quibbletown were less than one hour's march away [from Brunswick]. The teasing now occurred daily, and when they did not visit us, we rendered the honors to the Americans. Not only did the men have to stay dressed day and night but they had to be kept together, the horses constantly saddled, and everything packed."[19] This constituted an intense, nerve-racking form of warfare, with precious little rest or respite from fear, precisely the stressful environment the Americans hoped to induce by their constant pecking.

On January 23, a British unit of six hundred men and two cannons, while marching from Brunswick towards Amboy, was attacked south of Quibbletown. The Americans were led by Colonel Mordecai Buckner, his advanced elements under the direction of Lt. Colonel Richard Parker. Parker, leading men from the Sixth Virginia Regiment, immediately attacked the Crown troops, who were conveying wagons from Brunswick to Amboy. Parker continued the attack for some twenty minutes, reportedly inflicting heavy losses upon the enemy before having to withdraw due to a lack of support.[20] Reports of Buckner's failure to rapidly support his junior officer's attack made their way up the chain of command all the way to Morristown, where, once again, Washington was forced to act. "Had Colo. Buckner come up with the main Body," the commander in chief wrote, "Colo. Parker and the other Officers think we should have put them to rout, as their confusion was very great and their ground disadvantageous. I have ordered Buckner under Arrest, and shall bring him to tryal, to answer so extraordinary a piece of Conduct."[21]

An additional aggravation was repeatedly being brought to Washington's attention at the time: that being the confusion of loyalties and subsequent contrary behavior brought about by Howe's "Proclamation" of November 1776 upon the citizens of the region. Some were still abiding by Howe's terms; others actively agitating against the United States; others confused and operating in a state of limbo. So, under the authority granted by Congress, the commander in chief decided to issue a proclamation of his own, clarifying the situation and demanding loyalty to the United States only. Issued at Morristown, dated January 25, 1777, and printed in newspapers from Connecticut to Virginia, in part, it read:

> I do therefore, in behalf of the United States, by virtue of the powers committed to me by Congress, hereby strictly command and require every person, having subscribed such declaration, taken such oaths, and accepted protection and certificates from Lord or General Howe, or any person acting under their authority, forthwith to repair to Head-Quarters, or to the quarters of the nearest general officer of the Continental Army or Militia (until farther provision can be made by the civil authority) and there deliver up such protections, certificates, and passports, and take the oath of allegiance to the United States of America.[22]

In early January 1777, the British believed they had Washington's army cornered against the banks of the Delaware River, ripe for destruction, an end to hostilities clearly within reach. By the end of that month, however, it was the British who had been pinned essentially into the narrow environs of Brunswick and Amboy, and, even there, they were far from safe. The calculus of victory and defeat had been turned literally on its head, yet the British remained seemingly unfazed by this sudden and remarkable inversion of chess pieces. In late January, for instance, Stephen Kemble jotted this note in his journal: "*Friday, Jan 31st* Nothing Extraordinary."[23]

Around the same time, however, Captain Johann Ewald, out on the front lines near Quibbletown, seemed to have a decidedly different view of things. "Although everything necessary for the men was arriving in abundance from New York," he tells us, "nevertheless the horses also had to be fed, and the little fodder which we found in this area could not last long. For this reason foraging had to be undertaken, and since the Americans were close on our necks, we could not procure any forage without shedding blood."[24]

As February approached, that bloodshed would only escalate.

CHAPTER SIX
Drake's Farm

*I*n early February, the Americans increased their operations around Brunswick in an effort to starve the British of that one commodity they needed most: feed for their animals. "The foraging and scouting parties of the Americans through the country between Amboy and New Brunswick," writes historian Woodford Clayton, "effectually cut off all communication with the latter place during the month of February, excepting by the river Raritan. Lord Cornwallis had his headquarters at New Brunswick, and his detachment became quite short of provisions."[1] Like a screw being slowly tightened, this intensifying stress only served to heighten the tension and bloodshed. The British and Hessians, to remain an active fighting force, required forage. That meant larger, more heavily manned expeditions to try and counteract the rebel opposition.

On the very first day of February, the violence intensified, Redcoats emerging from Brunswick to forage in considerable force. Captain Archibald Robertson was marching with the column that morning, and he provides our narrative with his recollections. "Went this morning on a foraging party with Sir William Erskine towards Metuchen," about six miles northeast of Brunswick. This party, Robertson explains, consisted initially of about nine hundred troops but then subsumed another foraging expedition of about one hundred and eighty, bringing the total to roughly one thousand. The heavy snow that had fallen just days before was melting in the wintry fields as they approached Drake's Farm, a homestead near modern-day Metuchen.

This larger British party initially fared well, loading their wagons without interference and with the famed Forty-Second (Royal Highland)

Regiment, also called the Black Watch, standing guard as the foragers grabbed what they wanted. "The Black Watch stood guard over the fields where haystacks were still standing as Harcourt's men gathered the hay and loaded it into wagons."[2] This work went on unimpeded until about two-thirty in the afternoon, when "we were attacked by a Body of the Rebels," Robertson says, "consisting of about 4 or 500 who made a push at the Head of the Waggons where the 42d drew up in the Road and kept up a very hot fire for upwards of 10 minutes." This American force consisted of about seven hundred men of the Fifth Virginia and Connecticut troops under Colonel Charles Scott, who had marched from Quibbletown earlier that morning on a scouting expedition toward Metuchen. Elisha Bostwick from Connecticut was with Scott's troops, and he describes the action in his *Memoirs*. "On joining our army at Morristown, the enemy having withdrawn made it necessary we should have Strong Guards on our out posts," he wrote. "I was de-tach'd on one of them of 300 men for a fortnight tower [tour] under Col. Scott for a fornight during which time we all Slept on our armes & in our cloths a part of us lay at a place called Quibble town, had Sundry Skirmishes one of which was Severe."

Early on, Scott, accompanied by about ninety men, including Bostwick, went forward, where they ran into several British cavalrymen, who were also guarding British foragers. Scott's force promptly attacked the horsemen, then hastened down the road toward Drake's Farm, where they arrived just after two o'clock in the afternoon. Here, they located the main British foraging party on the hills nearby. Scott attacked the Black Watch, which was soon reinforced by about three hundred British infantrymen along with one fieldpiece, which was hustled into line, then promptly opened fire. Elisha Bostwick remembered the instructions Scott had given them before the shooting had started. Scott understood that, in the excitement of battle, men tended to fire high, thus often missing the target altogether. So he warned them to fire lower, insisting they "bring down your pieces and fire at their legs," because the musket tended to recoil and fire high. A heated skirmish ensued, in which Scott, after about fifteen minutes of intense musketry and now considerably outgunned, was forced back up the hill he had just come down.

At this point in the action, the remainder of Scott's Fifth Virginia appeared in three distinct columns atop the hill and began deploying. Unfortunately for them, they were deploying directly into the mouth of a trap laid for them by Erskine. Archibald Robertson recorded the moment: "The 1st Battalion Grenadiers advanced likewise on the right of the Hessians towards the Woods where the Rebels retreated, but all of a Sudden a Column of Rebels appeared within 250 yards coming to us over rising Ground in Front."[3] Erskine, thinking quickly, sent his light infantry and grenadiers on a flanking movement, which eventually forced the entire American force to withdraw to a tree line about one-quarter mile distant. Additional British artillery was then brought up and, sweeping the field, held the Americans at bay for the remainder of the afternoon.[4]

Had it ended there, the incident at Drake's Farm would have passed as nothing more than one more intense skirmish during a period of increasingly fierce skirmishes. But it did not end there. Bostwick describes the ugly after-action events at Drake's Farm: "We drove them at first but they brought a field piece to bear upon us & we having none re-treated, leaving our Wounded in the field among which our Adjutant, by the name of Kelley an active Charming officer. He was wounded in the flesh thigh by a musket ball & the Soldiers endeavored to bring him off but being prest [pressed] up on he told them to leave him Saying he must be a prisoner but horrid to tell, as soon as they came to him while asking for quarters they took his own Rifle & with the butt of it broke & Pounded his Skull to pieces plundered his pockets by cutting them off & a Soldier that belong'd to my mess Andrew Cushman, a pleasant youth was left among the wounded & with the rest was all murdered by repeated Stabs with the bayonet."[5]

Just as at Princeton, where Hugh Mercer had been savagely attacked and bayoneted repeatedly, far beyond even the violent norms of the day, at Drake's Farm, the same excessive violence was witnessed by many more Americans than Bostwick alone. For these eyewitnesses, the horrendous actions at Drake's Farm on the part of the victorious Redcoats crossed the line between legitimate warfare—no matter how cruel and violent—and murder. Five Americans had been left wounded on the field, while two officers, Lt. William Kelly and Lt. John Gregory, were being helped off due to their wounds. As reported by Bostwick, the British fell upon them all, repeatedly bayoneting the wounded and clubbing them to death with the butts of their muskets. It was a barbarous act and a gruesome scene. American Sergeant Tomas McCay seconded Bostwick's version of events: "They dashed out their brains with their muskets and ran them through with their bayonets, made them like sieves. Tis [this] was barbarity to the utmost."[6] Supporting both McCay's and Bostwick's reports, a Virginia officer's letter later appeared in Williamsburg's *Virginia Gazette* on February 28, which stated, "He [Kelly] was carried off the field with a flesh wound only, and five more Virginians; but the enemy coming on that ground, murdered them by beating out their brains, with barbarity exceeding that of the savages."[7]

Washington, painfully aware of the ongoing British atrocities across New Jersey, was naturally outraged when he received word of the incident at Drake's Farm and wrote accordingly to Samuel Chase:

> There has been another Instance of Barbarity in a Skirmish on the 1st of this Month. Lieut. Kelly of the 5th Virginia Regt was slightly wounded in the Thigh, but before he could get off the Field he was overtaken and cruelly murthered. Gen. Stephen sent in a flag to Sr William Erskine complaining of this savage Manner of carrying on war, but I do now know his answer. I have heard that orders were given at Trenton to make no prisoners, but kill all that fell into their Hands, but of this there is no proof.[8]

Washington then wrote to John Hancock, explaining that he had previously complained to General Howe of the British treatment of American prisoners at Princeton but had received no satisfaction. The problem—which the commander in chief well understood— was that if these barbarous actions continued, American troops would soon retaliate in kind, regardless of any orders to the contrary, and the war would very soon devolve into a murderous bloodbath with no end in sight.

> I remonstrated with Genl Howe upon the treatment of our wounded at princetown, you will see by the inclosed letter from him, that he disavows and detests the proceeding. But I fear that too much encouragement is given to such barbarous Behaviour by the British Officers, for in a late Skirmish in which Sr William Erskine commanded, Lieut. Kelly of the 5th Virginia Regiment was slightly wounded in the thigh, but before he could get off the field, he was

overtaken and murthered in a most cruel manner. General Stephen informed me that he would write to Sir William and inform him, that unless such practices were put to a stop, our Soldiers would not be restrained from making Retaliation.[9]

These were frustrating times for General Washington. Aside from the fact that his army was well below strength, thus limited in terms of what could be accomplished offensively, news soon reached him that the offensive feint (or full attack, if practicable) he had repeatedly urged General Heath to perform above New York had ended in fiasco. Heath had approached Fort Independence—the British bastion—on January 18 in three separate columns, totaling about six thousand effective troops. The position was defended by two thousand Hessians, and Heath immediately demanded the full surrender of the fort, threatening to put the garrison to the sword if his demand was not met within twenty minutes.[10] The Hessian commander, apparently unimpressed, declined Heath's offer and simply opened on the Americans with the fort's artillery, causing pandemonium in the American ranks. Heath was forced to redeploy and begin a cannonade of his own, which proved ineffectual. Orders were issued to surround the fort and cut it off from resupply or reinforcement from the city, but these orders had to be rescinded when the weather warmed and the troops could not cross over the creeks due to thawing ice. Eventually, the British responded, attacking the Americans in several locations and forcing withdrawals. On January 29, Heath, in fear of an impending blizzard and a British relief expedition supposedly moving up the Hudson commanded by Lord Piercy, withdrew entirely, having accomplished nothing other than making a spectacle of his own incompetence.

When General Washington got word of the debacle, he was naturally angered and responded accordingly:

> This Letter is in addition to my public one of this date
> – It is a hint to you, and I do it with concern, that your
> conduct is censured (and by Men of sense and Judgement who have been with you on the Expedition to Fort Independence) as being fraught with too much caution, by which the Army has been disappointed, and in some degree disgraced.

Summons, as you did not attempt to fulfil your threats [the ridiculous threat of putting the entire garrison to the sword], was not only Idle but farcical; and will not fail turning the laugh exceedingly upon us...Why you should be so apprehensive of being surrounded, even if Lord Piercy had Landed, I cannot conceive – You know that Landing Men – procuring Horses – &ca is not the work of an hour – a day – or even a Week.[11]

The real problem for General Washington—as it had been and would continue to be throughout the entire war—was that, while the American colonies had raised their own militia units along with the occasional provincial regiment, the art of fighting a war in the European style was not widely understood or practiced. As a result, Washington's top lieutenants consisted of a bookshop owner, politicians, farmers, businessmen, and the like, who had, in some cases, read a bit about war but had little practical experience in fighting one. Some had gained limited practice in fighting Indians along the frontier—Daniel Morgan and John Stark, as examples—but even that involvement proved limited when it came to fighting battalions of trained fighting men with experienced officers on the open field of battle. Issues that may have been glaringly obvious to professional soldiers were often fumbled miserably by the Americans or overlooked entirely by American officers. They may have been intelligent and industrious, but they were all learning on the job, as was Washington himself. Predictably, the results for such a cadre of leaders were mixed at best and, at times, painfully incompetent.

As a result of this lack of senior leadership, the burden for logistical and operational planning across the entire country fell principally upon George Washington, and he was often forced to formulate these operations down to the most meticulous details in hopes of avoiding a fiasco. In early February, Washington decided that removing the animals and forage the British coveted from the Jersey countryside represented a far better strategy than trying to locate and contest their expeditions, wherever and whenever they might suddenly appear. To accomplish this task, he turned to General John Sullivan, a New Hampshire-born lawyer who had been appointed general by Congress in the early days of the war. Washington trusted him—for good reason—and, on February 3, outlined the plan he had in mind precisely as he wanted it executed.

Upon considering the bests Mode of distressing
the Enemy and rendering their situation still more
disagreeable, as well as retarding their early Operations in the Field; I have determined to remove out of
their reach all the Horses Waggons & fat Cattle, for
which purpose I have appointed Thursday Morning
next early for you, Genls Putman, Warner, & Dickinson to do it. In the mean time you will, in the best
& most private manner, collect the necessary Information where these Articles are. I mean that you shd
take a sufficient party to remove them from the whole
country lying between Quibble Town & the Sound,
eastward; approaching as near the Enemy as you can
in safety; I would by no means have you grasp at too
much, lest the Attempt may be entirely frustrated;
undertake to remove no more of them than You can
with the greatest Certainty & Success accomplish –
The forage in the Circle above described I shall let
remain till another time.[12]

The plan was executed on Thursday, February 6, by all officers
involved. It went off without a hitch and, fortunately, just before the
British moved to confiscate those items in exactly the area Washington
had pinpointed.

In any event, General Washington would have precious little time
to wring his hands over Heath's handling of the Fort Independence
operation or his secretive foraging venture in Jersey, for Ewald tells
us that very soon after Drake's Farm, Cornwallis had set his sights on
far bigger game. "Early on February 5, I received orders to report to
Osborn's quarters," he wrote. "Foraging was to be undertaken near
Quibbletown, commanded personally by Lord Cornwallis. General
Grant would make a feint at Samptown with two English regiments,
and General Mathew would make a fake attack against Bound Brook
with the Jägers and the Guards Brigade."

This operation clearly represented a serious leap forward in
British tactical thinking, and Cornwallis's more aggressive response
may have been the result of his having been outguessed and rattled
at Princeton. The sophistication involved in this latest plan suggests
Cornwallis had finally come to grips with the violent reality his troops

were daily facing in the field. The operation described by Ewald was, therefore, no mere foraging party, or even a powerfully reinforced foraging party, but a large-scale operation involving a three-pronged advance commanded by Cornwallis himself, presumably to drive off or decoy American units operating in the area. Since Samptown, Quibbletown, and Bound Brook were all within marching distance of one another, the British units would naturally be operating within supporting distance should a nasty fight develop at any one point. This is the sort of plan that might be executed against a respected foe, say, Frederick the Great's Prussian infantry, and it implies British thinking at the highest levels had dramatically shifted, whether they cared to admit that or not.

The operation began on February 8, Ewald's Jägers leading the way out of Brunswick. The Hessian captain's description of the force, of its power and nature, provides a clear glimpse into Cornwallis's current state of mind. "At daybreak on the 8th Lord Cornwallis set out," Ewald recorded in his diary. "I formed the advanced guard with fifty Jägers, supported by four hundred light infantry. Behind them followed four hundred Scots, one hundred dragoons, a number of light 6-pounders, four hundred English grenadiers, two Hessian grenadier battalions, the foragers, and the wagons, and four hundred Englishmen drawn from several regiments."

The Americans were ready and waiting along the road to Quibbletown, undeterred by the noticeable strength of the approaching enemy column. Indeed, stiff fighting broke out soon after the Redcoats departed Brunswick. "The road leading from Raritan Landing to Quibbletown ran continuously through the woods," Ewald explains, "in which three devastated plantations were situated." This terrain was perfect for an ambush, and in this, the Americans did not disappoint. "At the first plantation I ran into an enemy post of riflemen," wrote Ewald, "who withdrew after stubborn resistance, of whom several were killed and captured on their retreat." Ewald's Jägers chased after the retreating Americans, shots ringing out in the woods, tree-to-tree, as the rebels fell back into town. "We followed this party so swifly that we arrived with them before Quibbletown at the same time," the Hessian officer explains.

The Americans had previously placed a detachment of six hundred to seven hundred Virginia and Connecticut troops in Quibbletown, and they were determined to hold their position or, if forced to withdraw, to at least inflict serious casualties on the approaching Redcoats. The rebels had posted themselves in houses, along walls, behind trees, and in gardens, waiting for the British advance. Ewald continues: "The place [Quibbletown] lies on two hills, between which a creek winds through a ravine that is spanned by two bridges. The stone walls around the gardens as well as the houses on both sides of the ravine were occupied by enemy riflemen, who abandoned the village after strong resistance when artillery was brought up, and withdrew into the nearest wood on the other side of the village." By this point in time, it was clear that Cornwallis's overwhelming show of force had failed to produce the desired effect and, in fact, appeared only to be egging the rebels on.

Once the Americans had abandoned the town for the nearby woods, the British moved in and took control, initiating foraging operations, grabbing everything of use, including the supplies the American troops had stored there. To accomplish this, the Scots and light infantry took up defensive positions in Quibbletown, while an artillery battery was established on a nearby hill, capable of sweeping the town, the bridges, and all approaches. "I occupied the stone walls between the village and the wood with the Jägers," Ewald tells us, "where I skirmished steadily with the enemy as long as the foraging continued."

As the gunfire persisted, the Americans extended their lines, however, eventually overlapping both flanks of Ewald's position. With the Scots and light infantry still behind him in the town for support, the situation remained stable but with dicey implications. "I took my position in the form of a semicircle," wrote the Hessian, "and discovered that the enemy was deployed along the wood to the right and left in such a manner that I was outflanked from both sides. But since Quibbletown was occupied, I did not run a risk of being cut off." But Ewald quickly discovered that, while skirmishing from behind stone-walls with the Scots behind him was one thing, abandoning those walls in retreat would prove quite another.

The rebels were in the woods in great numbers and were simply waiting for an opportune moment to attack. Heavy skirmishing went on into mid-afternoon, when, as the foragers pulled out, the Jägers received orders to fall back. "I received orders to retreat, which," says Ewald, "in full view of the enemy, was very disagreeable." In fact, as the Jägers stood and departed their cover, all hell broke loose. "I had hardly begun the movement when I was so heavily attacked from all sides by a vast swarm of riflemen that only a miracle of bravery by my men could save me." Here, Ewald and his Jägers Corps were forced to run a gauntlet of whizzing musket balls, trying desperately to get to one of the bridges and the safety beyond. "Nevertheless," he writes, "I reached the village where the crossing over the bridges were covered by the battery."

As Ewald's Jägers sprinted for their lives into town, the Americans reoccupied the buildings on one side of the ravine, dragging in artillery of their own while putting up continuous fire. "The enemy took possession of the outlying houses on the other side and erected cannon behind stone walls," Ewald recalled, "whereupon a stubborn fight occurred and many brave men were lost." The rebels may have respected the British artillery for good reason, but they appeared to have no problem going toe-to-toe with the Scots, Jägers, and light infantry—some of the cream of the British line—once their artillery had limbered up and moved off to a new position.

As the Redcoats pulled out of Quibbletown, their forage in tow, things grew increasingly hot for Ewald and his Jägers, who, as usual, were tasked once again with the dirty work. "I received orders here to form the rear guard and two companies of light infantry joined me," he wrote. "The road was not more than five to six hundred paces from the village up to the wood, where several cannon had been placed to cover my retreat." Which was all well and good, but the artillery once again limbered up and pulled back once the Jägers reached the woods, where Ewald and his rearguard "was left on my own." The Americans now pursued the British rearguard—skirmishing and firing from behind trees and rocks—all the way back to Brunswick, where at last, says Ewald—perhaps with a sigh of relief—"we reached our outposts."[13]

Casualty counts during these foraging engagements were decidedly unreliable, but it is clear from Ewald's account that the fighting in Quibbletown on the 8th raged for a good part of the day and was at times severe. Of this episode, while the Hessian claimed that "a stubborn fight occurred," Archibald Robertson later wrote: "on the whole we had only 4 men wounded."[14] Well, which was it? As stated previously, when it comes to analyzing British thoughts and intentions, it is probably best to set words and lists aside and focus instead on their ensuing actions. To that end, the measures they adopted after this clash on the 8th make it clear that, despite all the elite power that had been marshaled in hopes of staving off the rebels, the mission had been far less than successful. In fact, Ewald puts it plainly: "Since the army would have been gradually destroyed through this foraging, from here on the forage was procured from New York."[15] In other words, it was now emphatically understood by Cornwallis that no amount of British manpower would prevail while foraging in the New Jersey countryside against these angry swarms of rebel militia and that further attempts to do so would result only in the eventual annihilation of their army. Other lines of supply, no matter how difficult or cumbersome, would have to be established.

In mid-February, Washington wrote again to John Hancock, a letter in which he appears to express a certain level of satisfaction, at least as far as his operations across New Jersey were concerned:

> Since I had the honor of addressing you on the 5th Instt [Instant, meaning of this month] no event of an important and interesting nature has occurred, unless the Successes of our parties in foraging & bringing off Several Horses, Waggons & some fat Cattle, and Sheep, which were contiguous to, and around the Enemy' Lines, are considered as such. I then mentioned, that I had a Scheme in contemplation which was happily accomplished the next day without any loss. The Enemy, in turn, have made frequent efforts in that way, but with little success. When ever they made the Attempts, it never failed to produce a Skirmish.[16]

In January and February, the British desperately needed supplies and feed for their animals. As a result of American resistance, however, they had been forced to adopt the expedient of guarding their foraging parties with large numbers of troops and field artillery whenever they ventured into the countryside. The rebels, on the other hand, had adopted the simple policy of violent obstruction whenever and wherever the British might appear. Clearly, this forage war in New Jersey had become a bitter contest, not only of military power but of willpower. And as the smoke momentarily cleared in mid-February—whether gauging the results from Morristown or Brunswick—it appeared the Americans had taken round one.

CHAPTER SEVEN
Ash Swamp

*I*n mid-February, temperatures plunged, and the snows swept hard and deep across much of New Jersey. The widespread snow, deep drifts, and brutal cold imposed a natural hiatus on any plans for offensive maneuver, except in those outposts nearest Brunswick, where, by February, gunfire had become a way of life, regardless of the meteorological conditions. "From this time on until the end of March," writes Ewald, "nothing important happened due to the constant high snow, except for the daily skirmishing of our patrols and the continual alarms of the outposts on both sides."[1]

Meanwhile, at Morristown, the same wide-ranging list of troubles still plagued the American commander in chief, only now amplified by British reinforcements who recently arrived from Rhode Island. These additional troops added new weight to Cornwallis's force at Brunswick, in turn causing General Washington to fret anew as to Howe's future plans. Money—or the consistent lack thereof—proved for Washington as ubiquitous a fact as it was an unsolvable problem, and more than once, he complained to Congress: "It is with much concern," he wrote, "that the situation of our Affairs obliges me to mention so frequently the want of Money, especially when I am persuaded every means are used to furnish it. Our distress on this Account, is great indeed, and the injury the Service receives almost inconceivable. Not a day – an Hour or scarcely a minute passes without complaint & applications on this head. The recruiting the Regiments is most materially retarded by it."[2] Often, he could not pay the troops he had on hand, nor could the recruitment officers bring aboard fresh regiments without the money required to pay them. It was up to the states to raise capital through taxation, but often, the states—who alone could raise funds in this manner—were negligent in this regard. Hence, the "Continental army," like an invalid in need of medicine but lacking the funds to procure it, hovered at Morristown in a state of pathetic impotence, incapable of even defending itself should the British decide to pay them a visit. Mercifully for Washington and his army, Mother Nature had canceled all visits for the time being, but that good fortune, everyone knew, would not last forever.

As the snow flew, Elisha Bostwick, whom we last heard from during the ugly clash at Drake's Farm, served out his term of actual service and headed off to Morristown to collect his pay before setting off for home in Connecticut. "With this tour of duty my term of service in the Connecticut line & six weeks Service expired," he wrote, "I then return'd to headquarters at Morristown, Febry 15th 1777." Unfortunately for the men of the Connecticut Line—and underscoring Washington's complaints about adequate funding—when they "came back to headquarters at Morristown," Bostwick continues, "the Money had not come on to pay us off & one Morning Col Hinshaw came into a house where there was a roomful of us he took a Chair & Seated himself before the fire among us and gave us to understand that his Excellency had sent him to inform us that the Money was expected daily & hourly & that he thank's us for our Services & requested that none would go off without pay."

Whether their payroll had been delayed by heavy snows, cold, the British, or Congress was never made clear, but for Bostwick and his mates, the wait ended well. For after but a few days, he tells us, "The Money Soon come and we were all honorably paid off in Continental Money." Bidding the army farewell, he promptly headed out the door, "wading in the Snow returnd home on foot to my fathers house." Like many who fought in the war, Bostwick believed firmly in the Revolutionary cause and wanted to reenlist in the Continental service. But the troubles he discovered at home forced him to remain nearby in the local militia. He explains: "It was my choice to have Engaged again in the Continental establishment & I had offers as good as I deserv'd or desired, but alas the Situate of my fathers family, both father & Mother totally unable to provide for themselves & Samuel my younger brother in Yale

College who must leave his Education if he Should Stay at home any longer – I then accepted of a Lieut. Commission in my old company in the Militia from thence I per-form'd every duty & all alarms to close of the war in 1783."[3]

Despite the deep snow and cold, fighting continued around Quibbletown, and shots were exchanged on an almost-daily basis. On February 20, for instance, a party of rebels attacked a British foraging party on the outskirts of the village, driving off their guards and killing two dragoons. The rebels took twenty wagons loaded with feed from the Redcoats while suffering no casualties themselves. Then, the very next day, "The New Jersey militiamen beat back the Crown picket guard, killed eight men, and brought off fifteen loads of hay without losing a man."[4] The fighting in and around Quibbletown remained constant throughout February. "Scarcely a day passed when we did not have to stand under arms for hours in the deepest snow,"[5] Ewald wrote in his diary.

At Morristown, Washington fretted over what Howe and Cornwallis had in mind, and increasingly, he came to the belief that they intended to launch a major attack his way. On February 19, he wrote to General Horatio Gates, expressing his worst fear: "The enemy certainly reinforced at Brunswic, & the corresponding Intelligence from every Quarter, induce me to believe that They will no longer suffer themselves to be cooped up within such narrow, disagreeable Limits – Tis given out by them That they mean to move this way – but this may be a Blind to make their March towards the Delaware the more secure." By "Blind," Washington meant what we would term disinformation today, a cover for their real target, which might be Philadelphia, the American capital. After providing Gates with instructions to secure all boats along the Delaware River so as to impede any such movement by the Redcoats, Washington added this ominous P.S.: "Intelligence from several quartrs this Moment recd makes a Movement of the Enemy very soon almost absolutely certain."[6] From an operational perspective, at this point in the war, Washington's thinking had narrowed Howe's next move down to three possibilities: another strong foraging operation, a strike against Morristown, or lastly, a full campaign to seize Philadelphia.

From the 1777 map by William Faden, geographer to the King and to the Prince of Wales.

By February 20, the commander in chief's instincts appeared confirmed, and he wrote to John Hancock to clarify the situation, noting the drastic difference in strength then presumed between the two opposing forces in New Jersey.

> The principal design of this, is to inform you, that we have strong reasons to believe, that the Enemy are on the point of making some push. What their Object is, whether it be to beat up our Quarters and to extend their own – to make a large forage and collection of provender, of which they are in great want – or to turn their views towards the Delaware, is a matter of incertainty; But it seems probable, that One of these things they have in contemplation. Such of their Troops as have returned from Rd. Island, have landed at Amboy, and with them Several peices of Heavy Artillery. General Howe is come over too, & it is said Lord Peircy. Their number at Brunswic, & the landing place, before the arrival of this last reinforcement, was estimated from Seven to Eight Thousand.

I have ordered the utmost vigilance and attention to be observed at our Several posts, to guard against Surprizes, and every preparation is made, that the weak and feeble state of our little Army will admit of. At this time we are only about Four Thousand strong – a force You will suppose unequal to a successful opposition, if they were not Militia, and far too small for the exigencies of our Affairs.

It is clear from this correspondence that Washington considered his position at Morristown, if not untenable, at least difficult to defend, should Howe make a move in that direction. While the recent snows had made an immediate strike unlikely, March and warmer weather were rapidly approaching. Washington's gaze had to be increasingly focused on the coming spring, the time when European armies generally began campaigning activities. Once the snow melted, the roads dried, and grasses began sprouting green in New Jersey meadows, the British would no doubt be on the march; the only question being in which direction.

Equally as worrying as the current imbalance of forces was the disturbing news reaching Morristown that the new Continental regiments being raised across the states were not being equipped with muskets. This raised the very real possibility that the "New Army" might arrive on Washington's doorstep in worse than useless condition—mouths to be fed but with no fighting capacity. "I wish to be informed," Washington asked Hancock, "how the Regiments that are raising are to be Armed & the provision that has been made for the same. I have reason to fear, indeed I am convinced, that there is a great deficiency in many, if not the whole of the States in this Article [muskets]. Every Letter that I receive from them, mentions their want & calls for supplies."[7]

Meanwhile, the British were plotting bold schemes to bring the war to a rapid close. The overarching design in this regard was a campaign to sever New England from the other states by means of a three-pronged campaign. One of the prongs would move up the Hudson River from New York City under the direction of General William Howe. A second would march east from Lake Ontario under the command of General Barry St. Leger. Finally, the third movement was to proceed south from Montreal under General John Burgoyne, ultimately to meet the other two forces on the Hudson River some-where near Albany, New York, effectively cutting off New England from the other warring states. On a map in distant London, no doubt this appeared to be a sound and workable strategy. But no one in London really understood what the American wilderness between Canada and Albany was actually like. Here, few roads existed through miles upon miles of forest, and many of the virtually uncountable creeks and rivers that crisscrossed the countryside were unbridged. Confounding this strategic coordination was the sheer distance and time involved in communicating between policy makers in London and their field commanders in North America. Burgoyne would also discover, much to his chagrin, that the Americans were perfectly capable of felling trees over usable roads and destroying those bridges that did exist, greatly delaying his march.

While General Washington could correspond with Congress in weeks or even days only, communicating with London for the British high command—depending on the winds, fair or foul—could take weeks just for an express to reach London, then months more for a return response. Consequently, the situation on the ground for the British in real time could easily be entirely different than it had been when the initial strategic thinking had been put into writing, making much of their communication hopelessly outdated even before it arrived.

Exemplifying this unwieldy structure, in March 1777, Lord Germain wrote to Sir Guy Carleton in Quebec, explaining the details of the Hudson River expedition he wanted to be undertaken while simul-taneously demonstrating the profoundly unreliable nature of their system of communication. "My letter of the 22nd of August 1776," he wrote, "was entrusted to the care of Capt. Le Maitre, one of your Aide-de-camps. After having been three times in the Gulph of St. Lawrence, he had the mortification to find it impossible to make his passage to Quebec, and therefore returned to England with my dispatch." Then some eight months later, Germain wrote again to Carleton, hoping, it can be presumed, that this newest dispatch would find Carleton sometime within the next month or two—almost a year after the orig-inal instructions had been drafted. Nevertheless, since this was state-of-the-art at the time, no other options were available for the British to communicate across the vast Atlantic, a reality that was a decided disadvantage. Here, then, Lord Germain goes on to lay out the crown's thinking regarding the Hudson operation:

Upon these accounts, and with a view to quelling the rebellion as soon as possible, it is become highly necessary that the most speedy junction of the two armies should be effected, and therefore as the securing and good government of Canada absolutely require your presence there, it is the King's determination to leave about 3,000 men under your command for the defense and duties of that province, and to employ the remainder of your army upon expeditions – the one under the command of Lieut.- General Burgoyne, who is to force his way to Albany, and the other under the command of Lieut.- General St. Leger, who is to make a diversion on the Mohawk River.[8]

This communique did not reach Carleton until the spring of 1777; hence, the operation he outlined would not get underway until the late spring of that year. Burgoyne's force, numbering seven thousand—comprised of British and provincial regulars, Hessian and Brunswick auxiliaries, Loyalists, Canadian militia, and screened by parties from several Indian nations—would ultimately initiate his portion of the campaign on June 14, with a movement southward up the lake but with no knowledge of the whereabouts or intentions of the other commands he was supposed to rendezvous with near Albany. His initial objective was Fort Ticonderoga, at the junction of Lake Champlain and Lake George. Initially moving by water, Burgoyne's force was easily able to gain the southern portion of the lake. But, as we shall see, fighting in the New Jersey Campaign would have a significant impact on Howe's strategic thinking, thus leaving Burgoyne alone and helpless in the wilderness, ripe for failure and defeat. Howe believed Burgoyne would have no trouble defeating whatever American opposition he faced, but this miscalculation would have significant repercussions.

As Germain was thinking large at Whitehall, the New Jersey countryside erupted anew on Sunday, February 23. Archibald Robertson sets the scene: "A Strong Foraging party consisting of the 3d. Brigade and two Flank Corps from Rhode Island [British troops recently arrived from Rhode Island] went out from Amboy."[9] The British mission consisted of about one thousand, nine hundred troops accompanied by six pieces of artillery, and they headed out from Amboy through Spanktown toward Ash Swamp, a large bog near what is now modern-day Scotch Plains. Continental troops under General William Maxwell, along with local militias, soon got word of the expedition and raced to oppose it. Musket balls began flying around nine-thirty in the morning about two miles from the swamp as the British van stumbled upon scattered units of militia resistance.

Lieutenant John Peebles, marching with a company of the Forty-Second (Royal Highland) Regiment of Foot, had been tasked that morning by Colonel Mungo Campbell with leading the British advance. "I was ordered with 20 men to be the advance guard," he tells us. "When we had marched about a mile & a half to the Westward, I discovered a body of the Rebels on a hill." Peebles sent back word of his discovery to Colonel Campbell, but his advance party was immediately spotted by a small group of Americans, who began to close in. "I went up & met them & received their fire from behind a fence," Peebles wrote. "I moved on to a fence in front & order'd my men to fire, which we continued to do at each other for a few minutes when they gave way." Peebles then joined the main British detachment, which, after forming, began advancing toward the Americans, who were "...coming down through a Swamp & making straight for a wood." Again ordered forward, Peebles took a position along "...a fence at the edge of the wood with my little party which were reduced now to 14 or 15."[10]

The Americans, now outgunned, retreated into the swamp, followed by elements of the Redcoat vanguard, as the main body of the British detachment continued to come up. But the British advance became disjointed, unexpectedly offering their flank to American musketry. Peebles tells us that "...when they [the British] got up to the fence they soon found themselves gall'd by a fire on their right, & those [Americans] on our front being all posted behind trees almost flank'd the 42nd Company." Here, a significant exchange of musketry and cannon fire ensued for hours, rumbling the local area and ultimately setting many of the trees in Ash Swamp ablaze. Orders were eventually given for the forward British elements to withdraw, but Peebles, unaware of those orders, soon found himself essentially alone. "I remain'd at my post till I had not one man left near me, except Jno. Carr lying wounded, & fired away all of my Cartridges, when seeing the Rascals coming pretty close up I took to my heels and & ran back to the Company under a heavy fire which thank God I escaped."

Also engaged that morning was Lieutenant James Murray of the Fifty-Seventh Regiment of Foot, likewise operating in Colonel Campbell's detachment. Murray recalled that they soon discovered a large body of rebels ahead. He explains, "After a little of the usual prelude, firing betwixt the advanced parties, we were ordered to withdraw." This was when Peebles was mistakenly left alone out front and had to run for his life. But Murray also tells us, "In a few minutes our attention was awakened with a rattling of small arms upon our right, which we soon discovered to be our other Division driving the enemy before them. This was the signal for us to advance, which we did with all expedition inclining to the left in order to cut off their [the Americans] retreat." Murray's company then advanced into Ash Swamp. "The Grenadiers and soon after my Company pushed into a wood which they [the rebels] occupied in great numbers, and ought to have been supported by the 52 and 37th Regiment; by some mistake or other, the blame of which the Commanding Officers concerned endeavor to throw upon one another, they did not advance; so that the Rebels not only got off without any difficulty, but annoyed the Highlanders in particular, very much exactly from the quarter which these regts [regiments] ought to have covered." The British officers in command managed then to sort things out, and "the 52nd coming up soon thereafter," says Murray, "we advanced again into the wood upon which, after two [or] three pretty smart fires, the enemy thought proper to decamp, and I believe with very little loss."[11] With smoke billowing everywhere, the rebels eventually broke off the engagement and withdrew to a range of small hills west of the swamp, known then as the Short Hills.

The American force, now fully assembled and commanded by Maxwell, carefully observed British movements and soon realized they were withdrawing eastward on the road back toward Amboy, thus no longer posing an offensive concern. Maxwell subsequently sent Colonel Eleazer Lindsley and Major Joseph Morris off on a flanking operation shadowing the British right, which eventually caught up to the Redcoats near Woodbridge. The rebels promptly attacked the British rearguard, holding it in place until Maxwell, marching hard from Ash Swamp, arrived with the bulk of the American force. John Peebles describes the rearguard action, "...we moved on again, the men much fatigued & harassed a great many of them quite knock'd up; shortly after we got into the main road the Rebels appear'd in our rear & our rear flanks & harrass'd the Grenadiers that formed the rear guard very much. We were obliged to halt & fire some Cannon amongst them which set them a scampering."

At Woodbridge, a heated engagement ensued when the British discovered the Americans waiting in large numbers. Peebles describes the action when "...near Woodbridge we found a large body of them in a wood posted to oppose us in front. Upon discovering them we fired a few pieces of Cannon into the wood and then formed a line in front which moved on to the wood & pour'd in their fire which made them the Rebels quicken their steps to their right, to which they began to move when the front line moved on to charge them."[12] The fighting continued until nightfall, musket fire lighting the evening sky, until finally broken off by the rebels—according to American reports—when they could no longer perceive British movements in the dark.[13]

As to the clash at Ash Swamp, Lieutenant Peebles wrote candidly that "in this affair we had the worst of it for want of that support we had reason to expect from our rear, where the 52nd Regt. were drawn up but did not move."[14] Interestingly, Robertson, in his own understated fashion, supports the notion that this foraging expedition was roughly handled by the Americans at Ash Swamp, when they "Fell in with a Body of Rebels whom they drove. They [the Redcoats] at last retreated toward Amboy and the Rebels hung upon their rear all the way home."[15]

A portion of a letter written by an American officer, which appeared in *The Pennsylvania Journal* and *The Weekly Advertiser* on March 5, indicates the British sustained significant casualties during this outing: "The firing continued from that time [morning] with some short intermission until night, by the best accounts we can get the enemy's loss amounted to upwards of an hundred men killed and wounded; we took ten prisoners; our loss was eight killed and wounded. They came with fifteen or twenty wagons, a considerable part of which were employed in carrying off their dead and wounded; some of the wagons were so piled, that the dead fell off, and were left in the road."[16] But those figures appear sensationalized, for the following day, John Peebles recorded in his diary that, "In the affair of yesterday we have lost 69 killed & wounded & 6 missing, our Company has 2 Sergeants, 1 Corporal, & 20 wounded men & 1 killed."[17]

General Washington was clearly elated by the news of the American victory at Ash Swamp and reported as much to John Hancock on February 28:

> No military Operation of any consequence has
> occurred since I had the honor of writing to you last,
> except, that on Sunday, I recd information that the

Enemy were advancing in a manner, and in numbers so much greater than usual, that it looks like a prelude to an Attack upon our posts, which were immediately put in the best preparation to receive them. It turned out to be only a stronger foraging party than usual, and they were however opposed in so spirited a manner by our advanced parties, that they were checked, and retired in the Afternoon, towards Amboy, from whence they came. Their loss, in the Course of the day, from the best accounts I can get, amounts to about one hundred killed, wounded, prisoners and deserters. Some people who were near the scene of Action, and who have picked up accounts from those who have since been in Amboy, are sanguine enough to suppose that they lose five hundred altogether, but of this I have no conception. Our loss was only two killed and ten wounded.[18]

The day after the running engagement at Ash Swamp, the weather again turned decidedly foul—a boon for a weary General Washington, who was constantly on alert for aggressive British movements. Archibald Robertson tells us that "the greatest snow we have had this Winter" buried the region on February 24, once again limiting the threat of a strike toward Morristown. On that same day, however, as the snows piled up on the streets of Morristown, Washington wrote to his brother, John Augustine, restating his recurring fear: "I believe there soon will, as Genl Howe has withdrawn a great part of his Troops from Rhode Island in order to strengthen those in this State for I should think, (considering the Situation of our Army) some Offensive operation – If he does not, there can be no Impropriety, I conceive, in pronouncing him a Man of no enterprize, as circumstances never will I hope, favour him so much as at present."[19] What Washington did not know at the time was that General Howe had every intention of attempting to lure him down from Morristown in hopes of defeating the Americans in open battle, a story soon to be told.

Despite February's inclement weather and the ferocity and success of the rebel attacks on their foraging parties, the British trans-Atlantic supply line had been successfully extended from New York up the Raritan River. As a result, supplies of every description were being offloaded on landings, from Amboy upriver, finally making their way out to the outposts that dotted the front lines. While local skirmishing might have been a constant irritant, Ewald writes that by mid-February, "the men lacked nothing, for the most excellent provisions of salted beef and pork, peas, butter, rice, and flour for bread, along with the best English beer, were continually supplied during this time. Indeed, the concern of the English nation for its soldiers went so far that twenty overcoats of the finest English material were furnished free to each company, which were distributed to the sentries and the sick."[20]

As the last days of February slid off the calendar—and with the promise of a warmer March now on the horizon—George Washington still fretted over British intentions; the Hessian Ewald, although snug and well-fed, engaged in daily sniping with his American enemies, and the British army continued largely cooped up in that narrow corridor between Amboy and Brunswick. Washington's fear of a Redcoat thrust toward Morristown was at the time largely a product of self-induced anxiety produced by the pathetic state of his army and not actual British capabilities or intentions. One minor staff move did take place at Morristown, however, for the General Orders of March 1 noted the promotion of a junior officer to Washington's staff: "Alexander Hamilton Esqr: is appointed Aide De Camp to the Commander in Chief and is to be respected and obeyed as such."[21] Few knew who this young officer was at the time, but soon enough, he would make an impression. Operational viability continued to be hampered by cold and snow, for Kemble tells us that as March dawned, "very bad weather, the latter end of last and beginning of this month, prevents our General from Undertaking anything in Jersey, let his Inclinations be what they will."[22]

For the time being, at least, the British were going nowhere, flattened in barns and various buildings due to the recent snows. The Americans remained short of troops, money, and supplies of every description, it is true, but Mother Nature, at least, appeared to have smiled on their efforts.

CHAPTER EIGHT
Punk Hill

*J*ust how fearful British leadership had become of the speed, fire-power, and combativeness of the rebel resistance in New Jersey was vividly demonstrated by means of the elaborate plan and movements they concocted for March 9. Interestingly, the occasion bore no great military or political significance; indeed, the reason was nothing more than to allow General William Howe to travel from Brunswick to Amboy the distance of a mere ten miles. In that the British had established outposts to provide early warning of an attack, it might sensibly be assumed that Howe, accompanied by a troop or two of dragoons, might make that trip unmolested with ease, but that would be an incorrect assumption. In fact, so fearful of an ambush was the British high command that an elaborate operation involving thousands of troops had to be devised, then put into operation, simply to allow the general to scurry from one post to another.

The story began on Saturday, March 8, when General Howe traveled to Bonhamtown, an area in modern-day Edison Township. There, he personally took full command of an effort to reopen communications between that post and Brunswick, which had been cut by the Americans for some time. In this, he failed completely, but he was entirely successful in arousing the Americans into action, who began swarming the area in large numbers. On the 8th, Brigadier General William Maxwell, operating at nearby Quibbletown, attacked elements of the Forty-Second Highland Regiment, also out from Brunswick on a foraging expedition. Contemporary reports tell us that "General Maxwell attacked the enemy on Saturday last, near

Quible or Squable-town, as they were penetrating into the country for provender, most kinds of which are much wanted by them. We had three men slightly wounded, none killed or taken; the enemy left four dead on the field, and carried off numbers as usual, which, by accounts from prisoners, were twenty, and numbers wounded. Their rear was so closely pursued that they left one wagon behind; the three prisoners are just arrived, and say the 42nd, or Highland Watch, suffered greatly in the last action."[1] This skirmish was proof positive that Howe's mission had failed and that the region remained a dangerous hotbed of rebel activity.

Realizing that any trip back to Brunswick—or Amboy beyond that—would be hazardous in the extreme, Howe concluded that large-scale measures were called for to ensure his safety. So on Sunday, March 9, two to three thousand British soldiers marched out of Brunswick, making a great old ruckus as they did. With a "grand rattling of drums," they paraded out to Carman's, Punk, and Strawberry hills, three large knolls that dominated the terrain between Bonhamtown and Woodbridge. Here, they took up defensive positions, as noticeable as they could be, yet for no discernable reason as far as the locals could perceive. According to reports by General Maxwell, "the enemy brought out all their troops from Amboy &c. supposed to be about 3000, and posted themselves on Punkhill. They brought artillery and a number of waggons as if to forge, 'tho there was none left in that neighbourhood worth notice."[2] Maxwell watched all of this unfold from a distance, wondering what the fuss was all about.

William Maxwell was one of the few rebel officers who had significant prior military experience at a grade higher than a noncommissioned officer, and over the course of the Revolution, his know-how would prove invaluable. Born in Ireland's County Tyrone in 1733, Maxwell's family moved to America in 1747. They then settled on a farm in northern New Jersey in what is today Greenwich, Warren County. William served with a provincial American unit during the French and Indian War and rose to the rank of colonel—no small feat for a "provincial"—but resigned his commission in 1774 due to his political disagreements with the crown's repressive American policies. He was appointed colonel of the Second New Jersey Continental Regiment in 1775 and brigadier general in 1776. His successes during the New Jersey Campaign hardly went unnoticed, and Washington later appointed Maxwell leader of an American light infantry corps during the summer of 1777.

In that everyone knew the area around Strawberry Hill had been picked clean of forage long before the Redcoats' newest and most dramatic appearance, the sudden deployment appeared to smack far more of show, a grand diversion designed to draw off all those rebel bushwhackers lurking about, thus allowing General Howe to scurry off from Bonhamtown to Amboy; hopefully without incident. But things did not go quite as planned. Woodford Clayton writes that "General Howe himself subsequently attempted to open communications, but failed, narrowly escaping capture, and New Brunswick continued shut up until late March."[3] So what went wrong?

As the British marched out and took their positions—all the while making a grand spectacle of their movements—General Maxwell was closely observing their demonstration from a distant hill. Three thousand regulars well-posted on high ground were obviously a target too large to strike, so Maxwell began searching for a weakness somewhere along their lines that might be exploited. He first sent a feint off to his left, hoping this might draw off some of the British troops, then later detached a stronger party from the American right to try and determine if the Redcoats' left flank might be in the air. An officer who had read Maxwell's report, written on the 14th at Westfield, later wrote that: "About half a mile lower down between Carman's Hill, and Woodbridge, the two parties being joined, met a strong advanced part of the enemy [the British]. On the first firing Col. Martin and Lieut. Col. Lindley were sent to support them; they all behaved well, and kept their ground till they were supported from the main body, which imme-diately marched that way."

Both sides sent in reinforcements, and the fighting mushroomed, muskets cracking and smoke filling the morning air. Then, Maxwell spotted an opening—a gap between two British units—and ordered an American detachment to attack at once, driving a wedge through two units of the British line. This tactic worked, for the officer, previously mentioned, reported that "but on another regiment of ours being sent on the left to cut them off from their main body; the party [of Redcoats] gave way in great confusion; the flame catched [panicked] their main body, and all went together. Our people pursued them and took a prisoner and a baggage wagon – close in their rear, a good way down in the plain ground."

As the British retreated, the rebels snapped at their heels, but Maxwell feared that if he pushed his pursuit too far, a large detachment of British troops known to be at Bonhamtown might rise to the occasion and turn his left flank on the open ground. The Americans backed away, and the affair at Punk Hill went down as nothing more than another minor skirmish. Maxwell reported that the rebels killed twenty and wounded forty of the enemy, while the Redcoats claimed to have killed "a number" of Americans while taking fifteen prisoners.[4]

All the flamboyant show and maneuver did not spare Howe a distressing journey. Clayton explained that the general's large military party was still subjected to intense fire, and he came dangerously near capture. British officer Stephen Kemble noted the action: "The General left Brunswick for Amboy, his Escort comprised of three Battalions Infantry, one Light Troops, and one Grenadiers; the rear Guard attacked between Bonham Town and Amboy by near a thousand Rebels; the Enemy Repulsed, and 53d [52d] Regiment bore the Brunt of the Action; we had two Men Killed and 7 or 8 Wounded, the Rebels left 8 or ten Killed on the Field."[5] From Amboy, the general was ferried over to Staten Island; thence by carriage and ferry on to New York City, presumably having seen enough of New Jersey, at least for the time being.

While casualties at Punk Hill were minimal for both sides, the substantial operation of March 9 engaged in by the British—for no other reason than to allow General Howe to escape Bonhamtown for Amboy—demonstrated just how dangerous British leadership understood central New Jersey had become. Underscoring this were further notes from Maxwell's report: "Gen. Maxwell also mentions, that by a soldier taken [a British prisoner] about the 11th instant, he learns, that Gen. Howe was as Bonhamtown during the engagement, till he saw his troops make the best of their way home, and then thought it was time for him to go. That the enemy's real design in coming out that day was to secure the General's safe passage to Amboy, and that he has since gone to New York."[6] Clearly, by early March, New Jersey had become a hornet's nest of violent opposition for any British movement, no matter how powerfully comprised.

While all this fighting, maneuver, and travel were going on, General Washington was engaged in an interesting exchange of ideas with Robert Morris, who had remained behind in Philadelphia. Morris was a pivotal force during the Revolution due to his financial clout. He had moved from England to America when only fourteen years old and, over the years, had amassed a fortune through shipping and other business ventures. When war broke out with England, the Continental Congress turned to Morris—who adamantly supported the rebel cause—to help raise the capital, supplies, and manpower necessary to create both the United States' navy and army. Morris's financial support behind the scenes, along with his far-flung shipping interests, would prove instrumental in the eventual success of the American Revolution.

Having been informed by General Washington of his fear of an impending strike at either Philadelphia or Morristown, Morris—evaluating events a bit less pessimistically—had arrived at a different conclusion. On February 27, he presented his thoughts to the commander in chief, initially pointing out that, "from various Accounts I have been taught to believe that the Enemy have since Christmas lost so many Horses, are in such want of Forage, and their remaining Cavalry so worn down, that the defects in this department alone wou'd render any Movement of their Main body impossible without strong reinforcements."

Morris was well aware that, according to Washington's current strategic logic, Howe would either strike at Morristown or venture south across Jersey for a thrust at Philadelphia. But by means of the same impediments facing the British—from which Washington envisioned offensive schemes only—Morris deduced impotence, as if, glancing at the same coin, one man could distinguish only heads, the other only tails:

> Seems to me however that the enemy will be pressed with very great difficultys in their designs on this place [Philadelphia], allowing some degree of truth to their want of Horses Waggons and Forage, those wants will be infinitely more felt since the late fall of Snow than before for the Snow before it Melts will exceedingly impede the Motions of the Stoutest Horses, they will require more dry food as nothing can be got from the sod and the difficulty of obtaining such food, as I apprehend, will be greatly encreased by Your parties particularly the Rifle Men. When the Snow Melts it will render the Road totally impassable for the Carriages must then be dragged through Mud instead of Snow[.]

Morris had a point. The heavy snow, lack of forage, weakened horses, and so on, made it all but impossible that the British could launch an extended strike in any direction during early or mid-March, better yet across central New Jersey clear into the Watchung Mountains, for a poke directly at Washington. The fact that they could hardly get in and out of Quibbletown—only miles from Brunswick—without being savaged by swarms of rebel riflemen made Washington's repeated concerns appear, at best, overly concerned and, at worst, virtually paranoid. Morris made his point politely but clearly: "[In]short my Dear Sir I cannot help conceiving that General Howe's situation somewhat resembles that of a Strong Bull in Trammells, sensible of his own Strength, he grows mad with rage & resentment when he finds himself deprived of the use of it The Bull may not so well understand the causes of his disappointment & therefore may be more patient & I fancy if my picture has any resemblance to the truth patience wou'd be of great use to the British Commander."[7] Given the current road conditions and state of British supply, Howe would have little choice but to accept the reality on the ground that any significant movement was all but impossible.

A few days later, Washington responded to Morris, assuring him that he valued his frank opinions as a gentleman and stalwart believer in the cause. "Your favour of the 27th Ulto," he wrote, "came to my hands last night – the freedom with which you have communicated your Sentiments on several matters therein contained is highly pleasing to me, for be assured Sir, that nothing would add more to my satisfaction than an unreserved Corrispondance with a Gentleman, whose abilities and attachment to the Cause we are contending to support, I entertain so high an opinion of as I do of yours." Even acknowledging the overtly ornate literary style of the day, it seems clear that Washington knew well he was walking on eggshells if he disagreed too strenuously with Morris. It appears he took the time to lay down a careful and cordial preface before moving on to his own opinions. "The reasons my good Sir which you assign for thinking Genl Howe cannot move forward with his Army are good, but not conclusive – It is a descriptive Evidence of the difficulties he has to contend with, but no proof that they cannot be surmounted – It is a view of one side of the Picture, against which let me enumerate the advantages of the other, and see which preponderates."

The commander in chief believed that his side of the "coin" better reflected the facts on the ground, and he was not about to be disabused of them by a financier in Philadelphia, no matter how essential to the cause. Washington had delved—he clearly believed—far deeper into the situation than had Morris. Thus his strategic assessment represented a significantly more sophisticated evaluation than the businessman had previously pondered. Here, Washington lays out the strategic picture he had come to believe as accurate in more detail than previously disclosed, and it serves as a clear and valuable window into his strategic thinking at the time:

> Genl Howe cannot, by the best Intelligence I have been able to get, have less than 10,000 Men in the Jerseys and on board of the Transports at Amboy – Ours does not exceed 4,000 – His are well Officerd, well disciplined, and well appointed – Ours raw Militia, badly Officered, and ungovernable – His numbers cannot, in any short time be augmented – Ours must, very considerably (and by such Troops as we can have some reliance on,) or the game is at an end – His situation with respect to Horses & forage is bad, very bad I grant – but will it be better? No – on the contrary, it is growing daily worse, and therefore an Inducement, if no other, to shift Quarters – Genl Howes Informants are too numerous, & well acquainted with all these Circumstances to suffer him to remain ignorant of them; with what propriety then can he miss so favourable an oppertunity of striking a capitol stroke against a city from whence we derive so many advantages, the success of which wou'd give so much eclat to his Arms, and strike such a damp upon ours. Nor is his difficulty of removing so great as imagined – all the heavy Baggage of the Army – their Salt Provisions – Flour – Stores -- &ca – might go round by Water, whilst by their superiority of numbers, they might Sweep the Country round about of Horses, left by us.

The commander in chief continued: "In addition to all this Genl Howes coming over to Brunswick himself – his bringing Troops which cannot be Quartered, & keeping them on Ship board at Amboy, with many other corroborating Circumstances did induce me firmly to believe that he would move – and towards Philadelphia – and I candidly own, that I expected it would have taken place before the expiration of my Proclamation [Washington's proclamation dated January 25] – the longer it is delayed however the better for us, and happy shall I be, if I am disappointed."[8]

Ultimately, Washington would not be disappointed. Although it would be months longer than he had originally anticipated before the British would make their move, it *would* be just as he anticipated: by sea toward Philadelphia. But in March, the snow was still deep along the slopes of the mountains, and—beyond the narrow confines of Brunswick outward toward Quibbletown and Amboy—the British were incapable of going anywhere. Indeed, many of the Redcoats, now quartered in ships off Amboy, were being housed there simply because the British could not find adequate quarters; not because Howe was planning a seaborne excursion anytime soon, as Washington constantly fretted.

Despite the deep snow and muddy roads, life around Brunswick remained volatile and dangerous. On March 3, Continental troops charged with the bayonet and captured a picket party of approximately one hundred British troops without firing a single shot. Apparently impressed with the bayonet tactic, the rebels tried the same thing the next evening—this time, on a picket post consisting of Hessian Jägers and grenadiers. The Hessians managed to get off one round of musketry before beating a hasty retreat but lost two men as prisoners in the action.

Then, early on the 8th, two battalions of Hessians totaling one thousand men were shipped up the Raritan River to guard a foraging expedition loading salt hay onto boats for the return trip to Raritan Landing, near where Rutgers University football stadium stands today. Hessian grenadiers took a position along the Woodbridge Road to protect the operation but were soon attacked by a party of rebels numbering about four hundred. The firing continued for two hours before the Americans were forced into retreat. The Hessians reported five or possibly six men killed and wounded, while American casualties were unknown, and these three actions represent but a sliver of the number of skirmishes taking place between Elizabethtown and Brunswick during this period.[9]

On March 24, the *Pennsylvania Gazette* reported: "On Sunday Morning the 16th Instant, a party of the King's Troops under the

Command of Major General Vaughan, marched from Amboy as far as Spanktown in order to surprise a party of the Rebels who had been plundering in that Neighbourhood for some days. Col Mawhood was appointed to cutoff their Retreat, while the others attacked them in Front, but the Badness of the Roads prevented the Design from being put into full execution. However, the main Body fell in with a Detachment of the Rebels, killed some, and took 15 prisoners, who were taken to Town the day they were taken."[10] According to reports in the *Pennsylvania Evening Post*, however, the British remained virtual prisoners at Brunswick at the time, as noted on March 25. "By accounts from New-Jersey we learn, that the deserters daily come over from the enemy, who are penned up in Brunswick, so that they never peep out, but our people have a knock at them, which as often turns out in our favour. One of which skirmishes happened on Tuesday, the 18th instant, where we took several waggons, 8 prisoners, and found 4 or 5 dead in the field; and another happened on Friday last, when the enemy made the best of their way into the town to tell, that they could not get any forage for the rebels."[11]

Not all newspaper reports concerned themselves with fighting, however, as noted in this piece from the *Pennsylvania Gazette*, which seemed to indicate that life—at least in parts of New Jersey where the British were not prowling in force—had at least a hope of returning to normal:

> The under graduates of the College of New-Jersey [modern-day Princeton University] are 'desired to hold themselves in readiness to assemble on the tenth day of May next, which is the first day of the Summer session according to the usual practice; and all who propose to enter into any of the Classes are requested to observe the utmost punctuality as to the time; for it is proposed by assiduous application to recover what has been lost by the public confusions, and therefore it will be impossible, by extra attendance, to bring up those who fall behind their Classes.[12]

Meanwhile, at Morristown, General Washington still commanded an understrength army. Desperate for the recruits, his recruiting officers—recently dispatched to the various states—continued to promise him, but, seeing none appear, he became increasingly anxious as the cold days of March slipped away. He would also be frustrated with a mounting flurry of unreasonable requests from a Congress that had little comprehension of his resources or ability to satisfy such demands. He responded pointedly to John Hancock: "Could I accomplish the important Objects so eagerly wished by Congress, 'confining the Enemy within their present Quarters – preventing their getting Supplies from the Country & totally subduing them before they are reinforced, I should be happy indeed. But what prospect or hope can there be of my effecting so desirable a Work at this time? The inclosed Return, to which I solicit the most serious attention of Congress, comprehends the whole force, I have in Jersey. It is but a handful, and bears no proportion on the Scale of Numbers that of the enemy. added to this, the Major part is made up of Militia."[13]

Washington's woes were widely circulated throughout the region through newspaper accounts, only making matters worse, as this piece from the *Pennsylvania Evening Post* reveals: "Mr. Washington remains yet at Morris Town, with not above 4 or 500 Men. The rest of his People are stationed about Quibbletown, and other Parts the Country near the Troops, watching their Motions, and ready for Speed against the expected Time of their leaving Winter-Quarters. Most of the New England People are gone Home, some to their Farms and others to their Merchandize. The new Levies [men drafted from the militia to perform actual service to augment a state's Continental units for periods up to six months] have succeeded very ill; and Men are not to be had upon almost any terms."[14]

By mid-March, General Washington could hardly be blamed for believing the deck had been stacked against him and that he might never see a single recruit arrive before the snow melted and the roads dried. Nevertheless, he did receive a little help from a volunteer one day in the village of Woodbridge. According to the *Pennsylvania Gazette*, a young woman returning home through the streets spotted a Hessian soldier alone inside an abandoned house. Checking closer, she realized the soldier was drunk and had no doubt wandered off from his patrol. Thinking quickly, she rushed home, took off her garments, and dressed in the clothes of a man. Grabbing an old flintlock, she headed back to the abandoned house, slipped in, and got the drop on the drunken soldier, which apparently wasn't terribly difficult to do. She then disarmed him at gunpoint and marched him off, intending to hand him over to the local rebel authorities. On her way, she happened upon a small patrol from a New Jersey regiment, to whom she happily handed over her prisoner before departing once again for home.[15]

Unfortunately for the commander in chief, the cultural norms of the eighteenth century meant that a regiment of, say, two hundred and fifty such women was not a possibility, so his army continued throughout March, snowbound, greatly reduced in numbers, and waiting for all those new recruits, expected to arrive any day at Morristown.

CHAPTER NINE
Hudson's River

Throughout the winter of 1777, General Washington complained about the depleted state of his army, along with the ceaseless comings and goings of the militias. In all, they represented a sort of revolving door that made it all but impossible to develop any coherent plans. Indeed, the endless comings and goings made it difficult at times to obtain an accurate count of the army's manpower on any given day. Nevertheless, the clearest evidence we have of the army's strength during mid-March comes to us from a "Return of the American Forces in New Jersey," compiled on March 15, then delivered to the commander in chief at Morristown. While the total numbers are not as bleak as we might have expected—given Washington's consistent grumbles in that regard—the available strength was spread out across the state, which made it extremely doubtful that these forces could have been rapidly concentrated at any one point, should the British have launched a rapid attack. While even these numbers are probably less than precise, they do provide a fascinating window into Continental strength and clearly document the ongoing imbalance between British and American forces.

The return includes only those soldiers fit for duty, which is typical for any military organization. The first aspect of the count deals with Continentals only, the second militia strength. On March 15, 1777, the return indicates that there was a grand total of forty-six Continentals fit for duty at Morristown, these drawn from several Pennsylvania units. The Eighth Pennsylvania was stationed at Bound Brook, numbering 342, while Princeton had troops from Maryland and New Jersey, totaling 284. New Jersey and Pennsylvania companies made up the garrison at Chatham, numbering two hundred and sixty, while Pennsylvania riflemen were stationed at Rariton [Raritan, or modern-day New Brunswick], a force of ninety-nine. A total of 441 Continentals, consisting of Pennsylvania and New Jersey units, were quartered at Westfield, while Spank Town [Rahway] hosted a German battalion along with the First Pennsylvania Rifle Company, numbering 296. Lastly, the return reveals a smattering of different Virginia regiments posted at Whippany (in northern New Jersey), totaling 645. There were also one hundred and thirty Continental artillerymen scattered about, providing a grand total of 2,543 Continentals fit for duty.

Augmenting the number of Continentals, Quibbletown boasted 319 militiamen, mostly from Maryland and Virginia; Rariton [New Brunswick] quartered 423, Westfield an additional 234, bringing the total manpower available (Continentals & militia) to 3,519.[1] Subtracting the troops stationed at both Whippany and Princeton—in that they were too far distant to quickly cooperate in any sudden engagement that developed in the central part of the state—Washington had at his disposal two thousand, five hundred and ninety Continentals and militia to face a British force numbering (according to Stephen Kemble's numbers, previously reported) some 18,326 troops stationed nearby at Brunswick, Newark, Staten Island, and New York City. This represented a British force advantage of seven to one, not even including the recent British reinforcements from Rhode Island. Obviously, Washington's concerns regarding manpower were well-founded.

The most fascinating aspect of these numbers is just how incredibly successful the first three months of the New Jersey Campaign had gone for the Americans, despite the enormously lopsided advantage in manpower, supply, logistics, training, and so on that the British maintained. True, the snow and terrible road conditions had made maneuver trying for the Redcoats, but the Americans were traveling the same roads and appeared to be doing so with swiftness and dexterity. Somehow, a force outnumbered seven to one had managed to confine a vastly superior foe into a narrow strip of territory where local travel remained hazardous and any journey outside dangerous in the extreme. No doubt, Washington sat atop the chain of command, but it was not Washington who was pulling the strings. It was his officers commanding the frontline outposts who were responding to events as they developed, namely Maxwell, Stirling, and Dickinson, along with scores of their junior officers.

While the recent snow had imposed a hiatus on any major operations, the constant sniping and scraping in the villages and along the roads surrounding Brunswick continued apace. On March 18, for instance, rebels near Brunswick engaged in a heated skirmish with British troops, killing five and losing four of their own. Three days later, they were at it again when Redcoats attempted to return to Brunswick from a foraging expedition and were driven off by overwhelming numbers.[2] Then, on Sunday, March 22, a rebel regiment under Joseph Bloomfield attacked the British when "the enemy came out from Amboy, to bring in the property of one Barnes, who is gone over, when our people stationed near Woodbridge, attacked them and had a pretty smart shooting match, while they were retiring with the said effects: About the same time the enemy attempted to land from some boats on Woodbridge Neck and at Smith's Farm, to take off some cattle and hay; but in this they were disappointed, as our People distributed them, and took the cattle and burnt the hay."[3]

General Washington's strong belief that Howe intended to move on Philadelphia as soon as dry, campaigning weather returned had only become more firmly entrenched as intelligence reports supporting that conclusion continued to pile up on his desk at Morristown. On March 15, the general wrote to his brother, Samuel, suggesting, "as an opinion, that Genl Howe will move towards Philadelphia the moment the Roads become passable for his artillery and Baggage."[4] Then, on March 20, he sent a letter to officer Alexander McDougall, laying out the reasons to hasten recruits to Morristown. "The late collection of Waggons, by the enemy," wrote Washington, "upon Long and Staten Islands, some of which are already brought over to Amboy, plainly indicate a Move, whenever the State of the Roads will permit. Several accounts, by Deserters and others, also agree, that Materials have been brought from New York for constructing a floating Bridge, which can be for no other purpose than laying across the Delaware."[5]

As the warmer days of April approached, Washington became increasingly convinced that Howe soon intended to move and increasingly uncomfortable that he had not the means to oppose him once he did. He had been receiving reports from his recruiting officers that new regiments of Continentals would presently be on their way to Morristown, only to be disappointed time and again when they failed to arrive. Finally, he wrote to Congress, virtually despondent over this annoying problem, which was now verging on a crisis:

And that the colonels of the continental Regiments have been greatly deceived themselves – have greatly deceived me, or, the most unheard of Desertions, or most scandalous peculations have prevailed among the Officers who have been employed in recruiting: For Regiments, reported two and three months ago to be half completed, are, upon the Colonels being called upon in positive Terms for just State of them, found to contain less than one hundred Men, and this is not the Case of a single Regiment only, but of many – In Connecticut alone, by letter from Genl Parsons of the 6th instant, four Regiments are mentioned as not having more than Eighty Rank & File each.

No doubt about it, this was disastrous news for Washington, for his entire winter strategy depended upon keeping what little remained of his army together while awaiting the arrival of an entirely new force, hammered together by a staff of recruiting officers. That this now appeared mostly a fiction meant that any hope of impeding Howe's next move had been rendered fiction as well. "These Sir," Washington continued in his letter, "are melancholy Truths, but Facts they are, and necessary to be known to Congress, however prudent it may be to conceal them from the observation of others."[6]

Little did Washington realize at the time, but eastward across the state of New Jersey, in New York City, General Howe was dealing with problems of his own. In a letter penned to Germain in London, written not long after Washington's last to Hancock, the British commander in chief confessed his lack of progress—although he blamed it entirely on insufficient strength and weather and failed to mention the stiff opposition his troops were facing in the field. "My expectations of a move in the winter against the enemy in Jersey," he wrote, "upon the arrival of the troops from Rhode Island, as mentioned in a former letter, have been frustrated by a deep fall of snow which rendered the country impassable, and since the breaking up of the winter the depth of the roads forced me to relinquish the idea...Restricted as I am from entering upon more extensive operations by the want of force, my hopes of terminating the war this year are vanished."[7] No greater statement could have headlined a Whig newspaper at the time than Howe's ready admission that his "hopes of terminating the war at this time are vanished." Pity that no one beyond Germain would read it.

The essential stalemate of arms that existed in New Jersey at the time was perfectly reflected in the next two articles, the first of which appeared in *The Pennsylvania Journal*. Clearly reflecting a rebel tilt, it read:

> A Gentleman, late from Head-Quarters in the Jersies, acquaints us, that when he came away, both Armies seemed disposed to remain quiet.—That the enemy were lurking within the scanty confines of Brunswick and Amboy; surrounded by detached corps of our troops, whose advantageous situation enabled them to discover and repel any plundering party that hunger could force to sally out. Scarce a day passed without an attempt to forage and plunder, but the vigilance and bravery of our troops obliges the enemy to return commonly without plunder and often with a great loss of their men and baggage. The enemy too well know the fate that must attend their passing the woods and mountains which leads to Morris County, to hazard such an expedition...The Gentleman remarks, that he could not have believed it was in the power of any events to have made so great an alteration in the sentiments and spirits of a people in so short a time, as the enemy's rout and ravages made among the Jerseymen.[8]

In 1777—as has been historically the case—the sense one had of the fortunes of war depended a great deal on one's own loyalties and, consequently, the newspapers one preferred to peruse. Naturally enough, in Revolutionary America, different newspapers championed radically different views of the conflict, offering discriminating readers precisely the viewpoint they most preferred. A loyalist piece from a New York newspaper that ran contemporaneously with *The Pennsylvania Journal* article posted above seems to apprehend an entirely different state of affairs.

> The Philadelphia Newspapers are stuffed with continued false Accounts of Skirmishes; and other Exploits of their Raggamuffins in the Jersies,. in which they always obtain most wonderful and

"neverto-be-heard-of" Victories. The following may serve for a Specimen, taken from the Pennsylvania Journal of the 2d of April. In a Skirmish, in which is stated to have happened near Quibble-Town on the 24th of March, they say the British "must have lost some Men, as they were 22 seen carrying them off in the time of Action, which happened within lialf [half] a Mile of their Breast-works. We had two Rifles broke, but not a Man hurt in this Skirmish.[9]

The notion that Howe's hopes had been dashed by weather and insufficient strength—as he suggested in his letter to Germain—was, of course, an invention, but military leaders throughout history have always been loath to disparage their own actions in favor of a range of obstacles generally beyond their control. But if the British could not operate successfully in Jersey, they could still use the Hudson River to their advantage, which is precisely what they decided to do in late March. A British officer tells us that, on Wednesday, March 26, "The Detachment Commanded by Lieut Col. Bird returned to New York, having destroyed a quantity of Rebel stores at Peeks Kill as follows: four hundred Hogsheads of Rum, 20 pipes wine, some Brandy, a great quantity of Mo-lasses, Suorar [sugar?]. Coffee, Chocolate and Salt, about 600 Barrels oF Flour and Pork, 130 waggons with their Harness, a few Ox Carts, between 2 and 3 hundred boxes of Candles, a great parcel of Entrenching Tools, and two or three pieces of Cannon, and a great parcel of Smoked Beef and Dried Tongues."[10]

The plundering of stores at Peekskill upset General Washington a great deal, not only because of the loss of critical supplies but because it opened the prospect of future operations further upriver, potentially disastrous for the American cause. He wrote immediately to the feckless General Heath, who, it can be recalled, had recently turned the investment and siege of Fort Independence into a farse, mincing no words as to his concerns:

> The Situation of our Affairs again compells me to call upon you in express and positive Terms to hasten the Troops of your State (those inlisted for the continent I mean) to Peekskill and Ticonderoga, in such proportions as I have before directed, without one Moments loss of time. The Enemy have lately,

taking advantage of our weakness at Peekskill, made a descent there, burnt the lower Barracks, our Store Houses, and a valuable parcel of Stores. Perhaps elated by their Success, they may return up the River, and proceed as high as the Forts, which, if they do suddenly, and with any tolerable Force, I do not see what is to hinder them from making themselves masters of them.[11]

Visions of disaster seemed suddenly to be looming large. Whether north up the Hudson River or south toward Philadelphia, there were prospective calamities that Washington had few resources to blunt. Additional intelligence continued to filter in from New York, further hardening the general's belief that Howe intended to ship his army from New Jersey south for an attack on Philadelphia—a major campaign to take the American capital. A recent visitor to New York reported, as one example, that "the Enemy have built & are building a number of light flat Bottomed Boats, about Seventy of which were finished. Captn Desheild says, it seemed to be the general opinion & conversation, that the embarkation was for Chesepeak Bay with a view of makeing a descent on the Eastern Shore, or that the Troops were to proceed to Head of Elk [modern-day Elkton, Maryland], taking Annapolis & Baltimore in their way."[12]

Like trying to divine the future by sifting tea leaves, Washington was attempting to piece together British intent by scrutinizing a raft of intelligence reports: some reasonably valid; others wildly inaccurate. Reports of troop numbers and locations, casualty counts and unit identifications, and even victories and losses were often the product of little more than hubris, hysteria, gossip, and exaggeration. Adding an additional layer of fog to this entire enterprise, both sides routinely engaged in disinformation. False stories and fake documents were often planted wherever and whenever it appeared opportune to do so; in turn, sending wild tales cascading throughout the citizenry, windy rumors that flew across the state like gusts of wind. Despite all the difficulties involved, however, Washington's concerns regarding the Hudson River and the Chesapeake Bay would eventually prove uncommonly prescient, for, as we shall see, it was precisely in those directions the British had decided to move.

It can be recalled from Chapter Seven that the British had devised a grand strategy for severing New England from the other warring states by means of a three-pronged offensive. One of the prongs was to move up the Hudson River from New York City under General Howe. A second column would march east from Lake Ontario under the command of General Barry St. Leger. Lastly, the third movement was to proceed south from Montreal under General John Burgoyne; ultimately all three meeting on the Hudson River near Albany, New York.

But Howe—in operational command of British forces in North America south of Canada—had recently developed a deep concern regarding his ability to cooperate with this campaign and conveyed his thoughts in a letter to George Germain, then secretary of state for America in the British cabinet. In fact, Howe had left cooperation with Burgoyne up to General Clinton, his subordinate in New York, while opting instead for a different campaign of his own, precisely what Washington had predicted. Blaming it all—as usual—on a lack of sufficient military strength, Howe told Germain: "From the difficulties and delays that would attend the passage of the Delaware by a march through Jersey, I propose to invade Pennsylvania by sea, and from this arrangement we must probably abandon the Jerseys, which by the former plan would not have been the case."[13]

Howe also enclosed with this correspondence to Germain a letter written three days later and directed to Sir Guy Carleton in Canada in which he was a bit more specific as to his intentions. "Having but little expectation that I shall be able, from the want of sufficient strength in this army, to detach a corps in the beginning of the campaign to act up Hudson's River consistent with the operations already determined upon...and as I shall probably be in Pennsylvania when that corps [the movement descending from Canada] is ready to advance into this province, it will not be in my power to communicate with the officer commanding it so soon as I could wish." In other words, not only was Howe himself not going to assist Burgoyne in the Hudson River operation as planned, but he would not be able to advise him of the change in plans before Burgoyne had already departed Canada. Unknown to Burgoyne, he was going to be essentially on his own. Howe continues, "he [Burgoyne] must therefore pursue such measures as may from circumstances be judged most conducive to the advancement of his Majesty's service consistently with your Excellency's orders for his conduct."[14] Howe's decision would be the most critical factor in the greatest British defeat of the American Revolution prior to Yorktown—Burgoyne's surrender of an entire British army at Saratoga.

The previous December, the British army had romped across New Jersey, plundering, pillaging, and raping as they pleased. They then established a string of posts to pacify the region, the Continental army thought to be a thing of the past. Now—and only three months later— it appeared Sir William had had enough of New Jersey, and with the royal navy—under the command of his brother, Lord Richard Howe,— at his disposal, he was prepared to ship his entire command off by sea toward Philadelphia in hopes, perhaps, of finding a more compliant foe farther south. The reason for this radical alteration of strategy was because "the difficulties and delays that would attend the passage of the Delaware by a march through Jersey," as Sir William conveniently put it, had made such a passage dangerous in the extreme. Namely, his troops were being savaged by those same swarms of rebels that had made British travel in and around Brunswick so frightening, deadly, and next to impossible since the day they had arrived. Unknown to the Americans at the time, Washington's successful war over forage had already forced Howe into radical strategic changes; changes that would alter the face of the war.

It would be over a month before Germain received Howe's dispatches, and we can assume from his reaction that he was none too pleased with what he read. His response was long—touching upon a variety of topics—but the critical paragraph remained adamant regarding the Hudson River campaign: "As you must from your situation and military skill be a competent judge of the propriety of every plan, his Majesty does not hesitate to approve the alterations which you propose, trusting, however, that whatever you may mediate, it will be executed in time for you to co-operate with the army ordered to proceed from Canada and put itself under your command."[15] While obviously written in the cordial, aristocratic jargon of the day, Germain's instructions were nevertheless clear: Do what you please, but, without fail, you will cooperate with the Canadian expedition and take charge of our combined force at Albany. Howe had already made up his mind, however, and Burgoyne would march on his own.

In late March, fighting continued apace, with Rebel Major Ritney initiating a firefight with a British outpost just outside of Quibbletown. Ritney, largely outnumbered, put up a good fight, but other British units came running, and the Americans were eventually forced to withdraw. Soon, however, the rebels were substantially reinforced by a detachment of Virginia volunteers and Maryland militia, increasing their overall strength to one hundred and thirty. Feeling emboldened, they reentered the fray, attacking the Redcoats, who were then well-posted behind a line of trees nearby. "They drove the Crown troops into their breastworks, leaving behind them several hats, knapsacks, blankets and one bloody handkerchief. Several Regulars were seen carrying some of their comrades off the field."[16]

As the calendar changed from March to April, the weather warmed, and the heavy snow that had blanketed much of New Jersey began to disappear. The roads turned first to a brown, muddy stew but, over time, dried enough for military use. Likewise, the fields and meadows transformed from a barren landscape of frosty white to patches of green, and the skirmishing naturally intensified along the line of outposts that dotted the landscape near Brunswick. "With the end of the month of March," Captain Ewald tells us, "we watched the snow disappear, and everything was green in a few days. On the 4th of April, Wreden and I paid a visit to Bound Brook. We drove the enemy outposts across the causeway into the town, and returned without loss and with booty of fifteen head of oxen, which enemy soldiers had grazed on our side of the causeway."

The arrival of warm, campaigning weather was precisely what General Washington had dreaded the most during all those cold winter months, for it foreshadowed substantial movements by the British. Ewald wrote: "On the 10th we learned that a French major, Mr. Von Ottendorff, had arrived with a newly organized corps consisting of Germans and Frenchmen for reinforcements of the post at Bound Brook."[17] Here, Ewald's journal entries appear either slightly inaccurate or deliberately misleading, for it is hard to believe that Ewald believed someone with the title "von"—which meant "baron" in German—was anything other than of German extraction. Indeed, Mr. Von Ottendorff was no Frenchman at all but Nicholas Dietrich Baron de Ottendorf, a Saxon hired by Congress to raise an independent battalion of German-speaking volunteers from Pennsylvania to fight against the British.

So Baron Ottendorf took command of the German battalion posted at Bound Book in early April and promptly tried his hand at driving Ewald and his Jägers out of their position. Ewald describes the action in his journal but with a good bit more contempt for this new foe than ever before displayed as if he knew his opponent was no Frenchman but rather a Prussian like himself. Ewald was neither baron nor major; hence, a good bit of martial pride appears suddenly to have taken center stage, which the reader may judge for themself: "On the 11th this hero tried his luck against us," Ewald begins. "He attacked my post at daybreak, and I was forced to withdraw across a small ravine. At ten o'clock in the morning he came again, but since Captain Wreden came to my aid at once, he was driven back with losses and we escorted him up to the enemy outposts. But since he had firmly resolved to dislodge me today, he reappeared for the third time at three o'clock in the afternoon. Captain Wreden was on hand instantly, and the English grenadiers of the guards under Chevalier Osborn also came to our assistance, whereby the good Ottendorff was kept so warm that he had trouble getting away with his skin."[18]

The village of Bound Brook lay on the north or west bank of the Raritan, just eight miles west of Brunswick, the towns connected by two roads, one on the north side of the river; the other on the south. The Raritan River ran directly up from Raritan Landing—which was situated on the river, directly opposite Brunswick—allowing for waterborne supply and rapid reinforcement should the village fall under British control. Bound Brook was a central post in that widely scattered string of American posts, which guarded the approaches to Morristown while hemming Brunswick in, thus a natural, accessible target once the weather warmed. If Bound Brook could be taken, the American line might be fatally breached, opening the road to Morristown while simultaneously placing many of the remaining rebel posts in danger of being taken in flank and rear, thus rendered untenable. A swift, powerful strike just might achieve that end, promptly sending the Americans reeling backward in confusion, radically altering the chessboard of war in New Jersey. It comes as no surprise, therefore, that once the roads dried, Cornwallis promptly turned his gaze upriver.

CHAPTER TEN
Bound Brook

It is obvious that General Cornwallis had had his eye on Bound Brook for quite some time because Ewald tells us plainly that previously, on March 12, "I received orders to go to the headquarters, where Lord Cornwallis showed his confidence in me by entrusting me with drawing up a plan for a surprise attack on Bound Brook. But since it was necessary for a column to cross the Raritan above Bound Brook, the attack was postponed until spring."[1] March snows continued to keep Bound Brook operationally inaccessible. But by early April, all that had changed. The snow had melted, spring had arrived, and Bound Brook immediately became Cornwallis's target.

Washington had placed Major General Benjamin Lincoln in charge of the post at Bound Brook, and with the recent addition of the German battalion, by mid-April, Lincoln boasted a compliment of five hundred Continentals. From the heights along the river, the rebels could keep an eye on British activity at Raritan Landing or the bridge that spanned the river nearby. The garrisoning of Bound Brook allowed the Americans to deny the British easy access to the state's interior for foraging while protecting the farms and mills farther west in the Raritan Valley. It also served as part of the screen and early warning system for Washington's headquarters at Morristown.

Major General Lincoln seemed a fine choice for the command. Born into a prosperous farming family in Hingham, Massachusetts, in 1733, Lincoln joined the Suffolk County Militia as an adjutant in the regiment commanded by his father in 1755. And in 1776, he was promoted to major general in the Massachusetts Militia.

Joining Washington's army at New York, he served in the New York
Campaign, then returned to Massachusetts after the battle of White
Plains. He was then commissioned a major general in the Continental army in February 1777. "He was of middle height, broad shoulders and muscular build, with intelligent, pleasant features," historian T.E. Davis writes. "In manner he was easy, and unaffected, but
always courteous and polite."[2] Lincoln moved into a home owned
by Colonel Philip Van Horne along with other American officers,
a house located on the western fringe of Bound Brook. Nearby, he
had his men erect a blockhouse containing three field pieces, which
was then surrounded by earthworks. The blockhouse and guns
commanded the approaches to the village, including the confluence
of the Raritan River and Bound Brook, the stream from which the
town derived its name. The lower, or stone bridge (also referred to
as Queen's Bridge), spanned the Raritan, while the upper, or Van
Veghten's Bridge, crossed over Bound Brook (see map). The Raritan
River, along with the bridges, was considered the most likely avenue
for a British attack. To guard against this, Lincoln initiated a regular
patrol, extending southward from the Van Veghten's Bridge six miles
to the bend of the river from where Raritan Landing could be viewed
from the heights.

A sketch of Raritan Landing by British officer Archibald Robertson.

Lincoln immediately grasped the exposed position he was in—only eight miles from the British outpost of Brunswick—along with the uncomfortable fact that all the other American posts—from Princeton to Whippany—should the British strike any one of them quickly, were positioned too far distant for effective mutual support. He kept wagons at "morning stand to," ready for immediate departure, pointing out to the commander in chief that no American force was near enough to "render the least assistance to this post in case it is attacked."[3] Regardless, recognizing the need to detect any British incursion, Washington had to use what resources were available.

The Van Horne Home, Bound Brook, NJ, headquarters for General Benjamin Lincoln.

Having been embarrassed by Washington's victory at Princeton, Cornwallis constructed the Bound Brook operation leaving nothing to chance. Far more complex than even Washington's original plan of attack on Trenton, Cornwallis's design called for four separate wings. All four would depart Brunswick at different times and travel different routes, yet all were expected to converge on a single objective simultaneously in a coordinated attack. Designed not just for success, or even overwhelming success, Cornwallis's plan appears to have been devised to reestablish the superiority of British arms across New Jersey. The projected success of the Bound Brook operation would be proof positive that—after three months of lucky rebel victories and ruthless bushwhacking by ruffian militias—Howe, Cornwallis, and their superb British army were entirely capable of overwhelming any American post anywhere they chose.

With reinforcements from Rhode Island, British strength at Brunswick alone numbered seventeen thousand,[4] and only the most elite units from that overall force were selected for the Bound Brook operation. The first wing of the assault was to be commanded by Lt. Colonel William Harcourt. It was to consist of two battalions of British grenadiers, two battalions of light infantry, and fifty British dragoons. The second wing was to be commanded by Hessian Colonel Carl von Donop. This column was to consist of four hundred Hessian grenadiers, fifty British dragoons, and four light field pieces. The third wing would be commanded by General James Grant. It would consist of the Hessian Jägers, the Brigade of British Guards, two amusettes (light field pieces capable of being mounted on a swivel), and four four-pounder artillery pieces. The fourth and smallest wing was to be commanded by Major Thomas Maitland and was to consist of two companies of light infantry. Once assembled, the entire force would total four thousand of Cornwallis's finest fighting men, bolstered by ten light artillery pieces. Their opponent at Bound Brook—as Cornwallis knew—consisted of five hundred Americans, supported by three light field pieces. If the British plan worked as designed, the Americans would be outnumbered eight to one in terms of manpower and outgunned almost three to one in artillery. Clearly, Cornwallis was leaving nothing to chance.

While many historians seem to assume that Cornwallis had adopted Ewald's plan of attack, designed back in March, presumably because both included "a column to cross the Raritan above Bound Brook," there is clear evidence that suggests this was not the case at all (which will be discussed later) and that Cornwallis either devised his own plan or tweaked Ewald's considerably. At any rate, Cornwallis's plan called for Harcourt's wing to depart Brunswick first, head south on the road to Kingston, then turn west. From there, the column was to continue northwest on country roads that led through what is today Hillsborough Township, then overland to the Raritan, where it was to ford the river above (or west) of Bound Brook. This column was then to continue overland a short distance to the stream known as Bound Brook; cross that waterway below (or south) of Van Veghten's Bridge, thus entering the village from the west or rear. Clearly, Harcourt's wing had the most challenging task of all, given the length of the march, the two waterways they had to ford, and the fact that, to a great extent, they would be traveling through unfamiliar territory.

Von Donop's wing had a much less challenging task. Donop was being asked to simply lead his troops up the road that ran between Brunswick and Bound Book on the south side of the Raritan River. His objective was the stone bridge (or Queen's Bridge) that spanned the Raritan, leading directly into the village. Meanwhile, Grant's wing was ordered to march up River Road on the north side of the Raritan, which extended from Raritan Landing to Bound Brook. He was to enter the village from the east side, directly opposite Harcourt. Lastly, Maitland was to lead his wing northeast from Brunswick toward Quibbletown, ford two streams, then turn southwest until they reached the outskirts of Bound Brook, where they were to take up a blocking position. Their objective was to prevent the Americans from Bound Brook from retreating in that direction while simultaneously denying any reinforcements from either Quibbletown or Morristown to march to Bound Brook's support. Maitland was to travel entirely across unfamiliar country, which, again, could create delays and unknown difficulties.[5] Cornwallis's plan of attack was extremely sophisticated and required synchronization of the wings and their orders of march, making a breakdown in execution highly probable. The entire march was to take place during the dead of night, adding the most complicating factor of all.

The attack was scheduled for dawn on Sunday, April 13. Ewald writes that "toward evening on April 12th Lord Cornwallis sent his adjutant to advise me that the surprise attack on Bound Brook would be made during this night."[6] At eleven o'clock in the evening on the 12th, Harcourt departed Brunswick, Cornwallis traveling with this leg of the attack. Early the next morning, Donop led his contingent out of town, followed, in turn, by Grant at three in the morning. It is unclear when Major Maitland departed, but we can assume it was probably before Grant, for Maitland had the more difficult route. All four departures went off without a hitch. "The expedition was planned and carried out with so much secrecy, that the rest of the army and the people of the city did not know of it until Sunday morning."[7] All three of the attacking columns arrived at their attack positions before dawn without having raised a single alarm. There, they rested quietly in place, waiting for the signal to attack. Only Maitland's column would

fail to reach its objective on time, and this failure would have consequences. The operation's objective was to surround Bound Brook so
completely so as to either compel an immediate surrender or defeat
the defenders with an overwhelming assault.

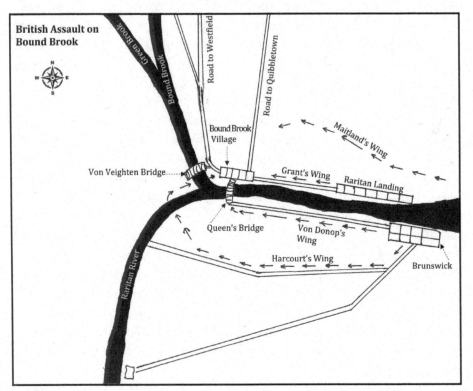

British assault on Bound Brook.

"Lord Cornwallis had ordered me to form the advanced guard
of General Grant's column," Ewald wrote. "For this I took Lieutenant
Trautvetter and thirty volunteer Jägers." As Ewald was preparing to
depart Brunswick, General Grant approached him and said: "Captain
Ewald, you know the area. I say nothing further to you. You know
everything else."[8] Unfortunately for Ewald, his original plan had
either been tossed out completely or altered substantially. Unknown
to him, the purpose now of his advanced guard was not to drive in
the American pickets but to act as a "feint" or demonstration to hold
the rebels in place, allowing the other two columns to storm the town.
Regrettably, no one had bothered to inform Ewald of this critical fact.

The night march continued west up River Road until, says Ewald,
"At daybreak I came upon an enemy picket on this side of the stone

causeway which led to Bound Brook through a marsh along the Raritan River for five to six hundred paces over two bridges." Naturally, Ewald immediately attacked. The Jägers fired, and the pickets promptly returned fire. Suddenly, just east of Bound Brook, the morning air was alive with musketry. "The picket received us spiritedly and withdrew under steady fire," Ewald tells us. Then, pushing his attack, "I tried to keep as close as possible to the enemy to get across the causeway into the town at the same time." The Jägers were able to push the outnumbered Americans back to a second bridge, which led from the marsh directly into Bound Brook, but there, they fell under the muskets of Continentals who were manning a nearby earthwork. "This succeeded to the extent that I arrived at the second bridge," says Ewald, "at a distance of a hundred paces from the redoubt which covered it and the flying bridge [the stone, or Queen's bridge that spanned the Raritan]." The rebels in the redoubt, now alert to the attack, responded with a blast of musketry, instantly pinning the Hessians down.

In Bound Brook, the Americans had been asleep, the guard patrols having failed completely to detect the approaching British. Historian Davis writes that "according to orders, the British waited until the American sentries cry 'All's well,' was heard and the morning gun fired, and then the two detachments simultaneously rushed upon them."[9] But this scenario appears doubtful, as Ewald states clearly that he attacked the picket east of town immediately and makes no mention of orders to hold his fire until the Americans' morning gun had fired. Far more likely is that the columns under Harcourt and Donop—concealed in positions across the river and brook—simply moved forward on the sound of Ewald's guns. Harcourt's column then forded the brook below Van Veghten's Bridge as Donop led his Hessians over the stone bridge (Queen's Bridge), both assaults overwhelming whatever meager resistance they encountered. In all probability, therefore, Ewald had unknowingly initiated an almost perfectly synchronized attack, precisely as Cornwallis had hoped for. Except there was one minor problem: The two companies of light infantry under Major Maitland had yet to take up their blocking position north of Bound Brook, failing to cut off escape in that direction.

Back near the marsh, however, Captain Ewald and his Jägers were still hugging the ground. "The day dawned and I was exposed to a murderous fire," he wrote. "When I looked around for my men, I saw that no one had followed me except the brave Lieutenant Trautvetter, my hornblower Muller," and seven other men, two of whom had already been severely wounded.[10] "We had no choice but to lie down on the ground before the bridge, whereupon I ordered 'Forward' sounded constantly [by the bugler, or hornblower]," but, despite the horn calls, none of the Jägers budged an inch. Ewald and his advance guard remained pinned down for another ten minutes until Colonel Donop's column stormed across the stone bridge to relieve them. With that, the Americans in the redoubt, now threatened front and rear, took off running.

As Ewald was ducking for cover, Harcourt's column suddenly appeared behind the Horne house, where General Lincoln and General Wayne were suddenly wakened by all the commotion. The Redcoats were spotted no more than two hundred yards off, and, leaping to their feet, the American officers had no time to lose. "Gen. Lincoln and his soldiers were startled by the fierce cry of his sentries, 'To arms!' Hastily arising, without time for dressing, they made a rapid retreat, passing through the fast enclosing lines of the two detachments of the enemy's army, firing a few shots aimlessly as they ran."[11] Harcourt's men pressed forward, engaging the guards around the house. "The guard was partly cut down," says Ewald, "and partly captured, the three cannon seized, and the two generals fled without their breechees."

So overwhelming was the British attack that, taken by surprise, the Americans had virtually no hope of defending either themselves or the village. As Donop's column was successfully running off what few Americans remained in the redoubt, Ewald and his men joined the advance into the village, hot on the heels of the fleeing rebels. "We arrived in the town with the garrison of the redoubt amidst a hard running fight," wrote Ewald," and the greater part were either cut down or captured." As Harcourt's troops pressed forward to join Donop's, those Americans who could get away fled for the hills behind the town. Fortunately for the Americans, many managed to escape because Maitland's troops had not yet arrived, leaving a gap through which many raced to safety. "Had the sentries alarm come only a few minutes later, or had Cornwallis' plan for surrounding the Americans been more speedily effected, the entire body of the Americans would surely have been captured by the superior force. It was in fact a very narrow escape from total destruction or capture. After reaching the higher ground, the Americans made a stand and began a brief firing, but the British line reforming, and returning the fire, they were compelled to fall back to the mountains in rear of Bound Brook for safety."[12]

While the British attack did not accomplish everything Cornwallis had planned, it was nevertheless a remarkably well-executed operation that killed and captured scores of rebels while sending the remainder scurrying for their lives. General Lincoln had escaped, apparently leaving his pants and personal papers behind, and for the Americans, it had been a short, desperate, embarrassing affair. The British were quickly in complete control of Bound Brook, but for all their remarkable planning and execution, they failed to exploit their victory. For a few hours, they took part in what the British army had become particularly expert—pillaging. "Afterward the place was ransacked and plundered," Ewald readily admits, "because all the inhabitants were rebellious-minded, and then the entire corps withdrew along the road from Bound Brook to Brunswick."[13]

General Washington soon got word of the attack and sent orders to Nathanael Greene at Basking Ridge to respond with force. Greene complied at once, rushing his detachment ten miles to Bound Book, but by mid-afternoon when he arrived, Cornwallis's troops—already well down the road toward Raritan Landing—were nowhere to be seen. Greene reoccupied the village while sending a small detachment off to harass the British rear, but little was accomplished. "The Jägers formed the rear guard," wrote Ewald, "and the enemy, who had rushed support from Basking Ridge, showed himself only at a distance."[14] A few shots were exchanged before the Americans withdrew. The Battle of Bound Brook was over.

Typical of Revolutionary actions, both the casualty figures and reports of the engagement varied widely. Howe, in a letter to Germain, boasted, "Lord Cornwallis, ever watchful to take advantage of the enemy's situation, surprised and defeated on the 13th instant, at break of day, a corps of rebels at Bound Brook, killed 30 and took between 80 and 90 prisoners including officers with three brass field pieces... The loss on our side was only three Yeagers and four soldiers of the light infantry, slightly wounded."[15] Ewald, on the other hand, made no mention of British losses but insisted that "three hundred men were captured, among whom were the adjutant of General Lincoln, one captain, and two officers."[16] Archibald Robertson noted in his diary that eighty American prisoners had been taken, along with two cannons,[17] while Stephen Kemble wrote that the "rebels were surprised, and ran off in their Shirts and hid in the Woods near; a few were killed, about 80 taken, with three field Pieces...Our Troops returned then to Quarters quietly."[18] As for the American version of events, the *Pennsylvania Packet* reported two days after the engagement as follows: "We hear that on Sunday morning last a party of the enemy attacked about 200 Continental troops, under command of Gen. Lincoln, near Bound Brook, New-Jersey. They fought them for some time, under great disadvantages, in point of numbers and situation, and at last retreated, with the loss of two men killed. The enemy had three men killed."[19]

Captain Ewald, as was often the case, had led the British vanguard into Bound Brook and the rearguard back out, and he later discovered that he was being accused of disobeying orders by bringing on a general action when his orders had been to create a feint or demonstration only. Curiously, he discovered this from the scuttlebutt circulating in camp, not a direct exchange with a superior officer, which would have been the proper avenue of reprimand had he actually done something wrong. "About noon I arrived back at my post," the Hessian wrote. "I learned later that I was accused of attacking too rashly, for General Grant's attack had been a feint. But I had not heard a word about it. I should have been advised if this attack was to have been a feint, for then I would have only skirmished with the enemy picket."[20]

It is obvious from reading Ewald's journal that he was an exceptional soldier who would never have deliberately disobeyed an order. Why else had he been selected to repeatedly handle the point leading into many actions and the rearguard during withdrawals? Cornwallis had enough confidence to include him in drafting the original battle plan for the attack on Bound Brook. If Cornwallis was, in fact, using Ewald's plan during the April 13 operation, then Ewald would surely have known that his mission was simply to create a demonstration, thus holding the Americans in place while allowing the other British columns to enter the town unopposed. But Ewald had no idea this was the case. So it seems a safe bet that Cornwallis was not using Ewald's original plan but something of his own design; in which case Ewald should have received direct instructions regarding his role in the attack from General Grant or an officer from Grant's staff. But this did not happen.

General Grant, on the other hand, had a long history of contempt for the fighting capabilities of both Americans and Hessians and, on more than one occasion, had blamed others for his own command failures, and this indirect slight of Ewald suggests the same sort of low blow.[21] It was Grant, after all, who, as a prewar member of the House of Commons, boasted that, given five thousand British troops, he could march from one end of the American continent to the other, presumably ending any talk of rebellion as he did.[22] Now that Howe had seventeen thousand British troops in Brunswick alone—and was routinely requesting additional reinforcements from Germain—Grant had been revealed as little more than egotistical and disparaging.

Nathanael Greene's detachment immediately began restoring order in Bound Brook. Lincoln promptly returned with what remained of his command, and supplies were shifted from other American posts to make up for what the Redcoats had pillaged. "Upon the return of the American soldiers to their camp at Bound Brook, they looked with dismay upon the devastation perpetrated by the enemy. Immediate steps were taken to restore order and repair damages." As this was going on, General Greene began a detailed inspection of the ground surrounding the post as to its defensive practicability. "Supplies were sent from other divisions of the army. Gen. [William] Alexander, also known as Lord Stirling, wrote to Gen. Lincoln from Basking Ridge. 'It has just occurred to me that a little refreshment for your men will be no disagreeable acquisition to you. I have therefore ordered 600 pounds of beef, three barrels of flour, and twenty gallons of rum to be sent you immediately.'"[23]

General Washington was rightly concerned over the ease with which the British had overrun Bound Brook, and Greene's studied report only increased his concern. What Greene discovered was a post that was essentially indefensible due to the implications of the surrounding territory. In short, Bound Brook should never have been selected as a key position in the first place. Moreover, short of massive improvements, which the Americans were incapable of effecting, the post could not be properly defended. Washington carefully digested Greene's report and would take the appropriate action soon enough, ushering in a new phase in the New Jersey Campaign, soon to be told.

Given the fact that the Americans were already back in Bound Brook by midafternoon, what, overall, can we make of the raid itself? The British military hierarchy at Brunswick, after all, appeared entirely pleased with the result, having achieved most of the sophisticated tactical objectives the operation had been designed to accomplish. To be fair, the attack on Bound Brook was a complex, tactically demanding operation. That it was executed almost flawlessly gives credit to Corn-wallis, along with the officers and men of the British army. Rarely, indeed, does a mission requiring a nighttime march across unfamiliar ground, with four uncoordinated columns descending simultaneously upon a common target, ever come off without a hitch. That Maitland's small part of the design was fumbled appears but a minor hiccup because I suspect—had Maitland's troops even been in place—most of the escaping Americans would have found easy ways through the woods to avoid them. From a tactical perspective, therefore, the British raid must be rated a spectacular success.

From a strategic perspective, however, the British raid on Bound Brook appears dramatically less impressive. To begin with, confiscated stores, homes plundered, three cannons taken, along with a few rebels killed and captured seems a measly prize for such a spectacular opera-tion involving four thousand of the king's finest troops. Bound Brook, a critical post in the American line, had been taken with ease and could have been held with ease, given the number of British troops and artillery involved. Moreover, there were important advantages to be gained. From Bound Brook, for instance, roads ran directly northeast behind Quibbletown, Woodbridge, and even Spanktown and West-field, which meant that a strong troop movement up any one of those roads would have placed all those American posts in immediate stra-tegic peril. Nathanael Greene—hardly a trained military engineer—seems to have grasped the implications of the surrounding ground and road network immediately, but Cornwallis appears not even to have glanced beyond the village itself. And yet, we know Cornwallis was perfectly aware of the roads that led from Bound Brook to Quib-bletown and beyond to Washington's headquarters at Morristown. That is precisely why he tasked Maitland with blocking those roads in the first place—not only to capture fleeing Americans but to prevent rebel reinforcements from arriving.

Cornwallis had four thousand troops at Bound Brook and another thirteen thousand still behind at Brunswick. The two roads between the towns were now entirely open for British use, as was the Raritan River for the Royal Navy. Early Sunday morning, it would have been easy to have had an additional four thousand troops rapidly marched to Bound Brook, still leaving nine thousand behind in defense of Brunswick. Then, two decisive actions could have been achieved. First, we know that Cornwallis was mindful of rebel reinforcements being sent to Bound Brook, so why not prepare a trap to ensnare them? After all, Cornwallis had one hundred dragoons with him at the time, so it would have been entirely feasible to use them to patrol the roads in and out of Bound Brook. No matter what troop numbers Washington responded with, Cornwallis was sure to outnumber them significantly, so why not use that overwhelming force to further advantage? With two quick punches, then, Cornwallis might easily have walloped two of Washington's principal outposts: first Bound Brook and then Greene's detachment arriving from Basking Ridge. But from events alone, it is apparent Cornwallis had no interest in anything beyond the British troops' customary looting.

The second action Cornwallis could easily have taken—as previously mentioned—was to send two strong detachments down the roads toward Quibbletown and Westfield. This would have placed powerful British forces *behind* the American post at Quibbletown while threatening Woodbridge, Spanktown, and Westfield with potential envelopment. Such a move would have made Quibbletown instantly untenable, forcing an immediate withdrawal, lest Quibble-town be cut off and taken front and rear. With Bound Brook taken and Quibbletown quickly evacuated, Cornwallis would have fatally breached Washington's entire forward line (even more so had Greene's supporting column been attacked in detail while coming up), placing the remaining American posts in strategic peril. Given Washington's repeated fear of a major British strike, there is every chance he would have immediately withdrawn all Continental forces back to the passes in the Watchung Mountains in something resembling a state of panic. In other words, a terrible strategic setback for the Americans, essentially accomplished through maneuver alone.

This is not speculation based on historical hindsight. These strategic possibilities were open and obvious and hardly required the offensive mind of an Alexander the Great to comprehend. It required only knowledge of the ground, road network, and location of enemy forces, all of which Cornwallis had at his disposal. A significant British breakthrough was there for the taking. But to be taken, it had to be seen, and from events alone, it appears Cornwallis had no interest beyond the myopic pillaging of Bound Brook itself. Consequently, by late afternoon, the Americans had reoccupied the village, General Greene had assessed its defensive liabilities, and the British had returned to Brunswick with their booty, artillery pieces, and eighty prisoners.

A mission that had been excellently planned and superbly executed had accomplished little, if anything, in the end. By the afternoon of April 13, both sides were back where they had started, as if nothing of consequence had occurred—because nothing of consequence *had* occurred. Nevertheless, the British appeared pleased with their day's work. The strategic leaps that might have been accomplished were never mentioned because they had never been envisioned in the first place. Cornwallis can be credited as an excellent tactical thinker, but of his strategic vision, precious little can be said—and he was one of the king's best. Howe would be recalled to London in the spring of 1778 after years of overcaution, and Cornwallis would march on until trapped into disaster at Yorktown, a defeat that effectively ended the war. Many reasons have been cited for British failure during the American Revolution, but an unimaginative senior military leadership that routinely underestimated the Americans' willingness to fight on might well be added to the list. And no more compelling evidence of that shortsightedness can be pointed to than the now largely forgotten Battle of Bound Brook.

CHAPTER ELEVEN
Danbury

A few days after the affair at Bound Brook, General Washington had enough valid information on hand to sensibly appraise both the tactical and strategic implications of the British operation. Four days after the Redcoats had returned to Brunswick, he mentioned the facts in a reasonably straightforward letter to General Alexander McDougall while sidestepping the ease with which the British had taken the post:

> In the morning of the 13th Instt Lord Cornwallis in person with Majors General Grants & Skinner attempted to surprize our post at Bound Brook and to take off the Troops we had there. Happily his Enterprize was not attended with the Success he wished; however, before our little force could withdraw to the Mountains in their Rear the Enemy advanced and possessed themselves of two or three pieces of Field Artillery which we had there. We lost in prisoners & killed, by the best accounts I have obtained, from thirty five to forty men. The last has been partly compensated for, in a small number of prisoners taken from them on Monday morning – The Enemy lost the post at Eleven O'Clock the same day, & our people took possession of it again. Fortunately, Our Stores there were trifling and not worth mentioning.[1]

While Washington may have passed the Battle of Bound Brook off to McDougall as a trifling incident of no great concern, in a letter to General Maxwell—also penned on April 17———it was apparent he had digested a great many strategic lessons from the engagement and was resolved to make whatever changes necessary. "That the Enemy are upon the point of opening the Campaign can scarce admit of a doubt – where, or in what manner, is yet uncertain; it behooves us however to be as well prepard as possible, & keep every thing in such order as to move at an hours warning." These, of course, were boiler-plate instructions—like keeping your powder dry or the horses fed— but then the commander in chief began to reveal specifically what he had discerned from the recent British strike. He continued, "one step toward this is, to have the number of our Posts reduced – the Men drawn a little more compactly together – and Scouts to supply the places of Stationary Guards, along the Enemy's Lines." There is nothing in warfare that focuses the mind more clearly than failure. And the British, by successfully attacking Bound Brook—but then departing within hours—had handed Washington a gift: a failure of no great consequence and yet which clearly revealed the alarming fault lines in his frontline defenses. General Lincoln had previously pointed out the fact that, if attacked, no other American post was near enough to rush to his support. Now, Washington had glaring evidence supporting the validity of Lincoln's complaint. Not only that, but what was now painfully true of Bound Brook was equally true for the other American posts. The situation screamed for repair. Washington continued: "By this means we shall have it more in our power to move quick; shall be less liable to suprizes; and can give aid much quicker than in cases where Men upon any alarm, or Move-ment of the Enemy are to be assembled from Several different Posts, at a distance from each other."[2]

The inability for mutual support—now so glaringly obvious— had gone previously unnoticed at Morristown because the Ameri-cans, from January through March, had not been seriously tested as they had at Bound Brook. They had been fighting aggressively on the defensive, attacking British foraging operations wherever they appeared, content to simply drive them back into the confines of Brunswick. But now, spring had returned, bringing with it the warm, dry conditions necessary for serious campaigning, the very season Washington had been dreading all winter.

Fortunately for the rebel cause, Cornwallis had just provided Washington a tutorial regarding the vulnerabilities of his defensive postings, and all at the bargain price of a few plundered stores, eighty prisoners, and three captured cannons. As a military leader, George Washington would eventually lose more battles than he would win, but he was learning on the job, while both Howe and Cornwallis were the supposed professionals. Yet it was Washington who immediately grasped the flaws in his defensive scheme post-Bound Brook and moved to sensibly correct them, while the professionals appeared to slumber through the entire episode. Significant strategic objectives were there for the taking after Bound Brook had been seized, had Cornwallis the willingness to simply take a glance at his map. It had taken hours for Washington to respond to Cornwallis's attack on Bound Brook, yet this sluggish response seems never to have registered on the British general. Were other American posts equally as distant from one another, and might those distances be taken advantage of? This seems the most obvious question imaginable, but it appears Cornwallis could not see beyond a few plundered stores, eighty prisoners, three captured cannons, and a quick return to Brunswick.

Recognizing his good fortune at Bound Brook, Washington informed Maxwell of the immediate steps he was taking to consolidate his frontline posts. But that hardly meant good fortune would continue to bless him. While Bound Brook had shined a light on those flaws in the American defenses, it had also vividly demonstrated the fact that Cornwallis was now willing to move secretly, rapidly, and in great strength; precisely the sort of British operation Washington feared most. Campaigning season may have arrived, but the new Continental regiments were nowhere to be seen. "I wish I could see any prospect of an Army, fit to make proper opposition, formed any where," he wrote John Hancock. "You will perhaps be surprised at this, after the public Reports of the great Success of recruiting in all the States, but to convince you that these have been but bare Reports, I will give you the best information I have been able to collect, from actual Returns and other accounts."

The commander in chief then listed the true state of the "New Army," according to the actual recruiting figures, state by state. In New Hampshire, there were no new verifiable enlisted men; in Massachusetts, four hundred; in Rhode Island, three hundred and sixty. Connecticut boasted one thousand, eight hundred, but these were scattered throughout the state and, by and large, uninoculated for smallpox, hence useless. New York had raised only two hundred per regiment, and none of those regiments were ready to come online. New Jersey reported two to three hundred per regiment, but many difficulties prohibited these from joining the main army. Pennsylvania reported zero new enlistments, Delaware, the same, while Maryland had only two hundred men ready to march. Lastly, Virginia—Washington's home state—reported the possibility of raising only six new regiments, but those six were little more than a hope.

Washington had done everything he could think of to encourage recruitment from across the entire country, but every effort he had employed had failed. "If the Men that are raised, few as they are," he continued to Hancock, "could be got into the Field [field], it would be a matter of some Consolation, but every Method that I have been able to devise has proved ineffectual."[3] In April 1777, Revolutionary zeal across the United States appeared flat. Aware of this malaise then seemingly rampant across the states, in early April, Washington had sent General Arthur St. Clair off on a mission to Philadelphia with strict instructions to try and rectify the situation—at least in that city. "You will repair immediately to Philadelphia," he wrote, "and use your utmost endeavours to hasten the Troops on to this place – nothing but vigorous exertions – strict attention – and even rigour towards the Officers, will enable you to accomplish this purpose in proper Season, for I have too good reasons to believe, that the whole time of many of them, is spent in dissipation and extravigance – examples must be made of such."[4]

The lack of new recruits, amplified by worries concerning General Howe's next move, routinely tormented the commander in chief. Shortly after Bound Brook, he again expressed these concerns to General McDougall. "The views of the Enemy and the Schemes they mean to prosecute this Campaign," he wrote, "are not yet certainly unfolded. There is strong reason to conclude from a variety of combining circumstances that Philadelphia will be the first Object of their attention: However, as the Stratagems of War are many, and notwithstanding appearances, their real designs may be up the North River, it behoves us to be prepared at all points, as well as we possibly can."

The commander in chief then outlined several tasks he wanted McDougall to perform within the Hudson Valley to make that region less susceptible to incursion. As to the immediate future, Washington confided "that in few a days the Enemy will commence their Operations & their designs will be fully understood." Better consolidating the Continental army, just as he had pointed out to Maxwell, was still very much on his mind, no matter in which direction the British moved. "If Philadelphia is their Object," he continued, "The Militia, except such as the State has thought proper to raise for a longer service, may be permitted to return to their Homes without injury." On the other hand, "If the North River [Hudson River] is, All the Continl forces will be drawn together as soon as they can. At present they are too much divided, and if they become more so; we shall not be equal to the smallest resistance in any Quarter – do urge these things – the situation of our Affairs call loudly for every aid and for every exertion."[5]

An unknown aspect of Howe's evolving plan to move on Philadelphia was to leave New York City defended by a command of seven thousand British and provincial regulars under Lt. General Sir Henry Clinton and William Tyron, then royal governor of New York, then major general of provincial (Tory) troops. It had been Tyron who had led the April raid at Peekskill that had destroyed much-needed stores, and by late April, Tyron had turned his eye north toward much bigger game. Born to English aristocracy, he had risen to the rank of lieutenant colonel in the British army and later served as the royal governor of North Carolina before being appointed governor of New York in 1771. During the later months of 1776, the commissioners of the American army had designated Danbury, Connecticut, as the location for a supply depot to service the needs of the Hudson River Valley.[6] The location made sense in that the depot was established in western Connecticut, far from the Redcoats in New York City or potential raids along the Atlantic Coast. Unfortunately for the Americans, word of the depot's location had been obtained by a British spy in April 1777 and forwarded on to Howe in New York.[7] In that the depot contained enormous supplies of food, clothing, and armaments, it was immediately designated a target, and Tyron promptly planned a raid to be initiated on April 23. The hope was to injure Washington in New Jersey by bloodying his nose in Connecticut.

Archibald Robertson tells us that on April 20, "Upon Information that the Rebels had Collected a Great Magazine of Stores and Provisions at Danbury in Connecticut a secret Expedition was set on foot to destroy it." This expedition numbered one thousand, eight hundred troops, including cavalry, six pieces of field artillery, and a Tory detachment of three hundred foot soldiers. It was to set sail from New York City, proceed up the Atlantic seaboard, and ultimately disembark along the Connecticut coast. From there, they would rapidly march twenty-five miles inland to Danbury. Robertson explains that on the 21st, "about two o'clock we sail'd up the East River and pass'd Hellgate with a fair Wind, which fail'd and we came to an Anchor in the Sound off City Island." The winds momentarily left the ships bobbing motionless for a few days before turning favorable again. On April 25, the expedition finally arrived at its destination on the Connecticut coast. "About 5 o'clock in the Evening," wrote Robertson, "Landed on Cedar Point about 4 miles East of Norwalk and 8 west of Fairfield on the Connecticut Shore."[8]

But the Americans had lookouts all along the coast, and it had not taken long before such a large flotilla had been observed. "There were twenty transports and six war vessels in the fleet. The object of the expedition was kept a secret by those in command. The next morning, from a point of observation at Norwalk, the fleet was first discovered by our people [rebels]. Its destination was, of course, a mystery. The fleet passed Norwalk and stood in for the mouth of the Saugatuck river. In that harbor it dropped anchor. It was now four o'clock in the afternoon of April 25."[9] The British infantry immediately marched inland about one and a half miles, where they took possession of two dominating hills. The weather was warm and balmy, but a hard rain lay just over the horizon. On the hills above Cedar Point, the infantry awaited the artillery to be disembarked as the sun disappeared, and raindrops began to splatter the ground. Once the artillery had been disembarked—just after eleven o'clock that night—the entire column began marching northwest through a steady rain on the road to Danbury, which passed first through the village of Reading.[10] As the long column moved farther inland, rebel couriers were dispatched to warn of their approach, particularly toward the towns of Danbury and New Haven.

According to Stephen Kemble, the British moved with haste; realizing, of course, that any delay would give the rebels time to remove the stores the expedition had been designed to either appropriate or destroy. "When the Moon rose; pursued their march till 11 o'Clock the next Day," Kemble tells us, "when they Halted at Richmond, within six Miles of Danbury, till one; resumed their March, and arrived at Danbury about six in the Evening."[11] A courier had galloped into New Haven, where American General Wooster was quartered, along with General Benedict Arnold. Responding to the alarm, they ordered all militias to converge on Reading in hopes of stopping the British advance. These orders proved ineffective, however, for the rebel militias could not muster rapidly enough to counter the threat. Thus, while the British column suffered a few wounded from minor ambushes along the way, they marched into Danbury largely unopposed. "We halted an hour and a half [at Richmond]," says Robertson, "and then march'd forward to Danbury where we arrived at 5 o'clock in the Evening, having pass'd through a very mountainous difficult Country."[12]

Danbury was but lightly defended at the time, with a combined force of fifty Continentals and one hundred militiamen under the command of Colonel Joseph P. Clarke—a resident of the town—forming the only opposition. They managed to fire a few volleys but were no match for a such a massive invasion force and were quickly dispersed.[13] Robertson, marching in with the British troops, recalled the moment: "The Rebels Appeared about Danbury in a Body of 200 Scattered, they fired a few Shots at a Distance. Wounded 3 of the 23d while were taking possession of the Rising Grounds about the Village, When we entered the Street 7 Daring Rascals fired at us from a house that flank'd the street we were drawn up on. Two Companys of the 15th Attack'd them and put them to Death Burning the house." The Redcoats then went about carting off the supplies housed in the depot. "We immediately began to Collect Stores," Robertson wrote, "our men very much fatigued."[14]

General Tyron moved into the home of Nehemiah Dibble on South Street, while his men went about their business. But for various reasons, it would soon become an uncomfortable night for him. The British had been long on the march, and amongst the stores, they discovered a large stash of rum, which was immediately put to good use. While Tyron "had met with a complete success in reaching Danbury and destroying the stores, which was the object of his mission;" it was later reported, "the great bulk of his force was helpless in the strong embrace of New England rum."[15] Many of his weary troops were drunk, but that was not the worst of it. Those responding militias, which had failed to gather in time to oppose the British advance, were now reported swarming over the hills only miles away. In fact, by early morning, Tyron had received credible reports that American Generals Wooster, Arnold, and Silliman were already in Bethel, moving rapidly toward Ridgefield, where they determined to make a stand. "A heavy rain setting in, which continued all afternoon, the progress of the Americans was retarded, and they did not reach Bethel until eleven o'clock at night, the men were fatigued, their muskets rendered unserviceable by the wet. A halt was as necessary as it was prudent, and preparations were made to put their arms in a serviceable condition, and to refresh the men."[16]

At Danbury, General Tyron had thus been forced to alter his weekend plans. He had originally counted on passing a peaceful Sunday in town, but that idea had to be shelved. Around two o'clock in the morning, therefore, the destruction began, the homes of the Tories being marked by a cross, applied with lime to spare them the torch. That accomplished, the burning of Danbury began and proceeded throughout the early hours of Sunday, flames lighting the sky for miles around.[17] Robertson was on hand, noting that "by Day break set fire to all Stores and March'd about 8 o'clock on our Return to the Ships by way of Ridgefield. Had information that the Rebels were Collecting in Numbers to oppose us and Molest our Rear."[18] The damage inflicted on Danbury was severe, Kemble writing that the Redcoats "burnt about 20 Houses with a large Quantity of Medicines and Stores of different sorts in them, with a great quantity of provisions in the Streets, piled up on the borders of the Street."[19] As the British departed the village, the only structures left standing were the Episcopal church and the homes of the Tories. The town would be rebuilt before the end of the war, but the burning of Danbury would be long remembered throughout the region.

Major Archibald Robertson.

As the sun rose in the east, Generals Silliman and Arnold departed Bethel with about four hundred men, intent on confronting the Redcoats at Ridgefield. Wooster, with a mere two hundred, moved off in another direction, tasked with attacking the British rearguard as it approached the town. Six hundred militiamen against one thousand, eight hundred of the king's finest were not terribly good odds, but the Americans had come to fight, and fight they would. According to Archibald Robertson, the first shots were fired about five miles south of Danbury at a place called Ridgebury Hill. These were aimed at the rearguard but were fired from such a distance that they fell harmlessly to the ground.

The Redcoats then halted three miles short of Ridgefield for breakfast. As they were eating, Wooster struck the rear of the column in a quick, hot skirmish, killing two and taking forty prisoners. British reinforcements rushed to the scene, and Wooster retreated with his militiamen but returned about an hour later. The British, now aware of both his presence and intentions, were far better prepared to receive him. This second stroke ended poorly for the rebels. The Redcoats had wheeled three of their six artillery pieces into position and opened fire as soon as they spotted the Americans advancing. Wooster went down in a spray of musket balls and grape, imploring his men to follow, crying: "Come my boys! Never mind such random shots!"[20] He was taken to Danbury, where he lingered for five days before passing, his militiamen scattering in the wind after he had fallen. Nevertheless, Wooster's two attacks had delayed the British advance long enough for the other rebel force to reach Ridgefield.

It was now nearing noon, and Arnold and Silliman had barricaded the north end of Ridgefield's main street with anything and everything they could get their hands on, having been joined by another one hundred militia. Behind the barricade, they positioned three hundred men, and they placed one hundred on each flank, just outside the village. Entering the town from the north, Tyron quickly spotted the American barricade and brought his long column to a halt. After looking the situation over, he decided to send his main column directly at the rebels barricaded in the village and dispatch two detachments to circle round and envelop the Americans in flank and rear. The three attacks were conducted in a disjointed fashion, however, and the Americans were able to stand firm for over an hour, despite the numerical odds against them. The main attack on the barricade was led by General Erskine, supported by artillery, and under this intense cannonade, the rebels were eventually forced to give way. Hand-to-hand fighting ensued as the Americans withdrew down the street, the British hot on their heels.[21] Benedict Arnold attempted to rally his men at the south end of town but was soon caught up in the British pursuit. An article published in *The Connecticut Magazine* in 1906 captures the moment:

> A he rode on to the front of his troops, a battalion of British advanced and fired, his horse fell, pierced with nine bullets, but Arnold miraculously escaped, his foot however was caught in the stirrup and while he was endeavoring to extricate it a Tory rushed toward the general with his bayonet, "Surrender, you are my prisoner," the Tory shouted. "Not yet," exclaimed Arnold as he sprang to his feet, drawing his pistol he shot the man dead and bounded into some bushes followed by a shower of bullets."[22]

The Americans retreated down the road toward the Atlantic, beaten once but still determined. The British, having been severely tested, stopped to gather their dead and wounded. Rattled by the intense resistance, they spent the night in Ridgefield, deployed for defense. "In three severe Skirmishes," Robertson wrote, "we had about 50 or 60 Killed and Wounded and 4 or 5 officers, Major [Henry] Hope, Captain Rutherford, etc. We lay near the Village all night, 4 Battalions in line and two on the Wings."[23]

The Redcoats departed early the next morning, leaving six homes and the Episcopal church—which had been used as a rebel supply depot—in flames, determined to reach their fleet at Cedar Point. The Americans had rallied during the night as well, fresh militia units having arrived from across Connecticut and New York under the command of Continental Colonel Jedediah Huntington. These men had taken up positions behind walls, fences, trees, and barns all along the British line of march. Reminiscent of the New Jersey militias around Brunswick, they continually fired, withdrew, then fired again as the British marched toward the ocean, exacting a heavy toll throughout the day.

Farther south, General Arnold—unfazed by his encounter with the Tory infantryman—had assembled another five hundred men on Compo Hill, a prominence that dominated the approach to the Saugatuck River, where the British fleet rode at anchor and one mile from modern-day Compo Beach on the Atlantic. There, he was joined by a company of Continental artillery commanded by John Lamb, the two forming a daunting impediment to any British advance. The British pressed on, taking fire from all sides, until they came to within five miles of the beach, where they stopped on a hill that overlooked the surrounding plain. This is what Archibald Robertson saw: "When we got within 5 miles of the Shore we got upon a high hill call'd Chestnut hill, from which we could discern our Ships and the Rebels drawn up about 2 miles in front to oppose our Passing a Bridge over Sauketuk [Saugatuck] River."[24] Like Robertson, the British commander could see, even from a considerable distance, that to dislodge the Americans in Arnold's position would require an enormous sacrifice in dead and wounded, and—continually pressed from all sides by swarms of militiamen—he sensibly sought another route to the beach. Good fortune then arrived for the British in the form of a Tory who "directed him to a place where the river could be forded some two miles north of the bridge."[25]

Kicking up dust, the British hustled down to the ford, then crossed over rapidly, fearful of being surrounded by the pursuing Americans. According to Stephen Kemble, William Erskine led the troops across the river, then immediately back up the steep slope on the other side, hopeful of gaining the commanding ground at the summit before the Americans could get there. Says Kemble, "they pushed for the rising grounds near the Landing; we did the same, and happily seized them first; the 4th Regiment in the rear upon this occasion very near being cut off, but happily escaped."[26] The British may have won the race to the top of the hill, but that small victory hardly ensured their survival. Erskine, after placing the troops in a defensive posture, galloped downhill to the landing to alert the navy to the predicament above and grab whatever troops were available to follow him back.

As Erskine was leading a group of British marines and sailors back to the top of the hill, the Americans formed for an assault, hoping to drive the British into the Atlantic. Lamb's Continental artillery was blasting away, wreaking havoc along the British lines. "Four field pieces [Lamb's] on the enemy's right, within an enclosure of stone fences exceedingly annoyed the provincials [Tory infantry] where Lamb was engaged. Leaping from his horse he proposed to carry them by storm. The troops readily assented, advanced bravely receiving unterrified the grape which was plentifully showered around them."

Standing in the British ranks, Archibald Robertson had a good look at the Americans as they swarmed forward and later described their charge. "Rebels advanced from Wall to Wall keeping up a very heavy fire of Musketry and two pieces of Cannon."[27] The Redcoats were formed behind a stone wall, which the Americans intended to take. As they neared, Erskine hustled the sailors and marines into position, adding their muskets to the British defense. Still, through a withering fire of musketry, the rebels came on. "Lamb encouraged them onward, and they advanced to the fence with great resolution."[28]

For the Redcoats, the situation had become perilous, as Americans, in great numbers, began to envelop the wall. The two sides collided, and "as Lamb mounted the fence, he was struck with a grape-shot, and fell, both armies supposing him to be mortally wounded." Muskets and cannon were cracking and roaring at such a pitch that it was almost impossible to hear. The Americans drove the British from two stone walls back to a third, where the British, now seriously pressed, resorted to the one tactic that generally worked well against American militia—the bayonet.[29] Continental troops carried muskets equipped to carry a bayonet, but militiamen, using a variety of weapons brought from home, generally did not. So an overpowering bayonet charge commonly sent militiamen scattering for the hills in that once they had discharged their weapons, they had no further means of defending themselves. Robertson: "At length they came so near that it was thought advisable to charge them with fix'd Bayonets, which was done with 4 Regiments."[30]

As those four regiments charged the Americans, the remainder of the British column headed for the beach. Limbering up their artillery, they raced down to the fleet, where the guns of the warships could cover them. The momentum of the rebel attack had been blunted by the bayonet charge, and it would take time for the Americans to recover. Meanwhile, the British quickly reembarked their equipment and men on board the transports as the rebels closed to within musket range once again. "Arnold pressed on with every available man to cut off Tryon from his boats; so fiercely did the patriots assail the British, the ground was strewn with the wounded and dying. Arnold escaped unhurt, but his horse was shot, and a ball passed through the collar of his coat. The patriots continued the struggle until the last ship weighed anchor and passed out to sea."[31]

Casualties for the extended fighting—from Danbury to Ridge-field to the Atlantic—are, as usual, difficult to ascertain with precision, given the length of the British march and the distances involved. Nevertheless, by most accounts, it appears the British suffered far more severely than the Americans. Archibald Robertson lists British casualties as one hundred and forty men of the line killed or wounded, with another fourteen officers wounded and forty men taken prisoner. He lists American casualties as one hundred men killed and two hundred wounded, but it is entirely unclear where he got those figures, and they appear to be estimates rather than definitive counts.[32] The most accepted figure for American casualties is twenty killed and forty to eighty wounded,[33] but given the duration and intensity of combat, that figure is probably low.

The British were pleased with their raid on Danbury, but over time, it would cost them far more than they gained. They did destroy large quantities of rebel stores, which were much needed and hard to come by, but the wanton destruction they inflicted aroused the people of Connecticut—a state that had seen little action and was evenly divided in its loyalties—to a fever pitch of resentment. A brief listing of the stores burned provides insight into why the British fancied their raid a success but fails, as is to be expected, to even hint at the loyalties that had been shattered forever. The major items destroyed were seven thousand barrels of pork and beef, one thousand barrels of flour, eighty hogsheads of biscuit, one hundred barrels of rice, sixty hogsheads of rum and brandy, twenty barrels of wine, ten casks of medicine, one thousand tents, sixty iron kettles; five thousand pairs of shoes, along with smaller amounts of bedding, tools, axes, sugar, corn, and various arms.[34] In particular, the tents and shoes proved a terrible loss, for the Continentals were in dire need of both.

The burning of Danbury and Ridgefield would be remembered solemnly for over one hundred and fifty years. What had once been an essentially passive region had overnight been turned into a hotbed of rage against the British, an inversion of loyalties no amount of charred pork, biscuit, rice, and so on could justify.

CHAPTER TWELVE
Bonhamtown

After their raid on Danbury, the British did not get their troops back to New York City until April 29.[1] Nevertheless, General Washington had a first—if somewhat murky—report of the operation in his hands by April 28. This speaks well, at least, for Continental communications, no matter how disappointing the news. Awoken at three o'clock in the morning by a dispatch rider, the general's aides opened a letter from General McDougall, which contained three quickly penned reports from Jedediah Huntingdon describing what he knew of the British incursion at the time. From the meager facts they contained, Washington could only presume the worst, but all three had been written only hours after the British had landed in Connecticut; the last as they were entering Danbury.[2]

In fairness, all of Huntington's letters were written hurriedly in the field on the 26th as the British were closing on Danbury. In fact, his first letter contained correspondence dashed off by General Silliman on the 25th, imploring militia officers to join him as soon as possible. It read: "The Enemy from 24 Sail of Shipping have landed at Campo their Number is yet unknown but it is of the last Importance to be ready to oppose them you will therefore immediately muster your Regiments & march Day & Night till you get here as soon as you get Twenty Men of a Company together." Huntington, grasping the grim situation at Danbury, added this note of his own: "there are about one hundred continental Troops in this Place double the Number marched from this the 24th on their Way to Peeks Kill – there is great Want of Amunition....P.S. Flints are wanting."

Huntington's second letter was written at seven o'clock in the morning on the 26th, as the British were marching toward Danbury. Still trying to muster the strength to oppose the Redcoats, he wrote: "Lt Col Sherman will march immediately for Peeks Kill with 40 or 50 Men being one half of all that are here at present – I hope, about 100 men now on the Road, will be here this Night or Tomorrow Morning – the Militia in this Neighbourhood are on the Move towards Fairfield in Consequence of the Express from General Silliman – I am sending an Express eastward to hasten Troops and Militia to this Place & Peeks Kill." The colonel's last report was written at four o'clock in the afternoon of the 26th, as the British were entering Danbury. Rational in tone and realistic regarding his options, it read: "The Enemy are just entered the Town [Danbury] & I am reduced to the hard Necessity of leaving the Plain & the greatest Part of the Stores & repairing to the Heights with about 50 continental Troops & as many again Militia – I had sent Expresses every Way for Succours [help] but none has come worth mentioning the Enemy are said to be 2000 – I did not think it prudent to stay in the Town to make any opposition as the Place is encompassed with Heights & the Numbers of the Enemy so superior. I hope some continental Troops from Massachusetts now at or near New Milford will be here Tomorrow."[3]

Just as at Bound Brook, the British had organized and executed a secret mission employing overwhelming force with remarkable precision, and there was no American force nearby that could have stopped them. To have expected local militia to have somehow collected and opposed a force of one thousand, eight hundred well-trained troops trailing a heavy compliment of artillery within the time frame involved is fantasy, pure and simple. That there was no adequate guard at Danbury, or plan for arousing one quickly, was just one more example of the regionalized, disjointed, ill-thought-out American war effort that had plagued the endeavor from top to bottom for years and would continue to do so until the end of the conflict.

Upon receiving the letters from McDougall, Washington promptly reported the situation to John Hancock as follows:

> At three OClock this morning, I received a Letter from Genl McDougal inclosing three from Colo. Huntingdon, Copies of the whole of which, I have transmitted. By these you will perceive, the impres-

sion which a part of General How's Army has made into Connecticut, and the prospect they had of destroying such of our Stores as were deposited in Danbury, which unfortunately, were but too large & considerable, if the Event has taken place...I have no other information upon the Subject, than what these papers contain, but we have little ground to expect, that they have not accomplished their purpose.[4]

Fortunately, Congress would learn promptly about the ruinous raid on Danbury and craft an appropriate response. On April 30, they resolved to correct the situation—and not just at Danbury but across the board. All the depots would have to be moved to safer locations, Washington explained to Generals Clinton and McDougall: "They [the depots] cannot, under the Terms of the Resolve, be deposited nearer the River, than Twenty miles; For my own part, I would wish them to be placed, Thirty miles off or more, if circumstances will admit it. they would be more secure against the designs of the Enemy, should they attempt to destroy them. It will be absolutely necessary that some Work should be thrown up to cover them & a Guard of Militia posted for their protection."[5] Remarkably—given the glacial pace at which Congress usually moved when responding to problems, much less solving them—the difficulty had been rectified this time around with a quick and sensible solution.

Out of a virtual universe of intractable problems, at least one of them had now been solved by Congress, leaving the commander in chief essentially where he had been prior to the Danbury raid—at wit's end. Desertions were mounting daily, recruits were not coming in, and money for necessities remained nonexistent. Enthusiasm for the war effort amongst the people, soldiers, and even Continental officers themselves continued to hover at low tide. While the desire for liberty had not waned, the *rage militaire* was certainly ebbing. Writing to General John Glover, for instance, Washington lamented that, "I have with great concern observed the almost universal Listlesness, that prevails throughout the continent," a condition he attributed, in part, to the indifference of his own officers, who, once moved by the spirit of liberty, had since resigned their commissions in droves. "Can any resistance be expected from the people when deserted by their leaders?" Washington asked pointedly. "Our enemies count upon the resignation of every officer of rank at this time, as a distrust of, and desertion from the cause, and rejoice accordingly."[6]

True, Washington's officers were resigning, but his troops were deserting and not just a few here and there but by the hundreds. "I am well convincd that the amazing desertions which have of late prevail'd among our Troops, proceeds intirely from their not being regularly paid," Washington wrote. Congress, happy to write new instructions for the placement of army depots, as usual was nowhere to be seen when it came to raising the funds necessary for paying the troops, as if compensating soldiers what they were due, for the American political class, remained a concept beyond their ken. Moreover, the funds that had been raised, Washington suspected, were often pilfered when "the Officers have drawn large sums, under pretence of paying their men, but have been obliged from extravagance and other purposes, to appropriate this money to their own use." The army would disappear entirely if the men continued to go unpaid. Nothing could be more obvious than that. "There is a necessity at this time for the mens being paid up," Washington wrote, "as nearly as possibly."[7] Unfortunately, like a lot of details confounding the Continental army in 1777, that obvious fact remained far easier said than done, and in fairness to the officers and men, many had reenlisted in other units and were themselves off now helping to recruit.

While the focus may have switched momentarily from Bound Brook to Danbury, the fighting in New Jersey had not diminished, with much of the action now centering around Bonhamtown. Most consisted of skirmishing between picket posts, midnight raids, or shots exchanged during the night, often when least expected. On April 15, Colonel Edward Cook, commanding a detachment of the Twelfth Pennsylvania, attacked a picket post some five hundred yards from Bonhamtown at two o'clock in the morning. The fighting was brief but intense. The pickets were members of the Seventy-Fifth British Regiment of Foot, who were quickly forced to withdraw to their earthworks nearby, leaving nine dead and another sixteen taken prisoner. The Pennsylvanians reported only two wounded, neither seriously.[8]

Then, on April 20, a similar skirmish took place when sixteen Continentals under Lt. James McCabe attacked pickets at Bonhamtown. Despite the Redcoats being reinforced, McCabe and his men kept up a steady fire until dawn, when they finally withdrew. The British reportedly lost one dead and two wounded, while McCabe reported no casualties.⁹ The British promptly doubled the guard, but that had no effect. The very next day, on April 21, with a force of thirty-two, Lt. McCabe and Lt. Lodge again attacked the guard, driving them in. They then peppered the British troops all night, forcing them to remain under arms.¹⁰ These were all small-scale attacks for sure, unit-driven and designed to do nothing more than make the lives of the British and Hessian soldiers posted nearby as miserable and nerve-racking as possible, an objective that was routinely accomplished.

Back along the Raritan River—and keeping with this nocturnal, nerve-racking motif, often called bushfighting—the struggle for martial supremacy between Hessian officers Ewald and Von Ottendorf had resumed once again, as was to be expected of two men clearly determined to outduel the other. Ewald and his Jägers had been assigned a picket post on the north side of the river, between Brunswick and Bound Brook, where once again, bullets had begun whistling through the night, as he explains: "Although the surprise attack [at Bound Brook] had scared off the enemy for some time and he let us alone for a few days," he wrote, "he now began to harass us in a different manner. Since the 18th of April, Mr. Von Ottendorff had prowled about at night in the ravines across the river and had fired on our posts, through which several sentries were killed and wounded."

Just as with the nighttime skirmishing in and around Bonhamtown, these were minor clashes of no serious strategic consequence. For those involved, however, they were fierce and deadly encounters where death might strike suddenly; at any moment. Hiding behind trees, bushes, stone walls, or even in nearby outbuildings, combatants on either side would fire while unseen, cloaked within impenetrable darkness, wounding an enemy soldier or taking a life in a fraction of a second. So it was for Ewald and his Jägers. "The enemy had also hidden several times in the barn of the preacher across the river," Ewald observed, "and fired on my quarters through holes cut in the barn walls."¹¹

This was the sneaky, sinister form of warfare practiced by both sides called *petite guerre*, rarely if ever portrayed in the heroic portraits of the era. And Ewald, schooled in the finer points of sharpshooting, knew exactly how to raise the ante. "I decided to draw these guests into an ambuscade," he confided in his journal, a trap that would require both stealth and overwhelming firepower. "I put an amusette"—a small artillery piece that could be carried manually, then mounted on a swivel—"behind a false hedge which I had fashioned from bushes, placing it so that the barn could be pierced easily." Knowing Von Ottendorf often secreted his riflemen inside the barn, Ewald plotted to use their own tactic against them. "I sent Lieutenant Trautvetter with twelve Jägers to a small hollow on this side of the river across from the parsonage, with orders to keep hidden until the Americans were dislodged from the barn by the fire of the amusette. They were then to rise and accompany the piece with sharp rifle fire."[12] During the night, Ewald spotted the rebel sharpshooters—armed with the deadly long rifle—slipping into the barn immediately across the river.

The Pennsylvania long rifle was a uniquely created American weapon originally fashioned for hunting game in the wild but later adapted for use in war. Individually crafted, they featured a longer barrel than most military firearms, like the Land Pattern Musket or the "Brown Bess," the standard-issue firearm for the British army. Both the musket and the long rifle used similar firing mechanisms but, beyond that, were radically different weapons, each effective in its own way.

First, the long rifle: "The long barrel improved accuracy and range. Increasing the length burned a little more of the gunpowder before the ball left the bore. With this added push, the ball went faster (almost 2,000 feet per second at the muzzle) and farther (effective up to 200 yards or more). The faster bullet meant a flatter trajectory (or flight). It's much easier to hit a distant target if you don't have to allow much for the drop of a relatively slower bullet. The long barrel also put more weight out front, so the weapon was muzzle-heavy and hung nicely while you aimed. And since the front and rear sights were farther apart, your aim was more precise."[13]

There were disadvantages to the long rifle, however. It took longer to load than a musket; fired a lower caliber ball, which was generally crafted by the riflemen themselves, and naturally inflicted less damage than the larger musket ball. Each weapon was also crafted individually by gunsmiths, which meant all repairs required specially fashioned parts produced by a skilled smith, making the long rifle somewhat unreliable on campaign. The Continental army did maintain artificers and gunsmiths, but repairs for men in the field were generally inconvenient and slow. Lastly, it could not be fitted with a bayonet, which made the weapon impractical for the battlefield or hand-to-hand combat. In the hands of a skilled marksman, however—and in the United States, there were many highly skilled marksmen—the long rifle could be a frighteningly lethal weapon at distances unheard of for the musket. A British officer fighting in the Carolinas, for instance, remarked that he "never in my life saw better rifles (or men who shot better) than those made in America," noting that he had personally witnessed a marksman with a long rifle take down a target with a precise shot at four hundred yards.[14]

Muskets, on the other hand, were carried by most British foot regiments, Continental regulars, militia, and Hessian regulars. Muskets could be fitted with a bayonet and had a range of about one hundred yards but were wildly inaccurate due to their shorter barrels and smooth, interior bores. This explains why eighteenth-century combat generally took place at extremely close ranges—often within fifty or even twenty-five yards—and, even then, the weapons proved inaccurate. Firepower was gained not through accuracy but by marching detachments near enough an enemy to deliver a shattering volley, often followed by a bayonet charge. The advantages of the musket were that they could be loaded and fired faster than a long rifle—three to four times a minute—were often made of manufactured parts, hence far easier to repair, and did not require a skilled marksman to fire.

The inaccuracy of the musket is one of the reasons—along with smaller troop numbers involved—that many intense and lengthy Revolutionary War engagements produced relatively few casualties, at least when compared to later periods. The smooth bore musket would remain the standard American infantry weapon until the American Civil War, inadvertently reinforcing a rather romantic, less-lethal notion of warfare. By the advent of the Civil War, however, advances in weaponry had produced new, far more deadly rifled muskets, which both sides quickly adopted. These new weapons—namely the Springfield 1861 rifle and the British Enfield—were highly accurate up to six hundred yards and still lethal beyond that. Firing a much larger bullet than the ball used in the Revolutionary long rifle, they turned the Civil War battlefield overnight into scenes of mass murder, a fact neither the medical corps nor the population in general was prepared—either effectively or psychologically—to comprehend.

Back along the banks of the Raritan River, Ewald and his Jägers remained primed and ready, taking cover in the bushes across the river from the rebel riflemen who had taken their positions in the barn overnight. "All went well," the Hessian tells us. "Soon as day broke, the rifle-men began their harassing with their long rifles." Unfortunately for the Americans, the Jägers also carried rifled muskets, although the barrels of the Hessians' rifles were twelve inches shorter than the American long rifle; thus, at increasingly greater ranges, increasingly less accurate.[15] On this night, however, that difference in accuracy would not come into play.

When the Americans began firing, Ewald opened with his amusette, blowing holes through the side of the barn where the rebels were hiding, which naturally sent nasty wood splinters showering the occupants inside, turning the barn into a death trap. It did not take the Americans long to get the message. "After the third cannon shot," wrote Ewald, "the barn became silent and the enemy left it, whereupon he fell into the Jägers fire. Since the road ran up along the river, which was not over a hundred paces wide, the Jägers had the best possible range, and every Jägers killed or wounded his man."

Ewald's clever ambush had worked perfectly. "After several hours an officer with a trumpeter appeared and requested permission to take away the dead and severely wounded on a wagon. I permitted this and asked the officer"—presumably not Baron von Ottendorf—"if he would not visit us again soon. He shook his head, and they took away their dead and wounded in two wagons. There were five dead and two badly wounded."[16]

As all this skirmishing was taking place, in Morristown, General Washington was still fretting over the desertions that were decimating the ranks of his army. "The desertions from our Army of late have been very considerable," he complained. Making matters worse, General Howe had recently authored a proclamation authorizing a bounty to be paid to any rebel who deserted at any one of the British posts, carrying his weapon, an incentive that only increased the rate of desertion. Given that Washington could barely pay his own men, this added another dimension to the problem. "Nor have the base frauds practiced by several of Our Officers, contributed a little to this, in my Opinion," he insisted. "Many privates complain loudly, declaring they have not received either pay or bounty – Others not a farthing of the latter, and they have become so mutinous & uneasy in many cases, that I have been obliged to draw Warrants for Money on Account, to distribute among the men."

Not all recent reports had been entirely dispiriting, however, in that new information had trickled into camp suggesting the harm done at Danbury had been less than originally suspected. "The damage we sustained at Danbury," Washington told Hancock, "nor the Enemy's loss, have not been transmitted with any accuracy; but from the latest accounts from thence, The former was not so great and the latter more considerable, than was apprehended at first."[17] This may not have been much in the way of good news, but it was at least *something* that contained a positive spin. And one thing was evident: from the letters coming and going from Morristown in late April 1777, it was abundantly clear that the commander in chief had precious little to feel good about, as a world of problems continued to bedevil him.

In late April, Ewald received good news just days after the ambush he had so cunningly arranged. "On the 28th I received orders to maintain my post only in daytime," he wrote, "At night I was to withdraw across the sunken road, where the remainder of the company was stationed under Lieutenant Hinrichs, because the enemy had reinforced the two posts at Bound Brook and Quibbletown." Clearly, the British were now expecting trouble, no doubt in terms of increasing rebel offensive activity, and they did not want their outer pickets overrun during a major nighttime assault. Hence, the British began to throw up earthworks. In response to the reports of American reinforcements, Ewald ordered several defensive measures to be initiated. First, an earthwork was constructed in front of a small bridge that crossed a ravine nearby. Then, to support that earthwork, he also constructed "a rampart at the beginning of the ravine, and a small redoubt behind it on the hill."

These were measures taken to obstruct any American attack, and in this, Ewald was not disappointed. "On the afternoon of the 30th the enemy again attacked my post," he tells us, and the fighting instantly intensified. "Captain Lorey fought with eight mounted and ten unmounted Jägers, while I tackled the enemy on his right. I cut him off from the highway to Bound Brook behind a hill around his left flank, fell on his rear, cut down ten men, and took six prisoners."[18]

British intelligence had concluded the Americans were soon to launch an offensive somewhere in the area around Bound Brook and Quibbletown, and for this, they braced. Unfortunately, no assessment could have been less accurate, for Washington, properly digesting the fault lines in his outer defenses, was soon to move in precisely the opposite direction.

CHAPTER THIRTEEN
Piscataway

*T*hroughout the winter and spring of 1777, Washington was continually counseling the officers under his direct command in New Jersey while also contending with the Continental defenses from Massachusetts to Virginia. This required recruitments, promotions, demotions, courts-martial, and the punishments that were to be meted out. The army's dwindling numbers, the state of its commissary department, the training of recruits, conditions of magazines and armories, and so on were all issues that found their way to his desk. A review of the general's mail that winter reflects an astounding variety of difficulties, most of them worrisome; some virtually insoluble. And yet sprinkled amongst these bedeviling concerns were some that appear—at least from our distant, more fortunate perspective—borderline comical. There is no question that General Washington did not find these issues amusing at the time; more likely something between irritating and infuriating. Nevertheless, they provide the modern reader a glimpse into the catalog of problems General Washington was being asked to adjudicate on an almost-daily basis.

First, Washington had to endure the uniform color conundrum. This had its origin in a letter Washington received dated April 12 from James Mease, clothier for the Continental army. Among a range of topics covered that day, Mease included this line, which instantly grabbed the attention of the commander in chief: "Col. Moylan depends on the clothing of the 21 for his regmt wh. Is now in good forwardness & I have promised to get it for him if possible a long time ago wh. I hope will not be disagreeable to your Excellency."[1] While, at first blush, this might sound innocent enough, the twenty-one Mease was referring to was the Twenty-First British Regiment, which had had its uniforms seized on the high seas while in transit to Canada earlier in the war. In other words, Mease intended to outfit a Continental regiment in the distinctive scarlet uniforms of the British, an act which, to almost any conscious observer at the time, should have seemed obviously ridiculous in that this Continental regiment would then be indistinguishable from the enemy they were fighting. Moreover, Mease implied that many more Continental regiments—in fact, he had enough scarlet uniforms for two thousand men—were soon to be similarly outfitted, a fact which, if true, would only serve to increase the disaster exponentially. Washington promptly replied to Mease's letter, point by point, then added this postscript, underscoring the obvious: "P.S. I am convinced, that we shall experience many inconveniences, from our Soldiers being dressed in red; I therefore wish, to have all the Clothes now on hand of that colour dyed. I dont care what their colour is." To which I will add, as long as it's not *red*!

Those instructions seemed eminently straightforward, and there, the issue should have ended, but it did not. On May 11, an escort detail from Moylan's regiment guarding a shipment of funds on its way to Morristown rather naturally created quite a stir as it traveled cross-country, clothed, as they were, in their new scarlet uniforms. Washington—possibly not believing his own eyes when they arrived—responded at once, writing Mease: "Yesterday an Escort to money from Colo. Moylan's Regiment dressed in that [red] Uniform, alarmed the Country, and had they passed where the Enemy's Horse could possible have been, they certainly would have suffered." Indeed, had they been captured by the British, they could easily have been charged as spies, then tried and hung. On the other hand, had they encountered Continentals in blue or American militia who had no forewarning of their approach, Moylan's red-clad escort might have been shot right out of their saddles. Thus had the uniform conundrum already spiraled well beyond the merely ridiculous into the realm of insanely dangerous.

General Washington put his foot down emphatically: "Being more and more convinced, of the impolicy of any part of our Troops being Clothed in Red," he sternly advised Mease, "and that many injurious and fatal consequences are to be apprehended from it, I think it necessary to repeat my request, mentioned in my last, that you will have all the Clothes in your hands, of that Colour, dyed of some other, as soon as you can." Then, adding an exclamation point, the general pointed out the blatant stupidity of clothing American troops in the same scarlet worn by the enemy. "Unless the matter is immediately remedied," he wrote, "by changing the Colour, our people will be destroying themselves."[2] Fortunately for all concerned, the problem was thus sensibly resolved, despite the absurdity of the issue to begin with.

Next—and raising the comical ante a bit—during this same period, General Washington was approached by one of Governor Livingston's sons regarding a family issue that had recently spun up, causing considerable angst amongst the Livingston clan. It then became a delicate problem dropped, remarkably enough, directly into the lap of the commander in chief. William Livingston was then the governor of New Jersey and a political ally who Washington, of necessity, depended upon for help and cooperation. Seems that the governor's wife, Susannah French Livingston, had fled their home in Elizabeth Town due to the approach of the British, ultimately settling in with several of her daughters in the Basking Ridge home of General William Alexander, also known as Lord Stirling. Alexander commanded one of Washington's Continental divisions and had been born into a reasonably well-to-do family in New York in 1726, but due to his claim upon the Scottish earldom of Stirling, he preferred the aristocratic title of Lord Stirling to the more pedestrian William Alexander.

Alexander had inherited a substantial sum upon the passing of his parents and subsequently lived the lavish lifestyle of a Scottish aristocrat on his Basking Ridge manor. In battle, he had proved himself at the Battle of Long Island when, as the Continental position began to collapse, he took hold of the First Maryland Regiment and fought heroically with it in the rearguard, allowing Washington to escape with the main body. (The stand of the First Maryland on the old line that day was considered so critically important to the Revolutionary effort that the State of Maryland would take its first sobriquet from the event, naming itself the Old Line State). Taken prisoner, Alexander was eventually exchanged, and because of the skill and bravery he displayed on Long Island, he had become one of Washington's most trusted lieutenants. Stirling also happened to be the brother-in-law of William Livingston. Thus, Mrs. Livingston's move into his Basking Ridge manor house had made perfect sense at the time.

General William Alexander (Lord Stirling).

What initially had made sense, however, over time became trying, a situation not at all uncommon for families of any means, large or small. Perhaps Mrs. Susannah French Livingston was unaccustomed to being given orders, no matter how politely framed. Or possibly Lord Stirling was an overbearing stiff, unaccustomed to the niceties of high culture, no matter how gracious his guests, or maybe both were true. Or perhaps some other dynamic had put the two at one another's throats. But, whatever the cause, spun up they were and seemingly in need of arbitration. And who better to mediate such an earthshaking state of affairs than George Washington himself, a man who obviously had no other pressing issues to deal with? That the Livingston clan had turned to General Washington to resolve a simple family squabble was simultaneously ridiculous and impressive—ridiculous in that they should seek resolution of a family squabble from the commander in chief of the Continental army and impressive in that it demonstrated just how striking George Washington's reputation for fairness and good sense had become.

Washington wrote to William Alexander on May 6, perhaps realizing that he was stepping into a sticky situation, having heard but one side of the dispute. Nevertheless, after praising Lord Stirling's character, he offered his thoughts on the topic:

> The present situation of public affairs, affords abundant causes of distress, we should be very careful how we aggravate or multiply them, by private bickerings. It is not for me to enter into the merits of the dispute, that gave rise to the ill treatment complained of; but I must take liberty to give my opinion, that prudence and compassion equally dictated, all little differences and animosities, calculated to increase the unavoidable evils of the times, should be forgotten, or, at least, postponed; and that Mrs Livingstons Character, connexions, Sex, & Situation intitle her to a degree of respect and consideration, inconpatiable with the kind of deportment, which I am informed you have, in this instance, observed towards her.[3]

Yes, Mrs. Livingston was presumably capable of creating an unwanted stir if her ego was not properly assuaged; all valid points. Unfortunately, this was a *family* affair, and William Alexander remained unmoved by the general's logic. He had merely—according to him, at least—asked her to leave some six weeks before. So Alexander responded at once, obviously irked by the fact that his family's "dirty laundry" had somehow made its way all the way up the chain of command.

> I am extremly unhappy to find by your Excellency's letter of this date that any of my private Affairs should have taken up so much of your Attention; I could wish your Excellency had beleived the whole matter had been Misrepresented to you, Mrs Livingston was informed Six Weeks ago that I was in want of that part the house which she possesses. She had then no less than four other houses engaged, I yesterday in the most friendly Manner informed her that my family was under great inconveniences for want of Room and that I should be Glad she would make it Convenient

to Move as soon as possible; I conceived this to be but a Modest request, to enjoy my own property; and was not in the least governed by passion; she behaved very improperly and threatned to move the Next Morning. I told her she Might do as she thought proper.[4]

As Plato had warned centuries before: "Justice means minding one's own business and not meddling with other men's concerns." Fortunately for the commander in chief, events soon took on a more customary tone when, on Saturday, May 10, American Generals Maxwell and Stephen attacked the British near Piscataway, commanding some two thousand troops gathered from Westfield, Chatham, Samptown, and Quibbletown. According to *The Pennsylvania Evening Post,* "Last Saturday week Gen. Stephens ordered eight hundred men, from different regiments, to muster at Col. Cook's quarters, about nine miles from Matuchin meeting-house. In the afternoon they marched over Dismal swamp, and advanced to the place where the enemy kept their picket." Stephen struck first, attacking the British just as they sat down to dinner, turning their evening meal into pandemonium.

The British picket consisted of detachments of the Seventy-First Regiment of Foot, the Forty-Second Royal Highland Regiment, and the Thirty-Third Regiment of Foot, along with an additional six companies of infantry, posted on an arc from Bonhamtown to Piscataway.[5] Stephen hit hard where the Redcoats "had collected about three hundred, whom our advanced guard engaged for some time, and making a feint retreat over a causeway, turned suddenly upon the enemy and repulsed them with a considerable slaughter." British reinforcements rushed to the scene, however, and, joining the fray, pressed the Americans backward. Fortunately for the Continentals, at this point Maxwell came up in support of Stephen "with six companies of light infantry, and other troops, when the skirmish became general, was pretty warm for some time, and the enemy gave way."[6]

The fighting raged, both sides giving as well as they took, when suddenly the British—receiving still more reinforcements—were able to turn the tables on the Americans, driving them backward again. British Lieutenant John Peebles writes that "the Company's turn'd out to their support & dash'd into the Wood upon the Enemy – the Light Infantry Companys in that Qrs. came up to their Assistance & the 28th Regiment turn'd out briskly to the support of the 42nd."[7] Finally overwhelmed, the American line tumbled into reverse, causing the Continentals to flee in some confusion, the Redcoats right behind them. The pursuit continued all the way back to Metuchen Meetinghouse, where the Americans managed to gather themselves, and the British finally backed off.

The following morning, on Sunday, May 11, General Maxwell followed up the previous day's action by striking the British guards near Piscataway once more. Commanding five hundred Continentals, he drove the Redcoat picket back in some confusion until they were reinforced, allowing them to hastily form a line of battle, which slowed the American advance. Fighting raged for over a half-hour until the British, outnumbered and suffering under a withering fire, were forced once more into retreat. Maxwell pursued, but the Redcoats, being reinforced yet again, were finally able to halt Maxwell's advance. With the British now overwhelming his position, Maxwell broke off the action, withdrawing back to Metuchen.

The two days of action near Piscataway had produced particularly lethal results. On Saturday, the British had one major "three subalterns, three sergeants, and about 60 privates killed. Captain Stewart of the light infantry and 120 privates were wounded, 40 so critically that they were brought to New York." Stephen, however, reported only two infantrymen and one captain were killed. A subaltern (a British officer below the rank of captain) was wounded and taken prisoner, along with twelve of his troops; however, the British later reported finding almost forty dead Americans in the woods, along with the same number taken as prisoners.[8] The casualty count reported in Sunday's combat was equally as lopsided. A letter reprinted in *The Pennsylvania Evening Post* suggested that "this may seem very extraordinary, but when you consider that we had a number of good riflemen, and many excellent marksmen well posted in the woods, and other suitable places, the enemy in the open field, and frequently in confusion, I think you will be reconciled to the probability of their loss so far exceeding ours. This action was conducted by Gen. Maxwell, and the troops were Jerseymen, Pennsylvanians and Virginians."[9]

General Washington was pleased by both the aggressiveness and determination of the American attacks. He promptly reported to John Hancock: "On Saturday, a smart skirmish happened with a Detachment of our Troops, who attacked a Number of the Enemy near Piscataway, in which our Men behaved well & obliged the Enemy to give way twice, as reported to me, with loss. The Enemy received a Strong reinforcement, our people retreated to their post. I cannot give the particulars, as they have not been sufficiently ascertained. Their pickets were also attacked yesterday [May 11] by some of our parties from Bound Brook & forced within their lines."[10]

Unfortunately, despite the relatively good news from Piscataway, the drumbeat of vexing irritants continued undiminished for General Washington, as suggested by several general orders issued from his Morristown headquarters. Good discipline, essential for any military operation, appeared to be breaking down. On May 8, the general despaired of gambling amongst the men, which seemingly had reached disturbing levels:

> As few vices are attended with more pernicious consequences, in civil life; so there are none more fatal in a military one, than that of GAMING; which often brings disgrace and ruin upon officers, and injury and punishment upon the Soldiery. And reports prevailing, which, it is to be feared are too well founded, that this destructive vice has spread its baneful influence in the army, and, in a peculiar manner, to the prejudice of the recruiting Service, The Commander in chief, in the most pointed and explicit terms, forbids ALL officers and soldiers, play at cards, dice – or at any games, except those of EXERCISE, for diversion; it being impossible, if the practice be allowed, at all, to discriminate between innocent play, for amusement, and criminal gaming, for pecuniary and sordid purposes.

That stated, the general then went on to insist that his order regarding gaming be read frequently by all officers to their men; that his officers should spend their time training and disciplining the troops while encouraging the men to read military books in their spare time, a thought that seems fanciful in the extreme. His order was to be distributed to all the commands, even printed in the newspapers of the various states, so that there could be no confusion as to its importance. Lastly, he made it clear that anyone who might "disobey this order, shall be tried by a General Court Martial."[11]

With the gaming issue hopefully resolved, General Washington then turned his attention to yet another breakdown in regulations that had recently been brought to his attention. Washington understood that discipline was instilled from the top down, and he had every intention of instilling it. He may not have had much of an army to fight with at the time, but for that semblance of an army he *did* still command, he appears determined it would reflect the finest of military traditions in terms of order and discipline, and not appear the "rabble in arms" some British officers had derogatorily referred to their American foe. Thus, no breakdown in discipline would be overlooked.

> It having been observed, notwithstanding former orders to the contrary, that some officers make a practice of riding the Continental horses, as well as those, belonging to the inhabitants, in the neighbourhood, of the army; The Commander in Chief positively declares, that, if any officer, in the future, will dare to presume, to ride any horse, either public, or private, property, without leave first obtained from the proper officer, if a public horse; or from the owner, if private property, shall immediately be brought to trial, by a General Court Martial.[12]

These may appear petty issues to the modern-day reader, but Washington was desperately trying to fashion a professional army out of a stream of untrained, ill-disciplined men who were coursing in and out of camp, many of whom fervently believed in the American cause, while many others had signed on for less honorable reasons. During the smoke and frightful thunder of eighteenth-century combat, only the most trained and disciplined army could prevail on the field of battle, and General Washington had every intention of prevailing. Indeed, the strategic lessons he had distilled from the British action at Bound Brook the previous month had made a deep impression upon him, and—quietly and secretively—he was now planning for a full realignment of forces, a concentration that would correct the inability of his separated detachments to support one another in the face of a sudden attack.

In early May, Doctor Benjamin Rush had written Washington, concerned that he intended to break winter camp and begin campaigning much too soon. It was medicine, not the British, that concerned the doctor. It was Rush's understanding that army illnesses remained high until truly warm weather arrived, and he was justly concerned that a rash consolidation of forces might do far more harm than good. "The variable weather of the Spring and fall," Rush wrote, "have always been found much more destructive to the health of an Army than the uniform heat of Summer or colds of Winter."[13]

Washington understood all this, but he was equally aware of the disturbing fact that his army remained scattered, hence vulnerable to unexpected attack. On May 6, he responded to Rush: "I shall be induced to incamp the army, sooner than I could wish," he wrote, "from this powerful motive, that the more an army is collected, the better it is adapted, both to the purposes of defence and offence, and the better enabled, either to defeat the attempts the enemy may project against it, or take advantage of favourable conjunctures, which may offer, to annoy and injure them. I shall however endeavour to defer incamping 'till the weather becomes a little more settled and temperate."[14]

So there it was—the quick and successful British strike at Bound Brook had taught General Washington a valuable lesson. Every reason Washington laid out to Rush for consolidating the army made perfect sense, but every good plan always contains dark possibilities. The dark possibility for consolidating an army in one place has always been the same: Separated, an army can be seriously injured but rarely destroyed, while once consolidated, the potential for complete destruction becomes a possibility. Moreover, the individual unit movements required to concentrate offer an alert foe the opportunity to attack and destroy those elements in detail, a tactical reality that is as old as the hills. Put simply, an army in motion is vulnerable to attack, while an army consolidated is less vulnerable but hardly *invulnerable*. Thus, Washington would have to maintain great secrecy over his intentions, move rapidly once in motion, and consolidate at a position that offered great defensive features—no small list of difficulties.

Nevertheless, Washington intended to move, and in mid-May, those efforts began in earnest. The preliminary movements of Continental forces were quickly noticed by the ever-observant British, although they appear not to have fully grasped what was going on at the time. Captain Ewald added this interesting note to his journal just after the action at Piscataway: "On the 15th of May we received information that the enemy had abandoned Elizabethtown and Newark and had concentrated his army at Basking Ridge."[15]

No, the Americans were not concentrating at Basking Ridge, but something big was clearly afoot, and once completed, those movements would change the chessboard of war in New Jersey considerably.

CHAPTER FOURTEEN
Middlebrook

*W*hen George Washington wrote Benjamin Rush on May 16, he had already selected the ground upon which he intended to consolidate the army. It was a spot in the mountains, only fifteen miles southwest of Morristown, on the eastern bank of the Raritan River. Called Middlebrook, it was named for the creek that ran nearby, tumbling southeast out to the Raritan. The new camp was to be near Bound Brook, still only eight miles from the British encampment at Brunswick; nevertheless almost impervious to assault. Situated along the first and second ridges of the Watchung Mountains, the craggy ridgelines, narrow defiles, and looming heights formed a natural fortress while allowing rapid egress reward if ever required. Artillery positions established atop the heights would dominate the area and, with clear fields of fire, make an attack from the valley floor hazardous in the extreme. The camp was to be laid out in an arc, extending from Middlebrook westward to Pluckemin along the crest of the mountains. From the heights above the Raritan, virtually all of central New Jersey could be observed; hence, British movements could be spotted from a great distance.

Thus, if General Howe moved overland toward Philadelphia, Washington could observe the movement from Middlebrook as it was initiated. Then, he could notify all militia units to harass the march as it moved south while shifting his army down from the mountains to hang on the British rear with the hope of landing a significant blow. On the other hand, if Howe turned back with any portion of his army to confront the Americans, Washington could simply withdraw back

within the safety of the mountains at Middlebrook, a position he was
sure Howe would not dare challenge. From all military perspectives,
the Middlebrook encampment was an excellent choice.

The first step taken to prepare the army for its concentration came
in a circular sent out to all brigade commanders on May 20, designed
to get their brigades organized to move. The most salient portion
read: "You are desired, immediately upon the receipt hereof, to draw
together the men of the Regiments assigned to your Brigade. As soon as
they are assembled; you are to call for exact returns from the Colonels
or commanding officers, obliging them to render a particular account
of the officers and Men who are absent."[1] Washington had selected
General Nathanael Greene to lead the relocation effort at Middlebrook, for Greene had become the general's right-hand man. Greene
was then on another mission to Peekskill to oversee the defenses along
the Hudson River for the commander in chief but returned in late May
to begin the new consolidation. On May 24, he wrote to Washington
from Middlebrook:

> I arrivd at this place yesterday about Noon – and
> immediately issueed [issued] the necessary Orders
> for collecting the Troops together from the out posts.

> I fear without great exertion in the Commesaries
> department there will be a want of Provisions – I
> shall endeavor to learn the design of the Enemies
> collection of Waggons.

> We shall begin to lay off the encampment this
> morning – Coll Biddle arrivd too late last Night to do
> any thing more than to ride round the ground.[2]

The next day, Greene wrote again, the arrival of troops having
already begun, troubles mounting. Among a range of issues mentioned, he wrote:

> I find a great want of Tents in several Brigades –
> General Maxwell sais he has none neither has he had
> it in his power to get any. I shall endeavor to get a more
> particular state today and will notify your Excellency

upon the subject. A small detachment of Col. Lewis
Regiment came in last Evening without Blankets or
Tents and sais there were none to be had at Philadel-
phia. If that be true we shall be miserably off.

Upon enquiry I find the Camp feever begins to prevail
among some of the Troops. Nothing will correct this
evil like the free use of Vinegar – the men feed principally upon animal food, which produces a strong
inclination to putrefaction – Vegetables or any other
kind of food cannot be had in such plenty as to alter
the state of the habit – Vinegar is the only remidy.

Your own reputation, the protection of the Country
and the success of the Campaign are dependant
upon the health of the Army. Objects so important
in their consequences demands your Excellencies
serious attention.

Inclosd is an account of the state of things in Brunswick yesterday Col. Broadheads Piquet was attack
yesterday the Enemy took one foot century and one
Vidett [picket post] the latter was lost by attempting
too rashly to recover the foot Soldier which however
was recoverd but wounded in a most shocking
manner.

The Troops are encamping as fast as possible.[3]

The skirmishing near Brunswick on the 24th mentioned by Greene
is recounted in some detail by the ever-present, ever-vigilant Hessian
Captain Ewald, who was unfortunately wounded in the action. He
had gotten wind of various American movements, but since nothing
of significance had come of it, he decided to ride into Brunswick and
report to his British commanders. "Since nothing new had happened
for several days," he wrote, "I rode into headquarter on the 24th to
report to Lord Cornwallis what I had learned about the movements of
the enemy. I had to stay for dinner, during which time the news arrived

that the enemy would abandon Bound Brook at nightfall, having already withdrawn his outposts in front of this place." Thinking it was worthwhile to verify this new intelligence, Cornwallis decided to send out a reconnaissance mission under Ewald's direction consisting of a British officer and twenty dragoons. Their mission was to reconnoiter as far as Bound Brook to determine if the reports of American withdrawals were accurate.

The officer showed up at about ten o'clock that night with his detachment of dragoons. "He was a young man," Ewald tells us, "who seemed to have much good will, but no knowledge of this business." Perhaps thinking the young officer was likely to get himself killed—not to mention many of his men—Ewald decided to take full command of the patrol. "Therefore," he wrote, "I decided to conduct the patrol myself since I knew every trail in the neighborhood. I passed the defile, left ten foot Jägers there, and went by a roundabout way to the plantation, where an enemy picket formerly had been stationed." Ewald then sent a dragoon up to the farmhouse to summon the owner, simultaneously ordering the young British officer to dispatch two flankers forward to the bridge at Bound Brook and to follow behind them with great caution.

The farm was only some five hundred yards from the village, and Ewald was clearly uneasy regarding the possibility of ambush. The dragoon returned promptly with the owner, however, who walked very slowly and deliberately through an orchard down to the road, stopping abruptly on his side of the fence rail. The farmer assured Ewald that the village had been deserted by the Americans. So the Hessian demanded that the man climb over the fence and come to him so they could talk further. But for some reason, the man refused, and Ewald—angry now—threatened him with a severe beating. "I had hardly uttered these words," wrote Ewald, "when rifle fire coming from the orchard made the air hot around my nose." The British patrol instantly recoiled, receiving additional rifle fire from a second position along the road. Cleary, they had walked straight into an ambush.

Ewald yanked his horse's reins, desperate to escape. He galloped off for the safety of a sunken road he knew to be nearby. But his horse lost its footing in the dark and toppled to the ground, sending the Hessian flying. Stunned and now horseless, his troubles had just begun. Just up the road, the young British officer, along with most of his dragoons—probably in a panic—began dashing madly back toward Brunswick, galloping right over Ewald as they made their escape, severely injuring his right knee in their flight. Ewald's horse then scrambled to its feet and bolted after the retreating dragoons, leaving him behind, alone, and seriously wounded on the road. Ewald finally managed to crawl to the side of the road, where, he thought, he was at least out of harm's way. Just then, the two remaining dragoons who had been sent forward toward the bridge came galloping down the road and thundered right over him again. He survived this second trampling without further injury, but he was now completely alone on the side of the road in enemy territory. Unable to move, there was little he could do. As he later recalled, he simply lay still and "awaited my fate."

While the British dragoons sped off into the darkness, the Jägers left behind on the road spotted Ewald's panicked horse, grabbed it, and realized at once that their captain was in trouble. Three of them went back in search. "To my great joy, these faithful fellows appeared and found me in my wretched situation," wrote Ewald. Americans heard the commotion and began firing from a distance. So Ewald had Muller, his horn blower, sound "Forward." Hearing the bugle call, and now fearing an imminent attack, the Americans ceased firing and pulled back. The other Jägers then came up, loaded Ewald onto a horse, and led him back to camp, where he was promptly bandaged. But the Jägers were not finished. When they realized their captain had lost his hat in the fracas, they went back and found it in the road. The Hessian captain was overwhelmed by their effort. "Does not such love and loyalty of the soldier for his officer merit admiration and recording for posterity?" he suggested proudly.

Such was the action near Bound Brook General Greene referred to in his May 25 report, but there would be much more to come. The British now understood the Americans had not abandoned Bound Brook. General Lincoln was still there, lying in wait, perhaps hoping to settle the score for what the British had done to him and his small command earlier that April. If true, he would not have long to wait.

Ewald sets the scene. The very next morning, he tells us: "At daybreak on May 25, Colonel Abercromby arrived at my post with the light infantry. He had been ordered by Lord Cornwallis to talk to me about the incident." So the Hessian explained what had happened the night before; the positions from which the Americans had opened fire, ultimately describing his harrowing escape. Abercromby took it all in and determined to move off, initiating a substantial and immediate attack on Bound Brook. He did not get far, however, for General Lincoln had moved his force down to River Road, where he carefully positioned his men on strong ground. There, they waited.

"He [Colonel Abercromby] took the Jägers with him and had scarcely reached our sentries when he ran into a strong American corps," Ewald explains. "A hard fight ensued in the vicinity of the house where I was lying like Lazarus." The fighting became fierce, both sides feeding in reinforcements. Despite British detachments racing to Abercromby's support, the Americans stood firm, the contest raging for hours, both sides unlimbering artillery to add their weight to the battle. "This fight continued until three o'clock in the afternoon, "Ewald tells us, "and many men were lost on both sides."[4] Eventually, the fight went the Americans' way, as they drove the British all the way back to Brunswick before breaking off the attack.

General Washington got word of the action and wrote to John Hancock on May 28. "I am just moving to Bound Brook from whence I returned yesterday morning. On Monday Morning a Body of the Enemy advanced near that post; they retreated on seeing a detachment marched to Meet them, there was some firing at long shot, but without great damage, we had only three men slightly wounded – What their Loss was, I know not; Three of their Light Horse were killed."[5]

On June 5, *The Pennsylvania Evening Post* ran an extract from a letter of a correspondent who had participated in the engagement. He hailed from a village named Mount Pleasant, near Bound Brook, and his letter adds insight into the fighting.

> On Monday last a party of our men gave the enemy a pretty little threshing: The number on the enemy's side was superior to ours. Gen. Lincoln, who commands at this post, had information the night before of their marching a body of between 6 and 700 men towards Bound Brook, we were immediately ordered to face them, which was done in a regular manner; we met them about 100 yards from the bridge, and drove them near 3 miles, 'till they got within their lines: They left seven men and three light horse dead in the field; we had three

men wounded, one of them mortally. We expect every moment to receive orders to attack them, or to hear they are moving towards us; we are very easy which way, as we natter ourselves we are strong enough for them, and dare meet them when and where they please."[6]

After the fighting, Ewald was removed to Brunswick to recover, where "I was confined to bed for over fourteen days, and for more than half a year I had to do my service on horseback. All the general officers honored me with their visits," he recalled, "and reproached me somewhat because I had not been ordered to go with the party. However, such reproaches are pleasant to hear when one has done more than his duty."[7]

On May 28, the troops at Bound Brook were finally withdrawn to the new camp at Middlebrook almost directly behind their old one, and by the 29th, the main portion of Washington's army had also arrived. *The Pennsylvania Evening Post* reported merrily:

> We can with pleasure inform our readers that General Washington has now received such supplies of men, &c. that he has removed his head-quarters from Morris-Town to Middle-Brook, on the east side of the Rariton, within seven miles and an half of Brunswick, where his army, (which is not composed of soldiers, whose times of service are continually expiring, but of those inlisted for the war.) are now encamped and makes a show that must please every person who is not a Tory.
>
> From our posts, near Middle-Brook, we are able to see and watch the movements of the enemy, who are encamped on BmsWick-Hills, the west side of Rariton.[8]

The *Post*'s reporting was partially true, in that Washington's army had grown due to a recent springtime infusion of new regiments. A headquarters Enclosure of the Continental Army dated May 20 listed known strength by brigades as follows:

1. Greene..........1,731

2. Stephen........1,711

3. Sullivan.........1,308

4. Lincoln..........1,640

5. Stirling..........1,798

Total: 8,188,[9] of which 7,428 were stationed in New Jersey. Of this 7,428, an unknown number of men remained unfit for duty due to illness, lack of proper equipment, or dietary problems.

Regardless of the problems, the Middlebrook encampment appeared a vast improvement over the conditions the troops had faced during the previous campaign. Brigadier General George Weeden, a Virginian who had served with Washington during the French and Indian War, now commanded a full brigade under Nathanael Greene and wrote glowingly of the new camp at Middlebrook:

> The Army is now drawn together at this place, at least that part of it, which have been Cantoned all Winter in this state. The whole of them now Encamped in Comfortable Tents on a Valley covered in front and rear by ridges which affords us security. His excellency our good Old General, has also spread his Tent, and lives amongst us. Every Department of the Army is properly arranged, and strictly Attended to – so different in our situation in every respect, to what it was last Campaign, that a friendly heart can not help being highly elated on reflection. Our men all happily over the small pox, and remarkable healthy, well Armed, well Cloathed, and from our Commander in Chief down, to the private Centinal, in the highest Spirits.[10]

While General Washington established his headquarters at Middlebrook on May 29, much remained to be done. "As it is a matter of the greatest importance to have the Camp well secured; guards properly fixed;" he wrote, "their respective duties precisely pointed out, and proper regulations established, to enable them to act in concert, and support each other – Major Genl Greene is requested to assemble, as soon as possible, all the other officers, and take these matters into consideration, at large and report their opinion of what they shall think necessary to be adopted."[11] Wayne's and Hampton's brigades were posted at the gaps in the first ridge line, with two artillery positions posted nearby for support. The main encampment was directly behind Wayne on the second ridge, Knox's artillery in the center overlooking the valley, and the brigades of Muhlenberg, Scott, Connery, Wofford, and Maxwell pitched their tents in order nearby. The commander in chief's tent was also in the center of this encampment. The troops quartered on the second ridge were in position to rapidly support any attack along the first, which, given the panoramic view offered from above, would be spotted hours before it could be executed. Writing for the *Journal of the American Revolution*, author Adam Zielinski writes, "The Continental army built earthworks and used old Lenape [Delaware Indian] trails to spread out its presence within the hills and low mountains. With an established hold on the entire Watchung range, Washington held a commanding view of the British positions throughout the region."[12]

As the new encampment was coming together at Middlebrook, Washington turned his attention to the minutia of camp life. No matter proved too insignificant to escape his attention, from guard routines, latrines, the grazing of horses, and so on, to even the army's corps of musicians, with whom he remained less than impressed. "The music of the army being in general very bad; it is expected, that the drum and fife Majors exert themselves to improve it, or they will be reduced [broken in rank], and their extraordinary pay taken from them... Nothing is more agreeable, and ornamental, than good music; every officer, for the credit of his corps, should take care to provide it...The *revellie* to be beaten at day-break – the *troop* at 8 o'clock in the morning, and *retreat* at sunset."[13]

On June 4, General Lincoln noted extensive British activity in the distance and gave orders for his command to prepare to move at a moment's notice in that a major enemy movement appeared to be in the offing. Then, on June 6, Washington wrote again to John Hancock, confirming his suspicions once more as to what he thought the British were up to. "From Sundry Accounts from New York there is reason to believe the Enemy are on the point of making some expedition. Their preparation of Ships for Troops – Light Horse &c. indicates that they intend to go by Water. What their Object is, yet remains a Secret."[14] The next day, June 7, he explained his suspicions in a letter to General Sullivan. "An intelligent person who left New York the 5th says many Vessels were fitted up for Horses and that some were embarked. That the Transports were prepared for Troops and that some were to go on Board had come over from Staten Island. If so the Fleet is near sailing. Therefore desire Genl Forman to keep a look out and when they leave the Hook [Sandy Hook] see which way they stand."[15]

The general's suspicions were on the mark. On June 4, British officer Stephen Kemble jotted this note in his journal: "British troops to Embark with General Howe, [Brigade of] Guards, 2 Battalions Light Infantry, two Battalions Grenadiers, 1st Brigade, 4th., 23d., 38., 49th [regiments of foot]., 2d.[Brigade], 10th., 27., 40th., 52d. [Regiments of Foot], 3d., 15th., 33d., 44th., Reserve [Brigade], Chasseurs, 4 Battalions Hessians Grenadiers, and three Regiments Vizt. Grenadiers Linsing."[16] Meanwhile, new Hessian detachments had arrived from Europe, bolstering British forces near Brunswick. "On June 8 Lieutenant von Wangenheim arrived with seventy-five recruits from Hesse for the Jägers Corps," Ewald noted. "The entire recruit transport had consisted of one thousand men. With the same fleet had arrived at New York two Anspach regiments, each of 600 men under Brigadier Eyb and a Jägers company of 116 heads. The recruits for both companies consisted of a few adventurers and experienced Jägers, and they were generally fine looking men."[17] It was then when Ewald learned that the Jägers were to be reorganized into one distinct corps under Lt. Colonel Wurmb, Captain Prueschenck of the Hessian cavalry to be promoted to corps major. Neither Ewald nor Wreden cared for the new alignment as both realized they were soon to lose their independent commands and feared the overall professional quality of the new corps would not be up to their old standards. "Neither my friend Captain Wreden nor I liked this news because we would lose our independent commands,"[18] Ewald lamented. For them, the reorganization was not good news.

Intelligence reports, along with local observations, continued to confirm Washington's suspicion that the British were preparing a major move, perhaps toward Philadelphia or possibly farther up the

Hudson River. Whether the Redcoats would travel by land, water, or a combination of the two, remained a mystery. Thus, on June 8, Washington issued the following General Orders, preparing the army for potential action: "By intelligence from different quarters, there is much reason to believe the enemy are on the eve of some important operation – This makes it absolutely necessary, that the whole army should hold themselves, in constant readiness to move at a moment's warning; and for that purpose they are to be always furnished with three days provision, ready cooked – Officers to take care that their men carry their own packs; and to suffer none but invalids to put their arms, or packs into the waggons."[19]

The war in New Jersey was entering a new phase. The numerous, violent engagements over forage that had gone on since January were now in the process of evolving into a more widespread conflict: a confrontation between two maneuvering armies. The individual outposts and aggressive militia actions that had held the British at bay throughout the winter—inflicting so many casualties throughout the long winter months—were about to be replaced by something much larger in scale. Only nine days after encamping at Middlebrook, General Washington was preparing his army for a new campaign. Obviously, events were evolving rapidly. If Howe moved toward Philadelphia, it would be incumbent upon the commander in chief to march rapidly south to take up an appropriate blocking position in order to defend the American capital from siege and destruction, wherever that defense might best be achieved.

On June 9, British officer Archibald Robertson advanced the script still further, writing: "This day the General [Howe] left New York and went to Amboy, to take command of the Army in the Jersey's which now consists of all the Troops that could be brought together after leaving Proper Garrisons in New York and Staten Island, etc. Sir William Erskine likewise left New York this day. We arrived at Amboy about 10 that Night." He also added proudly that, the day before, he had been elevated to deputy quartermaster general, a seemingly well-deserved promotion. Throughout the following day, Robertson prepared the wagon train for the massive troop movement soon to be undertaken, and on the 11th, Howe departed Amboy, bound for Brunswick once again. The enormous column included over one thousand wagons and stretched across the countryside for over twelve miles.[20] What were the British up to?

If, indeed, General Howe intended to shift his entire army toward Philadelphia by sea, he was going about it in the oddest way imaginable. By this latest land movement alone, it had become obvious he had something else in mind, and that design became increasingly apparent as the long columns of British troops began taking up positions along the Raritan near Brunswick. Robertson tells us that "The 71st with Coll. Leslie were posted at Bonheim Town [Woodbridge]. The other 3 Corps went to Brunswick where the General Arrived at 2 o'clock. He immediately gave Orders for raising 3 Redouts on the East side of Raritan River opposite Moncrieff's New Bridge [a recent span erected across the Raritan by British engineer, James Moncrieff] in order to Contract the Extent of Quarters from the Landing." These were clearly preliminary defensive structures designed for a land campaign and had nothing to do with a seaborne adventure. British intentions remained unclear.[21]

June 12 dawned cool and wet, rain falling hard throughout the day, turning the mud and sandy roads into quagmires. Additional British forces slogged slowly through the mud and drizzle toward Brunswick; Robertson telling us that some "encamped between Brunswick and Bonheim Town," while others "moved from Pisscatawa [Piscataway] and Bonheim Town to Brunswick."[22] All this maneuvering entailed some sort of offensive scheme, but what?

As the long, rain-soaked columns of Redcoats and Hessians entered Brunswick that day, Ewald was there to greet them, proud of the striking appearance made by the newest Hessian detachments. Rumors were circulating throughout the officer corps of Howe's latest strategic intentions, and Ewald was typically up to date as to what they might mean. "On the 12th of June the commander in Chief, General Howe, and the commanding General of the hessians, Lieutenant General Lieopold Philip de Heister, arrived at New Brunswick with ten infantry regiments," Ewald wrote, "the 17th Regiment of Light Dragoons, the heavy guns, and a number pontoons, and encamped upon the heights around the town. The general rumor in circulation," he tells us, "was that we would cross the Delaware and march to Philadelphia, and, it was hoped, lure General Washington by a diversion out of his strong position in the mountains between Morristown and Basking Ridge, where his army had been concentrated."[23]

Before departing for Philadelphia—whether by land, sea, or a combination thereof—Howe had decided to take a crack at Washington. To accomplish this, he had determined to try and lure the American commander out of the Middlebrook encampment, presumably by dangling the apparition of a quick strike and easy victory before his eyes in the form of unsupported and vulnerable British units. But, of course, those units would be neither vulnerable nor unsupported, and when Washington slipped down from the mountains for a bite at the bait, Howe intended to crush George Washington and his Continental army once and for all.

CHAPTER FIFTEEN
Howe Tries to Ensnare the Fox

Peering down from the heights as the Americans were, the British activity near Brunswick had hardly gone unnoticed. On June 12, General Washington wrote General Sullivan, advising him: "Every account confirms the certainty of the Enemy's intention to move by land, and I think it will from appearances take place in a very short time."[1] One day, it seemed the British would move by land; the next by sea. Whichever they might eventually choose was irrelevant, however, for Washington put the Middlebrook camp on alert. "The break of day being the most favorable time for an attack," the General Orders for June 12 read, "a good officer will be careful to turn out his guard *under arms* 'till an hour after sunrise, and to have his visiting rounds, and patroles going them more than ordinary. From watching through the night, men towards morning grow drowsy, secure and listless; and are more liable to a surprise – An officer's reputation calls upon him to guard carefully against this evil."[2]

For Washington and the Continental army, vigilance became an imperative. Fortunately for the commander in chief, an officer who had the combination of know-how, stealth, and fighting spirit to aid considerably in that regard had recently returned to the army. The officer's name was Daniel Morgan, a colonel then commanding the Eleventh Virginia and someone who had already risen to near-legendary status in the early days of the Continental army.

In many ways, Morgan's was a uniquely American story. His place and date of birth are unknown (Morgan refused to discuss these issues, and to this day, his past remains shrouded in mystery), but he had wandered into Winchester, Virginia, in the spring of 1753 as a hardboiled young man perhaps eighteen years of age. Dressed in homespun clothes with hardly a penny in his pocket, Morgan was nevertheless a large and physically gifted man, fleet of foot and enormously powerful. Most importantly, he had the willingness to work and learn. He soon took on a job hauling goods over the Blue Ridge from Winchester in the Shenandoah Valley to Fredericksburg north of Richmond.

Carefully saving his wages, Morgan purchased a wagon and team and began his own business hauling goods between the two developing towns. Earning a decent living, he reveled in the lifestyle of the wagoner: He drank too much, fought too much, and caroused far too much, and may well have ended up on the business end of a rope had he not married and settled down. In 1756, Morgan contracted to haul goods for General Braddock's expedition into the Ohio Country and witnessed the calamity brought about by Braddock's refusal to adapt his march and methods to the North American wilderness. It was then, as well, when Morgan, apparently refusing to move fast enough to suit a British officer, received a sword across his back for sluggishness. Enraged, he reportedly knocked the officer out cold with a single punch and was then tried for the offense. The penalty was five hundred lashes across the back—which Morgan, to his dying day, claimed to have counted as they were administered—and an act that engendered a lifelong hatred of the British. In 1771, he was commissioned a captain in the Frederic County militia, and in 1774, he commanded a company fighting in Dunmore's War against the Shawnee, who were then rampaging across what is today West Virginia and Ohio, a period when the Americans developed a unique style of fighting called "bushfighting."

As the American colonies slowly edged toward war with Great Britain, Morgan's sympathies fell strongly on the side of the rebels. When violence broke out in Boston in 1775, Frederick County, Virginia was asked to raise a company of riflemen, then march them to Boston to assist in the expanding siege of the city. The county responded, and Morgan was voted unanimously to command the unit. Enlisted from the most expert riflemen in the county, they wore hunting shirts rather than uniforms, carried the long rifle along with a tomahawk and scalping knife, were equally at home in the forest as were the Shawnee, and were all fearsome fighters. At Boston, they drove the British picket posts crazy with their long-range marksmanship, and while they were surely a rough-and-tumble lot, they were also extremely well-disciplined thanks to Morgan's firm leadership.

So impressed was Washington with Morgan's abilities that after Boston fell, he selected him to help lead an American advance into Canada commanded by Benedict Arnold. Pushing the American vanguard through the unforgiving Maine wilderness—over mountains; often in freezing creeks up to his shoulders—Morgan drove his men to the expedition's objective: the fortress of Quebec. On December 30, with fresh snow flying, the Americans attacked the city in a sophisticated plan of feints and assaults that disintegrated almost before it had begun. Arnold led the main attack; Morgan right behind him. Unfortunately, Arnold fell seriously wounded, and Morgan was selected by the remaining officers to lead the assault forward due to his acknowledged experience. When the other American attacks failed to appear as designed, however, Morgan was left alone on the streets of Quebec and eventually surrounded. Furious almost to the point of madness, he refused to surrender and could easily have been gunned down in a hail of musketry had not a local priest offered to accept his sword. But Morgan did not go easily, and the ferocity of his defiance both stunned and impressed his British enemy. The American rifleman George Morison was nearby as Morgan fought on Quebec's snowy streets, and he would never forget the performance he witnessed that day. "Betwixt every peal the awful voice of Morgan is heard," he later wrote, "whose gigantic stature and terrible appearance carries dismay among the foe wherever he comes."[3] Captured, Morgan remained in captivity until August 1776, when he was brought to Elizabethtown, New Jersey and finally exchanged. (So impressed were the British authorities at Quebec that they offered Morgan a colonel's commission in the British army, which he considered a profound insult to his honor as an American and promptly rejected.)[4] Now, joining the Continental army once more, Colonel Morgan was uniquely qualified to handle an advanced corps of riflemen designed to scout, harass, and keep a clear eye on British movements. General Washington wasted no time, writing Morgan on June 13:

The Corps of Rangers newly formed and under your Command, are to be considered as a Body of Light Infantry and are to act as such, for which reason they will be exempted from the common Duties of the Line.

At present you are to take post at Van Veighters Bridge [Van Veghten's Bridge, Bridgewater] and watch, with very small scouting parties (to avoid fatiguing your men too much under the present appearance of things) the Enemy's left Flank, and particularly the Roads leading from Brunswic towards Millstone, princetown &ca.

In case of any movement of the Enemy you are instantly to fall upon their flanks and gall them as much as possible, taking especial Care not to be surrounded or have Retreat to the Army cut off.[5]

The new ranger corps under Morgan represented the formation of an elite unit led by an elite commander. Washington realized that few men in his army possessed both the skill and discipline to successfully lead a special corps detached from the main army. "Washington gave Morgan command of a specially created corps of light infantry composed of nearly 500 picked Continentals outfitted in hunting shirts and leggings. The troops were from the western counties of Pennsylvania, Maryland, and Virginia, most of the Virginians drawn from Morgan's own regiment. The corps, considered an independent unit..., was excused from all regular duties of the camp. Aided by his able lieutenant colonel, Richard Buster of Pennsylvania, Morgan procured rifles and requestioned pikes."[6]

Lt. Colonel Daniel Morgan.

The formation of the ranger corps came none too soon, for on the same day that Washington wrote to Morgan, Howe put his army in motion. Archibald Robertson tells us:

> At 12 at Night the whole Army after leaving a Garrison at Brunswick, march'd in Two Divisions on the Hillsboro' Road. The 1st Division under Lord Cornwallis pass'd the Millstone River at Schenck's Bridge [Manville] and took Possession of the high ground round Hillsboro', where they had a little Skirmishing with the Rebels.

> The 2d Division under General Howe took up their Ground at Middle bush, about 5 miles from Brunswick and 3 from Hillsboro'.[7]

British cavalry formed an extensive picket line from Brunswick all the way out the Amwell Road through Middle Bush to the village of Millstone on the Millstone River, covering about twelve miles. General Leopold von Heister was then left in command of the advanced division at Middle Bush, while Howe moved on to Millstone, where he established his headquarters in the home of Annie Van Liew on the east side of the river.[8] By the disposition of forces alone, General Howe's intentions can be discerned. The cavalry screen had been established to keep American eyes from observing the division posted at Hillsborough while hopefully detecting any American movements along a wide front. The Second Division—von Heister's, posted forward at Middle Bush—served as the bait. And the First Division at Hillsborough served as a reserve, ready to move around the right flank of Washington's army should the American general take the bait and attack von Heister at Middle Bush. Howe and Cornwallis, then on the extreme left of the British deployment, were in position to lead the First Division from Hillsborough around the American rear, thus cutting Washington off from his encampment at Middlebrook. At that point, Washington would be trapped and crushed in a double envelopment between two superior British divisions; a dramatic end put to the American Revolution. Such, at least, was the plan.

Captain Ewald, marching with the Hessian contingent under von Heister, recalls the march and subsequent deployment. "On the 13th at ten o'clock in the evening, the army set out toward Hillsborough, and on the morning of the 14th it pitched camp in square formation between Millstone and Middlebush. Captain Wreden, with the Donop Jägers and half of the Anspach Jägers, stood at the army's right on the road to the mountains, and I with my company and the other half of the Anspach Jägers, covered the left toward Rocky Hill near Millstone."[9]

As a defensive move, General Washington had ordered Morgan's new corps deployed "near the junction of the New Brunswick-Delaware road [NJ Route 27] and a route leading northward toward the Millstone River." Washington's thinking appears clear: If the British troops continued south, they were headed for Philadelphia. On the other hand, if they turned off toward the Millstone, Howe's objective was probably Washington's camp at Middlebrook. On the morning the British marched out of Brunswick, Morgan was already in the field along the Millstone Road before the sun had risen, observing the field from high ground. From there, "he sent out scouts who hurriedly reported that Howe was headed in their direction." Morgan sent a quick message back to Washington, then moved forward with his whole corps, taking a strong position in the woods overlooking Hillsborough Road. Morgan, dressed in his usual hunting shirt, assumed a position behind his men in the center of his line from where he could receive reports and personally monitor any action.[10]

At ten o'clock that morning, as Morgan was hustling his corps forward, Washington wrote to John Hancock, keeping him advised of the rapidly evolving events: "The enemy are in motion & a body is advancing from Milstone towards VanBecters Bridge – Another division is on the Road leading towards Coriels ferry [Lambertville]. We are packing up & making every preparation to act as circumstances shall seem to require."[11] Washington knew Morgan's small corps could not possibly stop Howe's strong divisions. What he wanted, rather, was an expert corps capable of intelligence gathering and harassment of the enemy. To this end, Washington had even suggested that Morgan "dress a Company or two of true Woods men in the right Indian Style and let them make the Attack accompanied with screaming and yelling as the Indians do, it would have very good consequences."[12]

Whether Morgan acted on the commander in chief's suggestion is not clear, but what is clear is that when the British vanguard appeared, Morgan's men opened on them with a vengeance. Five hundred crack shots armed with the long rifle, firing from concealed positions, brought the British column to an immediate and chaotic halt and with deadly effect. The firing continued until the British rushed reinforcements to the scene, at which time Morgan wisely broke off the engagement. "As the British, strengthened by their main body, pressed forward, they heard the shrill sound of Morgan's turkey-call, an instrument he blew to assemble his men. The riflemen gathered around Morgan, who then led them to higher ground. There he bivouacked and dispatched information of his encounter to Washington's headquarters.[13]" Stephen Kemble recorded the engagement as follows: "The Army marched in two Columns from Brunswick to Bushwick, about five Miles. At Hillsborough, a Battalion of Light Infantry fell in with a Body of Rebels, took a few Prisoners, and Killed five or six, with the loss of one Man Killed and three wounded ; Captain Lysaght, 63d. wounded. The Rebels remain in their Position above Bound Brook, strongly Erenched."[14]

Back at Middlebrook, things were getting intense, and General Washington was taking no chance of being caught by surprise. Detailed orders were issued, preparing the army for a rapid movement. Whether that would be towards or away from the enemy remained unclear, as British intentions remained murky. But either way, Washington would be ready:

> The whole army to be in readiness to march, exactly at the time appointed, in this position, to wait the orders of the Major General of the day for moving that the whole army may march together – The Vanguard to consist of 40 Light horse and one brigade of foot under the command of Brigadier Muhlenburg to advance about 2½ Miles in front of the Army – to march about an hour before the troops are order'd to be in readiness, Reconnoitring parties to be sent some distance in front and upon the flanks to examine all the roads and Suspected places where ambushes may be concealed – The pioneers to march between the light parties in front of the Vanguard and to make such repairs to the Bridges and roads as are necessary to afford an easy and safe passage of the army.[15]

On the same day, Washington suddenly feared for General Sullivan, whose division was operating far closer to Princeton than Middlebrook. The commander in chief had received reports from Morgan that the British were maneuvering out towards the Millstone

River, and he began to fear the worst. "I am uneasy at hearing nothing from you," he wrote Sullivan. "The Enemy have advanced a party, said to be two thousand, as far as Van Ests Mill upon Millstone River. They have been skirmishing with Colo. Morgans Rifle Men, but have halted on a piece of high Ground. Some Accounts say that their main Body has marched by the Brunswic Road towards princetown but neither seeing your Signals nor hearing from you I am intierly at a loss how to act. I beg you will the Moment you receive this, send me back a trusty fresh Express [report] with an Account of Matters in your Quarter."[16]

Fortunately, later that day, Washington received a dispatch from Sullivan indicating his division had not been threatened. Relieved, Washington ordered him to move toward Flemington to avoid being potentially cut off from the rest of the army. He also brought Sullivan up to date regarding the latest intelligence as to the enemy's movements along with potential offensive actions he was contemplating: "Our move must depend intirely upon that of the Enemy," Washington wrote. "We have parties near them to give us the earliest Notice of their Motions and as we shall intirely disincumber ourselves of Baggage can harass their Flanks and Rear or make a more general attack if we find an Opportunity."[17] Then, on the morning of the 15th, Washington had Daniel Morgan report to him personally at Middlebrook so that he might get the clearest picture of the enemy's movements as possible. Morgan had become quite expert at gobbling up British stragglers and deserters, then pumping them for information. He was subsequently able to tell Washington that General Howe had encamped with the troops near Somerset Courthouse (Millstone). Furthermore, the extensive British maneuvers appeared to be little more than a feint to induce him to leave his defenses at Middlebrook and open himself to the prospect of a major battle on the open ground below.[18]

The fact that Howe had encamped on the Continental's extreme right on the Millstone River only confirmed for Washington the suspicion that the entire British operation had been designed to entrap him. The British commander would naturally be where he intended the most critical action to be, and that could only mean a sweeping attack on the Americans' right or rear, should Washington be foolish enough to desert his fortress and descend to the flats below. On the 16th, the astute commander in chief wrote General Schuyler in New York, outlining his state of mind: "On the Night of the 13th General Howe began his March from Brunswick, seemingly with an Intentin to push directly for Deleware – In the Course of the Night his Front reached Somerset Court House or nine Miles from Brunswick where he halted and has remained ever since. His Rear is still at Brunswick. I do not know whether this was intended as a real Move towards Philadelphia or whether it was to draw us down from the Heights we occupy along his whole Front."[19]

So Washington wisely refused to budge from his encampment until the true intentions of the British movements could be discerned. Morgan was given orders to remain in the field, following and harassing the enemy, without becoming decisively engaged. Meanwhile, the British were actively constructing nine substantial redoubts along Amwell Road, from Brunswick to Middle Bush. These were defensive arrangements to keep their westward line of supply open or smother any American attack launched in that direction. Unfortunately for the British, their ostentatious display of strength had caught the eye of the New Jersey militias, who—now well-led and battle-tested—swarmed like a plague around the Redcoats for days as they marched and deployed, inflicting casualties and making their lives miserable.

Then, on June 16, another British column started off toward the Millstone and was spotted immediately. Was it an attack or feint? Washington cautioned Generals Wayne and Lincoln: "Major Campbell advises by Letter just now received that the Enemy are advancing toward Van Vacter's Bridge [Van Veghten's]. I wish you to send out fresh scouts immediately, and to make the earliest reports. If this report is confirmed by your scouts you will order your Tents to be struck, and put into the Waggons, and have everything in readiness to move."[20]

For several more days, the British marched, strengthened their redoubts, and maintained their long picket line from Brunswick to Millstone—all to no avail. General Howe could not get Washington to budge. "The diversions of Gen. Cornwallis near Somerset Courthouse and of the force moving near Princeton did nothing to convince the Americans that a major engagement was ripe for the taking. As the British marched, American pickets and swarms of local militia continued harassing the British supply lines and kept the moving columns of redcoats on high alert."[21] Ewald, watching all of this closely, wrote: "General Washington, who neither moved nor let himself be lured out of his strong position by this demonstration, sent out several detachments daily which observed and harassed our army, whereby constant skirmishing ensued."[22]

Archibald Robertson provides our narrative with a running commentary from the British perspective during this period of maneuver.

> General Washington with his Army suppos'd to be about 7 or 8000 Men Occupied a strong Camp about 4 miles North of Bound Brook on the Road to Basking Ridge Amongst the Mountains.

> I believe it was generally imagined upon our Armys making Aforesaid Move, He [Washington] would have quitted his stronghold and retreated towards the Delaware. However it proved other-wise, He stood Firm. No Certain Intelligence brought in of the Situation.

> 15h Provision brought from Brunswick. A Patrole of the 16th Light Dragoons from Hillsboro' were fired upon this night, 1 Sergeant Killed and 1 Sergeant and 1 Private taken prisoners.

> General Sullivan with about 2,000 Rebels who were about Prince Town moved towards Flemington in order to effect their junction when Necessary with Washington.

> 16th At Day Break Three Redoubts were begun near Middle bush, and one on the east side of Millstone River Opposite Hillsboro,' I suppose to keep open our communications with Brunswick when the Army moves forward. At 9 this Evening the Three Rredoubts stopped when half finished.[23]

On the 17th, Washington was still trying to determine if the British were attempting to move by land toward Philadelphia, or if all their maneuvering were the preliminaries of a major attack on Middlebrook. Still nervous over Sullivan's exposed position at Flemington, he ordered that division withdrawn to Steele's Gap (Bridgewater) in the first line of Watchung Mountains, about four miles from Middle-brook. He also ordered Sullivan to keep a particularly keen eye out for heavy columns of enemy troops accompanied by artillery and wagons moving toward the American camp—a sure sign of a major attack in motion. "Besides keeping out scouting parties endeavour to get some of the Militia Officers, who are acquainted upon the princetown & Cranberry Roads," Washington suggested, "to go and try to engage some of the Inhabitants to keep a good look out and watch if the Enemy advance upon either of these Roads in large Bodies with Cannon & Waggons."[24]

By June 18, however, it appeared General Howe had finally concluded that no amount of maneuver or martial display was going to induce General Washington to come down from his mountain fortress. Archibald Robertson noted the sudden change. "18th Orders were delivered in the Evening for the Troops to be ready to march by day break."[25] Ewald explains the events that followed. "At daybreak on June 19 the English army marched back to the heights of New Brunswick, because General Howe found that Washington would not let himself be deceived. Indeed, we already certainly believed, including the English Commanding General [Howe], that Washington had learned from England of the impending expedition to the south [toward Philadelphia]."

But it would not be enough for the British to simply withdraw to Brunswick when the citizens of New Jersey could be savaged still further and their properties reduced to heaps of cinder. "On this march," Ewald explains, "all the plantations of the disloyal inhabitants, numbering perhaps some fifty persons, were sacrificed to fire and devastation."[26]

Washington watched from the rocks above as the long scarlet columns returned to Brunswick, funnels of black smoke filling the sky; wanton destruction marking their march. On June 20, he wrote John Hancock, providing his best analysis: "This sudden and precipitate change in their Operations, has afforded matter for much speculation. We suppose their Original design was to attempt an impression on our right or to manuvre us out of our Ground – or to advance towards the Delaware. Whether these conjectures were well founded cannot be ascertained."

Yet one thing *had* become remarkably clear: the people of New Jersey and their various militias had risen up in instant and violent opposition, attacking British detachments wherever they marched, often with great effect. Consequently, General Washington seemed not only impressed but almost overwhelmed by what he had witnessed. "For I must observe," he told Hancock, "and with peculiar satisfaction I do it, that on the first notice of the Enemy's movements, the Militia assembled in the most spirited manner, firmly determined to give them every Annoyance in their power and to afford us every possible aid. This I thought it my duty to mention, in justice to their conduct, am I inclined to beleive, that Genl How's return, thus suddenly made, must have been in consequence of the information he received, that the people were in & flying to Arms in every Quarter to oppose him."[27]

The people were in & flying to Arms in every Quarter to oppose him. During the fall of 1776, General Howe and his British army had marched through New Jersey virtually unopposed; plundering, burning, and raping as they pleased. Seven months later, the script had been flipped completely. George Washington had always known the American Revolution would never be won if the people remained unwilling to win it. But now, as he gazed out over the New Jersey countryside in mid-June 1777, it had become apparent that that was precisely what had occurred. It must have lifted his spirits enormously.

A few days later, Washington wrote to his brother, Augustine, putting the latest British move into perspective:

> Be the real design which it would, certain it is, a disap-
> pointment, &much chagreen [chagrin] followed; for
> on the Night of the 19th a sudden retreat was made
> back to Brunswick, burning and destroying Houses
> &ca as they went – this Retreat, I am perswaded, was
> the effect of despair at finding the Militia of this, &
> State of Philadelphia turning out to oppose them;
> whilst they would have part of my force (if they had
> attempted to cross the Delae [Delaware River]) to
> oppose them in Front, at the passage of the River,
> whilst I should be laying at them behind -- & to attack
> my Troops, Situated as I am, they found impracti-
> cable, without great loss, and a probable defeat.[28]

Washington realized that the Americans—in particular, the militia—were coming of age. Perhaps even more convincing was that many British officers—those in the field who had to fight the war daily—had noticed the same change. "The rebel soldiers," wrote Lt. General Sir Charles Stuart, "from being accustomed to peril in their skirmishes, begin to have more confidence. The wounding and killing of many of our rear guards, gives them the notion of victory and habituates them to the profession."[29] By the end of May 1777, British actions in New Jersey, rather than defeating an incompetent and dispirited enemy, were, in fact, producing a strong, skilled, and motivated one. How long might such an upside-down strategy endure?

CHAPTER SIXTEEN
Samptown

*I*t is easy to understand why General Washington remained unclear as to what he had just witnessed. He had watched William Howe march thousands of troops all over central New Jersey yet to no particular or obvious purpose. Yes, intelligence reports asserted that it had all been a ploy, designed to lure him down from the mountains at Middlebrook. But was it? Or had it been a dress rehearsal for a British march south toward Philadelphia, intended to see how the Americans would react while laying down certain defensive emplacements for safety's sake? On June 19, the British had begun withdrawing back toward Brunswick, but who could really say what any of it meant? Were they really preparing to embark by sea southward, or was it merely the preliminaries of another trap? Washington, commanding a significantly inferior force, was in no position to gamble. The commander in chief then received troubling information from General Schuyler in New York, forcing him to put on hold several troops' movements he had previously ordered until Howe's true intentions could be clearly discerned. This he told John Hancock on June 20: "The uncertainty of Genl How's Operations will not permit more to be done at this time."[1]

From various points along the first ridge of the Watchung Mountains, Washington was able to closely monitor British movements from afar. One afforded a spectacular view of the area and, over time, became known as "Washington Rock." Today, that rock—twenty-five feet high and forty feet wide—has been preserved by the State of New Jersey as Washington Rock State Park. Historian Robert Mayers writes: "Washington Rock, located in present-day Green Brook Township, is the location of the best known of several Revolutionary War observation posts that may be found on the crest of the first ridge of the Watchung Mountains. Historians and local residents claim that General George Washington used all of these sites to scan the countryside and observe the movements of British troops on the plains of central New Jersey, Staten Island, and New York City."[2]

The view from the British side, however, while less spectacular, was nevertheless far more telling. Robertson explains their movements and dispositions, while Stephen Kemble focuses on General Howe's true intentions. "At Day Break [the 19th]" Robertson wrote, "The 2d Division march'd from Flat Bush Camp, towards Brunswick, followed by the 1st Division from Hillsboro.' They incamped from Brunswick to Bonheim Town. The Rebels never fired on the Rear until they came within a mile of Brunswick and only Wounded one Man. General Washington still continues in his stronghold."[3] So the Redcoats had retreated to their previous defensive positions surrounding Brunswick, and Stephen Kemble tells us what General Howe had in mind: "Howe's withdrawing his Army to Brunswick, the Rebels being so strongly posted that it was not thought proper to Attack them, and a request to Lord Howe [William's brother, in command of the British fleet] to order Shipping to Amboy, to receive the Troops, stores, &c., fear this will Elate the Rebels very much."[4] Clearly—according to Kemble, who was in a position to know— regardless of what the past few days of maneuver had intended to accomplish, Howe planned now to ship his entire army off from Amboy, either south to initiate a campaign to take the American capital at Philadelphia or perhaps north up the Hudson River. Loading eighteen thousand troops, along with all their wagons, stores, artillery, and so on, and embarking them safely in the face of a motivated enemy, however, represented no small task. Hence, the strong defensive positions recently assumed would serve the purpose of holding the Americans at bay, while the embarkation proceeded.

While the situation remained murky for Washington—if the British were, in fact, leaving Jersey by water—it behooved him to prepare several units to move down from the heights and harass their departure without, of course, risking a general engagement. The General Orders for June 21 demonstrate Washington's judicious response.

Col. Sherborne's detachment, at present with Genl Parson, is to join Genl Varnum's brigade.

Genl De-Barre's brigade to get ready to march to morrow morning, at 5'oclock – He will send to the Adjutant General for orders to march.

Genl Varnum's brigade to relieve the picquets at Van Nest's Mill, and Van Veghten's bridge, at 4 o'clock this afternoon.

A detachment of 900 men and twelve light horsemen, with proper officers, to furnish themselves with three days provisions, cooked, and parade at 2 o'Clock this afternoon, behind the park of Artillery, completely armed, acoutered and furnished with ammunition, and with their blankets slung – Brigadier General Maxwell will command the detachment – The Monmouth Militia to go with the detachment.[5]

Meanwhile, all along their front, the British were jostling units to solidify their defenses. Captain Ewald, as usual, had been ordered into the center of things. "The army arrived at its encampment in the afternoon [of the 19th], and the enemy watched our march with light cavalry in the distance," he wrote. "At this camp, all the Jägers were assigned their posts at the same place where they had been stationed during the entire winter. The right wing of the army stood toward Bonhamtown, which the light infantry covered." At Brunswick, the baggage was being defended by a British brigade, a battalion of Hessian grenadiers, and a battalion of Loyalists, while light infantry was covering the center of the British line at Samptown (now a part of modern-day Plainfield). Ewald and his Jägers were promptly tossed from the frying pan into the fire. "On the 20th I was ordered to relieve the light infantry of the English Guards at Samptown," he tells us, "with eighty Jägers and an amusette. This post was situated in front of the army's center and covered a defile which ran through the woods."[6] With General Washington ordering more and more units into the field, things at Samptown were about to heat up.

What had at first seemed a placid posting for Ewald and his Jägers quickly descended into constant turmoil. "On the 21st and the 22d all our outposts were alarmed and harassed by the enemy," he wrote, "both day and night." According to Washington's most recent directives, American advanced units were closing rapidly. "I had two men badly wounded in a skirmish on the 22d," Ewald complained. "General Washington had advanced with his army and ordered the exits of Bound Brook, Quibbletown, and Samptown occupied with light troops, by which one could see that he was well informed of everything that was happening."[7]

Washington was receiving reports indicating the British continued to withdraw their forces; hence, he dispatched additional units to press them, and on June 22, he brought Hancock up to speed: "I therefore detached three Brigades under the command of Majr Genl Green[e] to fall upon their Rear," he wrote, "and kept the main Body of the Army paraded upon the Heights to support them if there should be occasion. A party of Colo. Morgans Regt of light Infantry attacked and drove the Hessian Picket about Sunrise, and upon the appearance of Genl Waynes Brigade and Morgans Regt (who got first to the ground) opposite Brunswic, the Enemy immediately crossed the Bridge to the East side of the River and threw themselves into Redoubts which they had before constructed."[8] Washington was becoming more confident by the hour that he had the British on the run. Morgan, Greene, and Wayne were now cooperating against the retreating British. Sullivan was subsequently ordered to march from Rocky Hill to Brunswick with his division, while Stirling was sent forward from Middlebrook to reinforce Maxwell on the American left. Everything appeared to be going in the Americans' favor. "After flushing a Hessian picket near the outskirts, Morgan joined Greene and Wayne inside the town [Brunswick], and the three American commanders drove the rear guard across the river bridge into redoubts on the east bank."

General Nathanael Greene.

An enemy in flight, Morgan knew, was an enemy in fear, and the proper offensive response was to exploit the situation and keep driving, no matter the odds. Panic can spread through an army's ranks like wildfire, and once lit, it is almost impossible to extinguish. But were the British really in a panic, or were they simply executing a disciplined withdrawal? After all, British Lieutenant John Peebles recorded no such alarm in his diary for June 22. "The whole army quitted Brunswick in the morning, & cross'd over Moncrieffs bridge. The Grenadiers & Light Infantry in the Rear, halted for a little on the heights on Eastside ye River, when a body of about 1,000 of the Rebels appeared on the upper ground near the Landing with three pieces of Cannon which they played for some time at a mile distance & did no harm, the Line moved on." The Americans continued to harass the rear of the British Column until, Peebles tells us, "the Rear of the army arrived & encamp'd near Amboy about 4 P.M."[9]

As the Redcoats moved across the Raritan River toward the east bank, the Americans moved up behind them, then began to encounter increasing numbers of British troops. "Even so," writes one of Morgan's biographers, "Wayne and Morgan, both intrepid fighters, urged an assault, and Greene agreed." So the Americans pressed on, pushing right after the British. During the advance, Morgan's corps ran suddenly up against a unit of British grenadiers: some of the finest fighting men in General Howe's army. Opening on them with their long rifles, Morgan's men went toe-to-toe with the grenadiers, exchanging fire at close range. The engagement went on for quite some time before the Redcoats finally backed away, a fact General Washington virtually crowed about the following day.[10] "By some late Accts I fancy the British Grenadiers got a pretty severe peppering yesterday by Morgans Rifle Corps – they fought it seems a considerable time within the distance of, from twenty, to forty yards; and from the concurring Acct of sevl of the Officers, more than an hundd [one hundred] of them must have fallen."[11] Ultimately, Morgan and Wayne had to break off their advance, as the number of Redcoats became increasingly large, fighting from within large redoubts that would require far too many lives to carry. Nevertheless, the day's action had gone entirely in the Americans' favor, and rebel spirits were running high.

The entire British army then began abandoning their outer defenses, continuing their withdrawal toward Amboy. On June 22, Robertson wrote: "The Whole Army Evacuated Brunswick. About 1200 Rebels with 2 pieces of Cannon Attack'd the Rear but were soon Drove off. We had 4 or 5 Killed and about 20 Wounded. The Rebels suppos'd to lose many more. We all got to Amboy about 3'oclock."[12] The following day, Captain Ewald also withdrew from his post at Samptown as Washington's advanced units closed. "At daybreak on the 23d the army set out toward Amboy," Ewald tells us. "The enemy had alarmed all the outposts all night long, and a great number of riflemen, supported by light cavalry and guns, followed us so closely that we had to withdraw under constant skirmishing up to the vicinity of Bonhamtown. The Queen's Rangers had been assigned to cover the right flank, but it had strayed too far from the army, and was attacked so severely by a superior force that half of the corps was killed or wounded. During this retreat the detachment under Captain Wreden also suffered very much."[13]

Also, on the 22nd, General Sullivan began his movement from Rocky Hill toward Brunswick, as previously ordered. Accompanying him that day was Charles Willson Peale, whom, it might be recalled from Chapter Two, had marched with the Continentals that January from Pluckemin to Morristown. Peale had set off early that morning to catch up with Sullivan's Division before it departed, and he had "just arrived in Time, for the Troops were under arms to march to Brunswick – before we Reached that place we understood that the Enemy had decamped – this we understood when we had got within 2 miles of the Town." What Peale witnessed as he came closer and closer to Brunswick was a scene of utter devastation. "How solitary it looked," he wrote, "to see so many Farms without a single animal – many Houses Burnt & others Rendered unfit for use. The fences all distroyed and many fields the wheat Reaped while quite Green Others I suppose left for fear of our Scouting parties."[14]

As the British retrograde movement continued from Brunswick toward Amboy, Washington's top lieutenants became convinced that the moment for a major strike had arrived. Washington remained skeptical, however, but ultimately acquiesced to their enthusiasm, deciding to move the entire army forward to offer close support to the frontline units. Writing to Joseph Reed on the 23rd, he explained his thinking, explaining that, unlike his officers, he did not believe Howe's army was retreating in a state of panic, but "notwithstanding it is the prevailing opinion of my officers. I can not say that the move I am about to make toward Amboy accords altogether with my opinion."[15] So, while Washington remained distrustful of Howe's true intentions, his officers around Brunswick plunged ever forward, hot on the heels of the retreating British, knowing the main body was soon to follow.

Both sides were trying to outguess one another, and in response to the American pursuit, the British soon redeployed their forces to defend Amboy, to screen the troops slowly gathering there. "The army deployed in the neighborhood of Bonhamtown," Ewald explains, "to support the rear, since it was expected that Washington would make vigorous attacks with his entire army." But one of the British army's routes of withdrawal toward Amboy had been blocked at a nearby mountain pass by a detachment of rebels. "The Commander in Chief [Howe] received information that the Scottish mountains, over which the army had to march, were occupied by the enemy," says Ewald. "General Leslie was dispatched to this pass with the 71st Highland Regiment and my Jägers detachment where we discovered an enemy corps of six hundred men and several light guns. General Leslie immediately ordered it attacked by the Jägers, supported by the Highlanders, and we became master of the mountains after a hard fight despite heavy fire, whereby several officers and some thirty Americans were captured." From that point, Ewald, under Leslie's direction, moved on to Amboy, where he and his Jägers encamped "in a crescent on the plains around the town, and where both wings were covered by Prince's Bay. The Jägers received their post on the road to the Short Hills."[16]

American forces continued to close in on the British, from Brunswick toward Amboy and from Woodbridge, pushing south, but heavy rains suddenly swept across the Jersey coast, instantly disrupting the pursuit. This allowed the British the opportunity to begin preparations to cross the bulk of their army across the Arthur Kill to Staten Island, from whence they intended to embark southward, presumably to Delaware and from there on to Philadelphia. By June 23, General Washington had gained so much confidence from the unfolding events that he decided to release the New Jersey militia, a move that only days before would have been unthinkable. "The Militia of the State of New-Jersey, who assembled upon the late alarm by signals, are dismissed; with the cordial thanks of the Commander in Chief for the readiness with which they turned out, and the spirit and bravery they have shewn in harassing the enemy; and preventing their incursions." Washington now intended to press the British with his advanced units while moving the entire army forward to the Short Hills near Quibbletown. "The rain having prevented the execution of a part of the after orders of yesterday," he wrote, "every brigade and corps of the army is to parade to morrow morning at 4 o'Clock, if it should not rain."[17]

Meanwhile, Generals Greene and Maxwell had failed to strike the British rearguard at an opportune moment, probably because orders for Maxwell had not arrived in a timely manner, allowing the British to slog through the rain and mud toward Amboy largely unopposed. Washington had been disheartened by the confusion because opportunities to bag a large portion of the enemy's force came along but rarely, and this one had been botched. "It is much to be regretted, that an Express sent off to Genl Maxwell on Saturday night to inform him of Genl Green's movements towards Brunswick," he explained to John Hancock, "that he might conduct himself accordingly, did not reach him...If Genl Maxwell had received the Order, there is no doubt, but their whole Rear Guard would have been cut off."[18]

Even the British themselves knew they were facing a perilous state of affairs, their troops crammed together while marching into Amboy. "One of General Howe's adjutants later expressed the opinion that if General Washington had attacked the retreating column in force at several points simultaneously, they would have inflicted severe damage, as the column was too unwieldly and too cramped for space in the narrow road," but this, of course, was hindsight.

As with their recent withdrawal from Somerset Courthouse, fire and ruin accompanied the entire British line of march. As the British retreated, the rank and file, in a sudden, defeat-induced rage, began burning homes, barns, and outbuildings indiscriminately along the way.[19] On June 25, *The Pennsylvania Gazette* reported that Colonel Morgan's rifle corps had "rendered his [Howe's] stay there so disagreeable, that in a few days after his arrival, being seized with the horribles, at the sight of General Washington on one side, and General Sullivan on the other, he packed up his all and pushed off to Brunswick. In his rout he (Sir William Howe) stole every thing worth carrying off, burnt Somerset Court-House, meeting-house, and a great number of other houses, wlieat, &c. and hung up three women, (two of them by the feet, at the head of his army) whom he imagined were spies.—in short, his whole progress through this part of the country, is marked with devastation and cruelty, more like the savages of the wilderness, than that of Britons, once famed for honour and humanity, the characteristics of brave men." Another letter from a local resident noted: "Here we have been some hours viewing the retreat of the enemy. They have left Brunswick, and all the road from thence to Amboy is covered with smoke, which we have the best reason to believe, are the houses they have set fire to, as they go."[20]

On June 24, the rains finally stopped, and Washington moved down from Middlebrook toward Quibbletown, where he established his headquarters. Morgan and Wayne continued pressing the enemy near Brunswick, while Maxwell marched toward Westfield; Lord Stirling toward the Short Hills [the Short Hills referred to at the time were comprised primarily by the modern-day towns of Metuchen, Plainfield, and portions of Scotch Plains, and *not* the modern-day town of Short Hills, located some ten miles north] with a sizable force. On June 25, Washington wrote to John Hancock, bringing him up to date regarding the situation in the field:

> After the evacuation of Brunswick I determined with the advice of my General Officers to move the whole Army the next morning to this post, where they would be nearer the Enemy and might act according to circumstances. In this I was prevented by Rain, and they only moved Yesterday morning. I have advanced Lord Stirlings Division and some Other Troops lower down in the Neighbourhood of Metuchin Meeting House and intended to have posted more there, but found on reconnoitring the Ground, that it was low and disadvantageous – and still more unfavourable through a scarcity of Water. Those reasons added to that of there not being the smallest prospect of attacking the Enemy in amboy with a probability of Success, secured on their Flanks by Water and in their Front by strong Redoubts across the Neck, would not permit me either in my own Opinion or that of my General Officers, to keep any greater body of Men in that Quarter, where they would have been dispersed & of consequence extremely insecure.[21]

The state of affairs on the British side was looking increasingly grim, as their army—eighteen thousand strong—continued to cram onto the grounds surrounding Amboy, with advanced elements of the Continental army constantly slashing at their heels. Nicholas Cresswell, an English citizen who had been caught up in the evacuation of Brunswick, recorded the scene as the Redcoats marched from Brunswick toward Amboy. "All the Country houses were in flames as far as we could see. The Soldiers are so much enraged, that they will set them on fire in spite of all the Officers can do to prevent them."[22] Stephen Kemble, an officer who had a clear understanding of British dispositions at the time, reported that on June 23, some of the army was encamped at Amboy, while another part had already been ferried

across the Arthur Kill to Staten Island. An army so divided is an army
in potential peril, especially with an enemy closing rapidly. On the
24th, Kemble added this gloomy note to his journal:

> 24th. Transports Sailed for Princes Bay, Staten
> Island, to take in the Troops. Lord Howe Embarks
> to-morrow on board the Eagle ; supposed the Troops
> are to proceed to Sea, and the Delaware their desti-
> nation. The Retreat of our Troops from Jersey give
> the Rebels great Encouragement, and strengthen
> their Cause much.[23]

As daylight broke on June 25, the British were packing to leave
as rapidly as possible. Archibald Robertson recorded that there
was "information being given to the General [Howe] that the Rebel
Army quitted their Camp and come down to the Low Country about
Sam Town [Samptown], Quibble Town, etc., and that they intended
to possess the Short hills near Metuchen to Annoy our Rear, when
Embarking orders were given for the Army to pack all their Baggage
and Tents at Amboy and to be under Arms at 6 o'clock in Evening."[24]
As Robertson and his men were packing to embark, Washington
was informing Hancock of his intentions, which, given the recently
constructed British fortifications, appeared limited. "I have light
parties lying close on the Enemy's Lines to watch their motions & who
will be ready to act in conjunction with Lord Stirlings Division and
such Other Troops as it may be necessary to detach. Tho I think and
so do the rest of the Officers, that no Event is likely to take place that
will require more, since the Idea of forcing their Lines or bringing
on a General Engagement on their own Grounds is Universally held
incompatible with our Interest."[25]

The situation was increasingly fluid, hence increasingly dangerous
for both sides should a miscalculation be made. A letter, dashed off
from Brunswick by an unidentified American, captured the evolving
state of affairs:

> I wrote two letters yesterday, by different expresses,
> giving an account of our being in possession of
> Brunswick, and the enemy retiring to Amboy, where
> we now hear their main body have reached, and
> their advanced guard about 4 miles between Wood-

bridge and Bonam Town. General Maxwell was near them, also General Parsons with his brigade, and Lord Sterling, with his division, is between them and our camp here. Near 6000 of our troops remain in Brunswick. The enemy have thrown their bridge (destined for the Delaware) across the Sound from Amboy to Staten Island, by which it is clear, they design to retreat, if closely pushed. The weather last night and this morning has been so wet, that nothing could be done, otherwise I believe we should have moved nearer towards them. Their retreat has been attended with such a destruction of property, that marks their despair of possessing this country.[26]

As Washington was contemplating his options, and as Archibald Robertson was at Amboy preparing his troops to pack and embark, Captain Ewald was conducting a patrol along the outer limits of the British defenses. "Since I was duty officer today, I had to conduct a patrol with fifty old and fifty new men," he wrote. "Toward two o'clock in the afternoon, several troops of light horse were seen in the vicinity of one of our outposts with whom we skirmished. About four o'clock enemy infantry and artillery approached and a hard skirmish ensued. Several wounded Americans fell into our hands, from whom we heard that a corps of three thousand men was situated at Westfield."[27]

From Westfield—only fourteen miles northwest of Amboy—roads ran in all directions like the spokes from the hub of a wheel, allowing the Americans quick movement or reinforcement in any direction. Like ominous clouds looming darkly across the horizon, Washington's army was closing rapidly on the British at Amboy, a dangerous threat for the British commander. Howe's army was now divided across the water between New Jersey and Staten Island; in warfare, the classic moment for an enemy to strike. To ignore such a hazard was to invite disaster.

CHAPTER SEVENTEEN
The Short Hills & Westfield

What General William Howe decided next has been debated for almost two hundred and fifty years. The disagreement arises over whether his actions emanated from a sort of grand and superbly calibrated strategy to finally lure Washington down from his mountain perch to the flats, where his army could, at last, be attacked by Howe's overwhelming numbers and dispatched once and for all or, conversely, if his actions were simply the hurried response of a man suddenly aware of his army's vulnerability resulting from last-minute intelligence indicating Washington had emerged from his mountain fortress and was fast approaching Brunswick with his entire army?

Some historians believe firmly that the entire British withdrawal, from Millstone to Amboy, had been an elaborate ploy magnificently orchestrated by Sir William to entice Washington into a posture where he might be attacked on open ground. On the other hand, it is difficult to imagine that Howe's sudden about-face on the morning of June 26 resulted from anything other than a moment of sudden anxiety. But whether strategic or hurried, General Howe can most certainly be congratulated for grabbing the brass ring and marching that morning with both conviction and power to confront the approaching rebels. As such, he caught General Washington by complete surprise, and in a letter written a few days later to Lord Germain, he explained his reasoning for the sudden attack. Whether this correspondence was shaped by his failure to bring Washington to battle or not, we do not know.

The necessary preparations being finished for crossing the troops to Staten Island, intelligence was received that the enemy had moved down from the mountain and taken post at Quibble Town, intending, as it was given out, to attack the rear of the army removing from Amboy; that two corps had also advanced to their left, one of 3,000 men and eight pieces of cannon, under command of Lord Stirling, Generals Maxwell and Conway, the last said to be a captain in the French Service; the other corps consisted of about 7,000 men, with only one piece of cannon.

In this situation of the enemy, it was judged advisable to make a movement that might lead to an attack, which was done on the 26th in two columns.[1]

Archibald Robertson, marching with the British attack early that morning, explains that "the Whole Army was formed into two Columns, and Lying on their Arms All night, they march'd at 6 o'clock in the morning of the 26th." One of the two columns, under General Cornwallis, marched due north toward Woodbridge with the intention of turning west. The other column, under General Vaughan, accompanied by General Howe, marched northwest toward Metuchen, intending to turn due north and join Cornwallis's column somewhere in the Short Hills behind Washington's position. The goal of the operation was for the two columns— numbering some sixteen thousand troops with ample field artillery—to cut Washington off from the passes that led back into the Watchung Mountains, hence forcing him to fight for his life on ground in and around the Short Hills. By means of an early and rapid march toward Westfield—where it was known a substantial detachment of Americans were posted—Howe intended to catch the Americans by complete surprise and be behind them before they realized what had occurred.

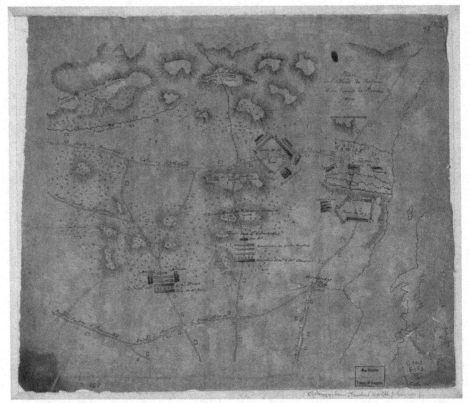

Battle of the Short Hills and Westfield from the 1777 map by Friedrich Adam Julius von Wangenheim.

It was, to say the least, an ambitious plan, and the operation began well. "The Right hand Column commanded by Lord Cornwallis," Robertson says, "march'd by Woodbridge and along the North side of the Short hills. The left Column by the Cross roads and Metuchen detaching the 28th, 35th and 2 Hessian Battalions to take post at Bonheim Town,"[2] in order to cover the column's left flank as it marched. The sudden appearance of strong British columns in the wee hours sent shock waves through Washington's advanced detachments. Charles Willson Peale, who had traveled with Sullivan's Division from Rocky Hill to Brunswick, recalled that "we expected to move down towards Amboy, but early in the morning we understood that the Enemy were moving towards us."[3]

The left column of the British advance under Howe marched largely unopposed. However, Cornwallis, on the far right, almost immediately stumbled headfirst into trouble upon entering Wood-bridge. Marching with Cornwallis was the ever-present Captain Johann Ewald, who tells us that his column consisted of "the Donop,

Prueschenck, and mounted Jägers companies, the Hessian grenadiers under Colonel Donop, the English Guards, and a part of the dragoons," and that they "took their route directly toward Westfield."[4] Previously, Washington had shifted William Alexander's entire division to a position on the American left near Ash Swamp in order to secure that flank, along with the passes leading into the Watchung Range near Scot's Plain (modern-day Scotch Plains) and Westfield. Alexander's division consisted of Maxwell's New Jersey Brigade, Conway's Pennsylvania Brigade, and Morgan's Rifle Corps, no longer operating independently. Alexander established his headquarters in Scot's Plain, while Maxwell and Conway deployed near Ash Swamp. Morgan's riflemen, covering the main force, had moved forward to Woodbridge.[5]

Morgan deployed on good ground overlooking the road leading north toward Westfield (now Green Street in Woodbridge). As the British van approached in the first light of day—the distinctive tramp of marching troops growing louder and louder—his riflemen took dead aim and opened on Cornwallis's vanguard, staggering the lead elements. The British had not bothered to scout their route northward, and the accurate blast of musketry from Morgan's marksmen sent them reeling. The long column was brought to an immediate halt, supports called up to dislodge whatever opposition lay ahead. But this took precious time, already compromising an attack that was fundamentally based on the element of surprise. Moreover, Morgan, grasping the strength of the British column he was facing, immediately sent dispatches off to Alexander and Washington, notifying both officers of the Redcoat advance.

Morgan's riflemen continued laying down heavy fire until finally faced with overwhelming odds. Then, he pulled back to a secondary position, opening fire once more and delaying Cornwallis's column until forced to withdraw yet again. Morgan's rifle corps continued to engage in a running battle with the British while backing away toward Ash Swamp. "The smoke from black powder drifted into the hues of dawn," as Morgan's skilled woodsmen repeatedly fired and retreated. "Using the cover provided by bushes and trees, the Americans opened fire once again. The British formed a line, and returned with penetrating fire from infantry and hessian Jägers. The Americans fell back over the hill into the woods."

As the sound of Morgan's gunfight crept closer and closer, William Alexander was preparing his division for action along the crest of one of the Short Hills, Ash Swamp to his rear. Behind him, and running parallel to one another, the foothills or Short Hills of the Watchung Mountains afforded still more defensive positions, should they be required. Artillery was being rolled into place, and the Continentals were hurriedly taking up positions behind trees, rocks, and fence rails for both cover and concealment. Just as he had on Long Island the year before, Alexander understood that time had to be bought for Washington and the main body to withdraw back to Middlebrook, and he intended to supply that time. Ahead, Morgan's riflemen were spotted—easily recognizable in their hunting shirts and leggings— firing and withdrawing, then ultimately falling in along Alexander's line. "Again, the British advanced and about half an hour later, they came upon a second hill where Stirling [Alexander] was positioned with twenty-five hundred Continental regulars."[6]

The report from Morgan, which reached Washington's headquarters that morning, put the commander in chief on high alert. He realized at once that the main body had to withdraw to Middlebrook as soon as possible or potentially fall prey to a developing design he still did not fully comprehend. Over the course of the Revolution, Washington had made many good decisions, some few poor ones, but in a pinch—once his natural combative instincts had been fully aroused— he was generally superb. Hence, the General Orders that morning were short and to the point:

> The troops are to complete three days provisions of bread and flour, as soon as possible; and but one day's provision of flesh, if it be fresh, or three days provisions of salt meat; if to be had, and to hold themselves in readiness to march at a moment's warning – They will lodge themselves in the best manner they can this night, near the gaps of the mountains – From every gap, proper picquets are to be posted and patroles sent out during the night.[7]

So, as Washington started the main body back toward the mountain gaps in the first ridge line behind Westfield, General Alexander stood his ground near Ash Swamp. He was now the American rearguard, trying to hold off a British advance of at least eight thousand troops accompanied by ample artillery—with at best two thousand five hundred men of his own. The odds, for the rebels, were far from favorable. As the Redcoats moved up through the woods and fields, Alexander's troops readied themselves, carefully loading their muskets. "The Americans opened fire with cannons from a distance of about eight hundred thirty yards before switching to muskets." As the British eyed the Americans for the first time, Ewald came forward and had a good look at the Americans arrayed across his front. This is what he saw: "The enemy [the Americans] had taken a position on the steep bush-covered heights; his right was protected by deep ravines and his left by a thick wood."[8] It was then about ten o'clock in the morning. The British promptly unlimbered artillery of their own, which began counter-battery fire from the flanks of the American position. After softening up the rebels with artillery fire, the British launched a full-scale attack straight up the hill into the teeth of Alexander's position. "They attempted a sweeping charge up the hill, but were driven back by relentless American firepower."[9]

More artillery was brought up to support the British attack, and the Americans responded with cannons of their own. The thunder of battle reverberated all the way across central New Jersey, so loud, in fact, that miles away on Staten Island, Stephen Kemble heard it clearly and jotted down this hopeful note: "Much firing heard this morning in Jersey, both of Cannon and small Arms, which we are told took its course towards Brunswick, we hope from thence a glorious issue to our Arms, and a total Defeat of Mr. Washington's Forces."[10]

Cornwallis, unused to seeing Britain's troops tumbling back downhill in the face of American volleys, marshaled still more units in a desperate attempt to sweep Alexander's division from its position on the heights. Ewald tells us that "the Jägers tried to approach the enemy in the rear through the ravines, and the Hessian grenadiers made an attack on the right, supported by the Guards."[11] Finally, facing a renewed assault and under an increasingly heavy cannonade, Alexander's line frayed, then broke entirely. Alexander, handling his division with calm and great discipline, led them back through the woods, although he had lost his horse in the action, and Maxwell had barely managed to escape capture. But both men were far from finished.

The British, unsure of the ground and just how many Continentals they were facing, pursued slowly and with caution, giving Alexander time to reform on another hill slightly behind his original position. Archibald Robertson, moving forward with the Redcoats that morning, wrote, "The Rebels halted again about a mile farther on and were Attack'd a 2d time."[12] Just as Morgan had done earlier,

Alexander realized he was not fighting to win—which, given the odds, was all but impossible—but rather fighting a delaying action, providing Washington time to withdraw. So, hill to hill, he continued fighting, forcing the Redcoats to move forward with great care and reconnoiter carefully. On this second hill, Alexander stood firm once more, perhaps fighting longer than he should have, for one of his officers recalled: "His Lordship [William Alexander] was in no hurry to retreat, but preferred engaging for a while, wherein he made a wrong choice, for he had been nearly cutoff by the right column under Lord Cornwallis."[13]

By now, however, the British realized they had overwhelming numbers in their favor and attacked Alexander's second position with vigor. "The enemy was attacked with the bayonet," Ewald writes, "and driven back, whereby colonel Minnigerode and his grenadier battalion greatly distinguished themselves, taking from the enemy three Hessian guns [artillery pieces] which had been captured at Trenton. The loss of the enemy in dead and prisoners was reckoned to be about 500 men, and on our side about one hundred and thirty dead and wounded, the Minnigerode Battalion having lost the most men." Alexander had put up a valiant fight, but the sheer power of Cornwallis's column had finally succeeded. "Grapeshot from the Continental Army's cannons took its toll, but the Crown forces had overwhelming numbers and firepower, compelling Stirling [Alexander] to give orders 'to Leave the Ground.'"[14]

As the Americans were initiating their retreat, a lone British officer made a bold move toward the rebel line, for which he would pay dearly with his life. One of the Continentals present recounted the event in a letter penned a few days later. "The fire growing hot, and our men beginning to retreat, a British officer singly rode up to a cannon that was playing on [firing upon] the enemy, and with his pistols and hanger [short sword], forced every man from it, then seeing Lord Stirling he cried, 'Come here you damned rebel, and I will do for you.'" While impassioned the officer's actions may have been, prudent they were not. "Lord Stirling answered him by directing the fire of four marksmen upon him, which presently silenced the hardy fool by killing him on the spot. Our men recovered the field piece which through want of small arms obliged them to abandon."[15] Many of Alexander's troops scurried off through the woods, making their way towards the mountains, while General Maxwell gathered what he could of his brigade and beat a path up the road toward Westfield.

It was now past noon, and the day was warming considerably. Many of the British columns had been on the march since before dawn, and the heat was beginning to take its toll. The Redcoats and Hessians, dressed in heavy wool uniforms, were particularly susceptible to the withering effects of the heat. After catching their breath, they began a slow march up the road toward Westfield, still hopeful of cutting Maxwell's brigade off from escape to the mountains. By now, both the left and right columns of the British operation had met and merged on the road to Westfield, General Howe leading them forward.

"We continued our march both Columns on the same Road towards Westfield in extreme heat," Robertson remembered vividly. That heat took a heavy toll on the marching column. "Since it was extremely hot, especially on the 26th," Ewald recalled, "some twenty men died marching, among whom were seven Jägers of the troop, who had to make this march on foot burdened with their hussar boots and hussar sabers [heavy cavalry boots and sabers]"[16] Despite the withering heat, by late afternoon, the massive column finally reached the outskirts of Westfield, where orders were given to encamp overnight. "The 1st Column Encamp'd near Westfield," according to Robertson, while "the 2d about 1 mile short of it." Unfortunately for the British, Howe's grand plan to envelop and destroy either all or most of Washington's army had failed completely. Even the reliably upbeat Robertson could do little but note the obvious: "The Whole Rebel Army decamp'd that were near Quibble Town and regaind the Mountain."[17] Washington had fled the Short Hills for Middlebrook once again, and in the end, the long British march through torturous heat and battle had accomplished nothing of significance.

Tradition has it that as the British marched toward Westfield, Mrs. Barbara Frazee was in her home on Raritan Road baking bread for the Continental troops who were then in retreat from the Short Hills. Cornwallis apparently got a whiff of the delicious aroma as he neared her residence, promptly dismounted in her yard, and approached the kitchen door. "My Lady," he asked politely, "may it please you to give to Lord Cornwallis the first loaf that comes from your oven of baking bread?" Mrs. Frazee dutifully acknowledged the general's request and went about her baking. Meanwhile, Cornwallis took a seat in the shade outside to escape the insufferable heat. Once the first loaves were fully baked, Mrs. Frazee took one out to Cornwallis and his officers, who were naturally gathered nearby. Handing him the freshly baked bread, she said, "Your lordship will please understand that I give the bread in fear, not in love." Cornwallis, apparently impressed by the woman's courage, rose in admiration of her bravery and responded, "Not I, nor a man of my command shall accept a single loaf."[18] While Cornwallis and his officers were reportedly content to ride off unfed, his soldiers were less inclined to depart in the same manner, happily plundering her livestock before renewing their march.

In 1777, Westfield was a prosperous community of a few hundred homes and farms nine miles west of Elizabethtown. Located along the old Minisink Trail, a pathway used by early Native Americans for their annual hunts, the village had naturally grown over the years due to its easy accessibility. As settlers—mostly Presbyterians—flocked to the area in the 1680s, primitive roads naturally began to stretch out toward other local settlements, over time turning the growing community into a small road hub. Strongly Whig in its politics, Westfield had become well known to the British as a center of rebel sympathy. As local historian Charles Philhower notes, "General William Maxwell held Elizabeth Town, with the British occupying Perth Amboy, during the first half of 1777. General John Sullivan was in command in the immediate vicinity of Westfield. At this time, there was much military activity in town. The enemy was constantly sallying forth from Amboy and Woodbridge, raiding the country south of the mountains. Continental troops were continually moving from Elizabeth Town to Westfield and Scotch Plains. This was in fact the line of defense."[19]

Throughout the first five months of war in New Jersey, Westfield had been behind American lines, thus not suffering the ravages other communities had endured when unfortunately visited by the British. Regrettably, all that was about to change. As the long British columns snaked up the road from Ash Swamp toward Westfield, the bell in the Presbyterian Meeting House began clanging its warning wildly, announcing the approach of the enemy. The warning was unmistakable, and, gathering what they could, the inhabitants fled down the roads toward the mountains, leaving the town virtually deserted as the British marched in.

As the Redcoats were approaching Westfield, "the battered Americans retreated through Scotch Plains to the gap in the Watchung Mountains at Bonnie Burn Road. From there they returned to the main army at the Middlebrook Encampment, through Watchung and Warren, using the protection of the first Watchung ridge."[20] There, they were joined by the residents of Westfield and the surrounding area, fleeing from what they rightly feared would be severe retribution. As time would prove, they were entirely correct in their assumptions.

Before settling in at Westfield, General Howe rode out to one of the short hills that paralleled the first Watchung ridge and took a long look at the mountain passes; particularly the American encampment at Middlebrook. The view was unsettling. One American soldier wrote: "Our army is encamped at the old spot [Middlebrook], only large bodies are posted at all the passes, and in some advantageous places below the mountains. It is suspected that the enemy would force our camp, if possible; but to attack us in the mountains is a thing devoutly to be wished by every one who desires the destruction of the British army."[21] There is little doubt that General Howe agreed with this soldier's assessment that any attack against the rebels in their mountain defense would be virtually suicidal, and he wisely declined, turning his horse about and riding back to Westfield instead. He later justified the decision to Germain as follows: "The enemy was pursued as far as Westfield with little effect, the day proving so intensely hot, that the soldiers could with difficulty continue their march thither; in the meantime, it gave opportunity for those flying [the Americans] to escape by skulking in the thick woods, until night favored their retreat to the mountain."[22]

Meanwhile, at Westfield, the British had already discovered they had a complete and unopposed run of the abandoned town. In that the village had the reputation as a hotbed of rebel activity, the resultant pillaging was sadly predictable. Homes and stores were promptly looted; thus rapidly escalating into a virtual riot of destruction. "The thirsty Redcoats continued their plundering after discovering and imbibing three barrels of applejack at Lambert's Mills on Old Raritan Road. In James Lambert's subsequent claim for damages he listed the amount stolen as 20 gallons. British troops also drank the Terry well, located at the intersection of Rahway and Cooper Roads, completely dry on that scorching day in late June."[23] As previously mentioned, Westfield was then primarily a village of Presbyterian settlers. Hence, the British took particular delight in camping on the grounds of the Presbyterian Meeting House near the center of town. Here, they at once began maliciously desecrating its sanctuary in extreme acts of vandalism, even considering the times. A local member of the militia reported that "the British filled the church with sheep and put a ram's head in the pulpit and slaughtered a great number of hogs, sheep, and cattle. They threw down the bell from the steeple and slaughtered sheep and cattle in the building."[24] British pillaging was widespread, affecting the entire area of their march but centering now on the areas in and around Westfield. "The British army burnt, stripped and destroyed all as they went along. Women and children were left without food to eat, or raiment to put on. Three hundred barrels of flour were sent down towards Westfield and Ash Swamp, by order of his Excellency, to be distributed among the poor sufferers. The enemy even destroyed all the books of divinity they came across."[25]

While one British column camped on the church grounds, the other bivouacked at the intersection of Mud Lane and Rahway Road (modern-day Grove Street and Central Avenue), drinking, pillaging, and acts of general destruction continuing throughout much of the night as the Redcoats took their revenge on the town. After the British had finally marched on, an inventory revealed the extent of the carnage. Over ninety homes had been either looted or destroyed, over eleven thousand individual items stolen, all the money in the town absconded with; some two thousand fence rails put to the torch—a stunning record of destruction for one small village. Soon after the British evacuated the town the following morning, American militiamen entered, Colonel Israel Shreve among them, and he recorded the almost astonishing level of devastation he witnessed:

> They made shocking havock, Distroying [sic] almost Every thing before them, the house where Gen. How stayed which was Capt. Clarks he promised Protection to If Mrs. Clark would use him well and Cook for him & his Attendance, which she Did as Chearful as she Could, just before they went off Mr. how [Howe] Rode out, when a No. of his solider Come in And plunder the Woman of Every thing in the house, Breaking And Destroying what they Could not take Away, they Even tore up the floor of the house, this proves him [General Howe] the Scoundrel, and not the Gentleman, Gen. Lesley took his Quarters at Parson Woodruffs Protected his property in Doors, the Doctor fled his wife and family Remained, the meetinghouse a Desent Building they made a sheep

pen of threw Down the Bell, and took it of..., they
Drove of[f] All the Horses, Cattle, Sheep & hogs they
Could Git, – I saw many famalys who Declared they
had Not one mouthful to Eat, bed or beding Left,
or Stitch of Wearing Apparel to put on, only what
they happened to have on, and [the British] would
not afoard Crying Children a mouthful of Bread Or
Water Duering their stay.[26]

Fortunately for the townspeople of Westfield, the sun would
finally rise on June 27.

CHAPTER EIGHTEEN
Amboy

*A*round nine o'clock in the morning of June 27, the British decamped at Westfield and began marching back toward Amboy, burning and looting as they went. Throughout the past few weeks of skirmish and maneuver, they had partaken in numerous acts of wanton violence and destruction, enraging the inhabitants, while failing, at every turn, to bring Washington and his Continental army to battle—a litany of failures with few redeeming features. Many British and Hessian soldiers had been lost to combat and heat exhaustion, all to no discernible purpose, and the exhausted, heat-worn troops knew they had been sacrificed for little if anything. For General Howe, who had marched twice from Amboy with the intention of luring Washington down from his mountain perch and destroying his army on the lowlands below, those twin operations had petered out in utter failure.

Marching his army south across New Jersey toward the Dela-ware River was now unthinkable for the British commander, given the recent response of the Jersey militias and Washington's marauding Continentals, who had recently stormed into Bruns-wick. No, a march across Jersey meant the destruction of his army, something General Howe had to avoid. Thus, for the British, only one course of action remained truly plausible: an evacuation by sea. Far behind the lines, and late on the 27th, an anxious Stephen Kemble, desperate for accurate reports of the most recent action in Jersey, wrote: "Accounts vary so strangely, that there is no confi-dence to be put in them, the only Authentic is, that Lord Cornwallis had met with Lord Stirling, commanding upwards of 3,000 Rebels, at or near Quibble Town, Attacked, and put them to a Total Route, and took three pieces of Cannon. This is all the Accounts we have this day at six in the Afternoon."[1]

While the British left Westfield around nine o'clock in the morning—presumably in good spirits after virtually wrecking the village—the devastation they left behind was appalling and something that would require months to rectify. Departure was slow, with sixteen thousand men marching off in unit order, taking quite some time to accomplish. Historian Charles Philhower tells us that, "at 3 o'clock on Friday June 27, the British retreated by way of Mud Lane, Willow Grove, and then to Rahway." American units quickly followed through Westfield on the heels of the departing Redcoats. "Scott's light horse and Morgan's rangers came through town in the afternoon and followed the retreat vigorously, attacking them on flanks and rear." Behind, in the village, "old residents spoke of the camp kettles of the British having been hung from the branches of walnut trees," near their encampment on Mud Lane and debris left scattered everywhere.[2]

The temperature rose throughout the long day, and, despite only six miles separating Westfield from Rahway, many more soldiers would collapse and die on the march due to the suffocating heat. Captain Ewald brings us up to date: "The entire army withdrew afterward upon the heights of Westfield Meeting House, where it remained overnight in bivouac. On the 27th the army withdrew in two columns to Rahway, where it was protected by the Rahway River."[3] The British column stretched out for miles on the march, a herd of livestock taken from the farmers of Westfield leading the way. Heat and the smothering dust of an army on the march made the journey almost intolerable. According to Major John Andre, who would later be hung as a spy for his part in Benedict Arnold's treasonous plot to hand over West Point to the British, "at 9 in the morning we marched by the left bringing with us about 60 prisoners picked up in different places and driving cattle we met on the road."[4] Archibald Robertson noted simply that "all the Army moved to the Banks of the Raway [River] about 6 miles and encamp'd without A Shot being fired at our Rear, had several men died on the March from the Excessive Heat."[5]

Having returned to the camp at Middlebrook on the 27th, General Washington remained naturally baffled as to Howe's intentions. Orders were subsequently issued preparing the army for combat, which Washington considered potentially imminent, should the British move toward the mountain passes. He also thought to fine-tune the passage of orders, an issue that had caused problems during the most recent operation. General Orders for that day reflect his concerns:

> The Commander in Chief earnestly desires, that the General Officers, in case of an action, or the appearance of one will (when practicable) send all their orders either in writing, or by an Aide-de-Camp, or Brigade Major – to prevent the unintelligible and contradictory directions, which are too often conveyed, and may prove fatal to the views and designs of the commanding officer.

> Intelligence of the enemy's movements, and approach they are also requested to communicate in the same manner to the officer commanding; otherwise it will be impossible for him to make a proper disposition.[6]

While several American units followed the British march, little in the way of serious fighting took place, the Continentals content to merely skirmish while determining the Redcoats' intentions. After camping for the night along the banks of the Rahway River, the British were up again early continuing their march toward Amboy. "On the 28th the army marched back in two columns to its former encampment at Amboy," Ewald wrote. "On this march an enemy party followed our rear guard, but it was constantly repulsed by the Jägers."[7] Back on Staten Island, Stephen Kemble was still impatient for information regarding the latest British operation, but once again, he would be disappointed. "Today, June 28th, Captain Mulcaster, this after-noon arrived from Jersey and Amboy, informs that General Howe came there last Night with the whole Army; that Lord Cornwallis had fell in with Lord Sterling between SampTown and Quibble Town, had put him to flight without loss, except that of Captain Finch of the Guards, who is most dangerously Wounded, but does not say how far General Howe proceeded, or anything more about him."[8]

It seems General Howe had now seen enough of New Jersey and intended to remove his army from Amboy to Staten Island, where it was to embark on a new campaign as soon as possible. On June 28, Archibald Robertson, no doubt exhausted from two days marching in the withering heat, wrote: "Arrived at Amboy at 10 in the Morning, Stirne's Brigade embark'd immediately. The 7, 26, 38, and 3 Battalions Hessian Grenadiers cross'd to Staten Island and encamp'd. The Rest of the Army remains on the old Camps at Amboy." When it came to logistics, the British army was nothing if not organized and efficient, and things continued moving smoothly. The very next day, Robertson wrote, "In the Morning 52, 35, Waldeckers, 2 Battalions Anspach, Kohler's, and Loos Battalions cross'ed to Staten Island and were encamp'd. Continuing to pass over all the Horses and Heavy Baggage of the Army."[9]

Moving eighteen thousand men with all their baggage, supplies, artillery, wagons, and horses was an enormous task that would take days to finally accomplish. As this was ongoing, Alexander Hamilton—who, it can be recalled, had joined General Washington's staff earlier that winter—described the recent failed British operation and their return to Amboy to the governor of New Jersey, Robert Livingston:

> They remained at Westfield till the next day, and perceiving their views disappointed have again returned to Amboy, plundering and burning as usual. We had parties, hanging about them in their return; but they were so much on their guard no favourable opportunity could be found of giving them any material annoyance. Their loss we cannot ascertain; and our own, in men, is inconsiderable, though we have as yet received no returns of the missing. I have no doubt they have lost more men than we; but unfortunately, I won't say from what cause, they got three field pieces from us, which will give them room for vapouring [bragging], and embellish their excursion, in the eyes of those, who make every trifle a matter of importance. It is not unlikely they will soon be out of the Jersies; but where they will go to next is mere matter of conjecture, for as you observe, their conduct is so eccentric, as to leave no certain grounds on which to form a judgment of their intentions.

Lastly, Hamilton expressed the great sense of failure many American soldiers felt, having watched the devastation wrought by the British—in particular, the fires and long trails of smoke rising toward the heavens—from the heights of Middlebrook, knowing that family, friends, and loved ones were suffering as they watched, powerless to help.

> In the mean time it is painful to leave a part of the inhabitants a party to their depredations; and it is wounding the feelings of a soldier, to see an enemy parading before him and daring him to a fight which he is obliged to decline. But a part must be sacrificed to the whole, and passion must give way to reason.[10]

Meanwhile, at Amboy, the British continued moving their troops across Prince's Bay in a constant stream. "During the night of the 28th and the early morning of the 29th the greater part of the army crossed over Prince's Bay to Staten Island," Captain Ewald informs us. "The rear guard under Lord Cornwallis, consisting of the Jägers, the light infantry, and both Highland regiments, crossed the bay toward evening on the 30th. The entire army took up camp from Billop's Ferry to Richmond," stretching across the island for miles. Seemingly pleased with the organization and speed of the process, Howe wrote Germain that "on the 30th at ten o'clock in the forenoon the troops began to cross-over to Staten Island, and the rear guard, under the command of Lord Cornwallis, passed at two in the afternoon, without the least appearance of the enemy. The embarkation of the troops is proceeding with the utmost dispatch, and I should have the honor of sending your lordship further information as soon as the troops are landed at the place of debarkation."[11]

Washington was watching all of this closely, having sent both Scott's and Conway's corps forward to observe the enemy's activities closely from Woodbridge, but he could still reach no firm conclusion. Up in the air as to Howe's true intentions, he brought John Hancock up to date on June 29:

> In respect to the Enemy's designs or intended move-ments, they are not to be determined. It is certain they got into Amboy Yesterday Evening and from advices this Morning from Officers sent to South Amboy to observe their Motions, there were strong reasons to conclude they were evacuating the Town, as their Horse had gone over to Staten Island and as

several Boats were also passing with Baggage and Others with Troops. There were further circumstances favouring this Opinion – such as Apparent breaches in some of their Lines – yet Genl Sullivan informs me by a Letter just now received, that from all the Intelligence he has been able to obtain to day, he does not think, they have any serious intention of quitting It, and that all their movements are a feint."

But then Washington enclosed this telling postscript on June 30: "From Intelligence received last Night, the Opinion that the Enemy are evacuating Amboy, seems to be more confirmred."[12]

On Staten Island, the British continued their preparations for embarkation, but room, even within their massive fleet of ships, was limited, thus new and restricted arrangements were called for. On July 1, Captain Ewald wrote that "today all the officers of the army were notified that they could sell their horses to the Hessian mounted Jägers and to the artillery park for ten guineas apiece, since no one up to the grade of colonel would be permitted to take a horse with him on the imminent expedition." For Ewald, who was but a captain, this new order presented an immediate challenge. It can be recalled that he had been recently wounded near Bound Brook and could still not walk well enough to perform in the field. "After the order," he tells us, "I proceeded at once to the headquarters to report that I was still completely unable of doing my service on foot because of my hard fall on my right leg, whereupon I was permitted to take a horse with me."[13]

Tradition suggests that it was during this period that the thirteen-star flag, the first official flag of the United States of America, was raised for the first time over the Middlebrook encampment, although the evidence supporting this claim remains somewhat murky. What is known is that on June 14, the Second Continental Congress passed the Flag Resolution of 1777, which stipulated: "*Resolved*, that the flag of the United States be thirteen stripes, alternate red and white; that the union be thirteen stars, while in a blue field, representing a new constellation."[14] There is evidence that this specific design had been suggested much earlier by Mr. Francis Hopkinson, a delegate to Congress from New Jersey who, along with several others, helped to design the Great Seal of the United States. While numerous flags had been created by several different seamstresses in Philadelphia prior to 1777, the flag that was raised over the Middlebrook encampment sometime between June 15 and July 2 was thought to have been sewn by Betsy Ross, although this has also been disputed. At any rate, by an act of Congress, the thirteen-star flag flies today over the Middlebrook encampment twenty-four hours a day, the only location in the United States where that is allowed.

By early July 1777, British intentions seemed to have finally been resolved—they were headed out to sea. Washington wrote to John Hancock, advising him that "yesterday afternoon the Enemy totally evacuated Amboy and encamped Opposite to it on Staten Island. General Scot entered directly after, and posting Guards to secure any Stores they might have left, he withdrew his Brigade & halted about Four Miles from thence."[15] Obviously, Scott had backed away a good four miles, not because he was confident the British were embarking soon for some other location, but because he was not, and he remained wary of a sudden strike back across the water toward Amboy. Nevertheless, the following day, July 2, General Washington's General Orders put the army on notice of an imminent move: "The whole army is to get ready to march to morrow morning, at 6 o'clock, with tents and baggage, all properly put up in the waggons."[16]

By now, Washington was sure that Howe intended to embark his entire army from New York. What he still did not know was where Howe was bound, and on July 2, he received intelligence that suggested that direction now appeared to be up the Hudson River to cooperate with General Burgoyne, who was then leading an army south from Canada. In fact, Burgoyne had departed Canada on June 14, sailing down Lake Champlain, his objective Fort Ticonderoga in New York, situated on a neck of land between Lake Champlain and Lake George. On July 2, Washington again wrote Hancock, advising him that he now had "a strong presumption that the Enemy have in contemplation a junction of their Two Armies by way of the Lakes & the North River [Hudson River]."

Washington, still trying to fathom Howe's intent, remained in a difficult spot, as he explained to Hancock: "Our situation is truly delicate and embarrassing. Should we march to Peeks Kill, leaving Genl Howe on Staten Island, there will be Nothing to prevent him passing to South Amboy and pushing from thence to Philadelphia or in short by any other Route...On the Other hand, if the North River and the possession of the Highlands are his Objective – Our remaining here till his views are certainly known may subject 'em to a risk, that we wish to avoid."[17] Until Howe's direction could be verified, Washington could do little but wait and watch.

The tactical situation in New Jersey was now reasonably fleshed out. On July 3, *The Pennsylvania Evening Post* reported:

> We have authority to assure the public that the enemy
> have totally evacuated the Jersies, and are encamped
> upon Staten-Island, opposite Perth-Amboy.[18]

But what did it mean? On Staten Island, the British army continued preparations for embarkation, but Stephen Kemble was suddenly hearing troubling comments from various British officers, displeased with the general situation, the appearance of defeat, and particularly General Howe's lackluster decision-making. It appears many officers still wanted to fight, while their commander had given up on that option. "Find from the general tenor of Officers Conversation that they are not well pleased with Affairs," Kemble noted in his journal, "but they often speak without thought. Asserted by several that Guides offered to Conduct General Howe by a Road where he might Attack the Rebels in their Entrenchments to advantage, but that he took no Notice of it."[19] But Howe had had enough of New Jersey, and his army was already loading onto a vast fleet of ships for the journey from Decker's, Cole's, Simonsen's, and Reisen's Ferries on Staten Island. Indeed, Captain Ewald informs us that "from the 4th up to the 9th, the entire army was embarked with everything that was necessary for the expedition."[20]

Washington could do little more now than wait and watch. Once the British fleet struck the Atlantic, if it turned south, then it would be presumed Philadelphia was Howe's objective. On the other hand, the fleet might sail directly up the Hudson and never pass Sandy Hook; hence, constant vigilance was of the utmost necessity.

CHAPTER NINETEEN
Sandy Hook

On July 3, General Washington broke camp at Middlebrook, sending General Sullivan's division north to Pompton, New Jersey, where it would be better positioned to march toward Peekskill, if and when necessary, while simultaneously shifting the main body back to Morristown, where headquarters were reestablished. These moves were taken in response to the British fleet moving "round from Prince's Bay towards the watering place and the Foreign Troops marched from the Ground opposite Amboy to the North End of Staten Island." So arranged, the British would be hard-pressed to move against Amboy again because "it would take him so considerable time to remove his Baggage and Stores back again, that we could be in our old Camp at Middle Brook long before he could effect this." Spies were working Staten Island for the commander in chief, providing daily reports, while two regiments and a detachment of cavalry had been posted between Newark and Amboy to prevent British raiding parties from crossing over the Arthur Kill, the stream that ran between Staten Island and New Jersey.[1]

Then, on July 8, the commander in chief received troubling reports regarding General Burgoyne's approach toward Fort Ticonderoga, which he immediately passed on to General Sullivan: "I find the Enemy had approached Ticonderoga and had taken post at Mount Hope. This Account comes by express from Colo. Trumbulls Brother and therefore cannot be doubted."[2] Facts were beginning to point to the Hudson River as Howe's true objective; ultimately, his cooperation with Burgoyne upriver. And if all that were true, Washington realized he

226

was in a poor position at Morristown to prevent Howe from operating along the Hudson; hence, a move farther north only made sense. For this, he prepared the army at once. On July 10, General Orders read: "The tents of the whole army are to be struck to morrow morning, at Gun-firing, and packed up, ready for marching, with the utmost speed; the line of march to begin afterwards as soon as possible."[3] A move into northern New Jersey was now entirely logical, even though Washington was still not entirely certain of Howe's objective. He explained both his decision and its logic to John Hancock also on July 10: "I shall, by the advice of my Officers, move the Army from hence to Morrow Morning towards the North River – If such should be his [Howe's] intention we shall not be too early as a favourable wind & tide will carry him up in a few Hours – On the other hand, if Philadelphia is his Object, he can't get round before we can arrive there, nor can he well debark his Troops &c. & proceed across the Land before we can oppose him."[4]

The Continental army was thus put in motion, and in two days, it made the trek from Morristown to Pompton Plains, despite rainy weather, which turned the roadways into rivers of mud. From there, Washington advised General Sullivan—who had already marched farther north—to cross over the Hudson once the weather cleared: "The army marched yesterday from Morris Town to this place, about eighteen miles from thence, and will proceed towards Peeks-Kill as soon the weather permits – You will also, at the same time, march through the Clove and cross the River at the most convenient and safe place."[5] Unfortunately for the Americans, the weather in northern New Jersey remained very soggy. Nevertheless, the army marched again on July 14 but covered only eight miles on the miserable roads and arrived at "Vanaulens" (believed to be Hendrick Van Allen's farm near modern-day Oakland, New Jersey) on July 14, from where Washington again reported his movements to Hancock: "I arrived here this After-noon with the Army after a very fatiguing March owing to the Roads which have become extremely deep and miry from the late Rains. I intend to proceed in the Morning towards the North River [Hudson River], if the Weather permits; At present it is cloudy and heavy and there is an appearance of more rain."[6]

The following day, the army moved on, crossing the Hudson River and finally bivouacking nearby at Clove, New York. Unsure what his next move might be, Washington had orders issued, preparing the army to move on a moment's notice: "Advantage is to be taken of the present halt to get the horses shod and waggons repaired – No delay is to be made in this matter, as it is very uncertain how soon the army may move again – And for the same reason, all officers and soldiers are to keep near their quarters, and on no pretence to ramble about the country, without leave first obtained by officers from their Brigadiers, and by soldiers from their Colonels."[7]

Meanwhile, back at New York—as the Continentals were going into camp at Clove on July 15—Archibald Robertson jotted this note in his journal: "Received Intelligence of General Washington having moved from Morris Town towards the North River, and a Letter from General Burgoyne dated 2d July that he had invested [began siege operations] Tyconderoga." Then, on July 17, Robertson at long last bordered a ship for the coming campaign. "Left New York at 8 in the Evening and got on board the *Fanny* Transport at 12. The General [Howe] embarked this Evening."[8] At the same time, Ewald explains that, "fifteen thousand men, and the generals accompanying them," had already embarked and were waiting for the fleet to set sail. But "Since the wind was constantly easterly, the fleet remained at anchor between Long Island and Staten Island in the vicinity of Denny's Ferry up to the 19th."[9]

At Clove, Washington was still in the dark as to where the British fleet was bound. On July 22, he wrote: "We have been under great embarrasments respecting the intended Operations of Genl Howe, and still are," although, by now, it surely appeared—from reports of those nearest the harbor—that he was headed out to sea. "By Authentic information there are only Forty Ships at New York," he continued. "The rest are gone elsewhere & have fallen down between the Narrows & the Hook [what is today called the Verrazzano Narrows, and Sandy Hook]Between these Two places, the Number, from the most accurate observation was about One hundred & Twenty on Yesterday." Then, he added, "As I observed before, their destination is uncertain and unknown."[10] The Verrazzano Narrows flows out of New York Harbor, emptying into Lower New York Bay, passing between Staten Island and Brooklyn as it does. Sandy Hook is a spit of land jutting out from New Jersey into the Atlantic Ocean overlooking Lower New York Bay. From Sandy Hook, an observer could immediately determine in which direction the British fleet was headed if, that is, it was put out to sea. If the fleet passed Sandy Hook and turned south, it was no doubt bound for Philadelphia. On the other hand, if the fleet sailed up the Hudson River, it would not be visible from Sandy Hook at all.

On July 20, the British fleet finally set sail, for Captain Ewald tells us that "on the morning of the 20th, about nine o'clock, a light wind arose, whereupon the fleet weighed anchor and put out to sea on the same day. The fleet consisted of two hundred sail," and on the following day, that "the fleet ran so deep in the sea that we lost sight completely of America."[11] Meanwhile, Archibald Robertson—a day behind on the *Fanny*—wrote on July 20, "Weigh'd Anchor and came to an Anchor at Sandy hook about 3 [o'clock] with the 1st Division. The large men of war obliged to come to an Anchor in the Narrows for want of Wind." But three days later, on July 23, all that changed, for the breeze picked up, and the remaining ships finally sailed off. "Early in the Morning," Robertson tells us, "All the Fleet got to Sea with a fair Wind."[12] It was abundantly clear now for anyone observing along the New Jersey shore that as the fleet sailed past Sandy Hook on a southerly course, General Howe's objective was Philadelphia.

On July 22, just before the winds off Sandy Hook had billowed, Washington wrote to Sullivan, advising him that "the greatest part of the Fleet have fallen down from the Narrows, but we have not been able to discover whether they have gone out to Sea."[13] Washington—with evidence mounting hourly that the fleet was soon to put to sea—immediately put his army in motion, recrossing the Hudson and marching to Ramapo, New Jersey. Then, two days later, an express rider galloped into headquarters with the message General Washington had been waiting for since February: specific news of Howe's intentions. Reading it over thoroughly, Washington knew at once what to do, and he wasted no time. He wrote first to Benjamin Lincoln: "I have just received information that the Fleet left the Hook yesterday, and as I think Delaware the most probable place of their destination, I shall immediately move the Army that way."[14] Lincoln was ordered north to serve as one of Gates's wing commanders and rally the New England militia, then Washington turned his attention to Daniel Morgan: "The Enemy's Fleet having left Sandy Hook & gone to Sea, you are, immediately on receipt of this, to march with the Corps under your Command to the City of Philadelphia & there receive Orders from the Commanding Officer."[15] General Howe had finally shown his hand, forcing the Continental army to concentrate upon Philadelphia as rapidly as possible.

While Washington headed south with the main body, other units in New Jersey were ordered toward the capital city. Orders naturally flew from headquarters, putting numerous divisions into motion. General Wayne was ordered to march to Chester, Pennsylvania, on the Delaware River below Philadelphia, where he was to organize the militias for an immediate defense, while Adam Stephen was dispatched directly to Philadelphia with his and Lincoln's old division. As to calling up the local militias, Washington wrote directly to Governor Livingston: "If the Fleet that has lately sailed is destined for Delaware, it will be necessary for the Militia of Burlington, Gloucester, Salem and Cape May to be assembled, as those of Pennsylvania; and I could therefore wish, that orders might be given for such a proportion as are usually called out upon Alarms to assemble immediately at Gloucester," a New Jersey village on the Delaware across from Philadelphia.[16]

On July 25, Washington returned to Pompton, receiving disconcerting reports along the way from the local inhabitants that they were being abused by the Continentals in passage. These reports always enraged the commander in chief, for he realized that the war effort depended upon the people, and if their loyalty were to be lost through foolish abuses, the war would eventually be lost. He wrote directly to General Sullivan, mincing no words:

> It is with no small concern, I am constrained to inform you, that I am constantly receiving Complaints from the People living contiguous to the Road of great abuses committed by the Division under your Command in their march through the Country. From their accounts, they have experienced the most wanton and insufferable injuries – Fences destroyed without the least apparent necessity, and a great number of Horses seized & taken away – in a word, according to them, they have suffered the flagrant violation of their property."[17]

So distressed was Washington by these reported abuses that the General Orders for the day addressed the issue in no uncertain terms. "How disgraceful to the army is it, that the peaceable inhabitants, our countrymen and fellow citizens, dread our halting among them, even for a night and are happy when they get rid of us? This can proceed only from their distress at the plundering and wanton destruction of their property." Under no conditions was preying upon the very people the Revolutionary movement was depending upon to be allowed, and Washington addressed these offenses in the harshest terms. "Two soldiers in General Sullivan's division found guilty of plundering the inhabitants, have lately been condemned to die, and one of them executed – At all events such practices must be prevented – for 'tis our duty to protect the property of our fellow citizens."[18]

By July 26, the Continental army had made the march back to Morristown, from where Washington wrote Adam Stephen again. "I arrived here this Evening, the division have marched five Miles beyond, from whence they will reach the Delaware [River] easily in two days. Let me know where you will be tomorrow Evening and when you expect to be at Howells Ferry."[19] Orders were also sent to Morgan, redirecting him to remain at Trenton unless he had conclusive intelligence that the British had been spotted in the Delaware Bay, or worse, sailing up the river. Then, he communicated with Alexander, who was also marching back from New York. "Genl Green's division will reach Morris Town this Evening," he advised. "Genl Stephen's and Genl Lincoln's march thro' Chester by an upper Road. I have no objection to your Lordship's taking the Rout you mention, and as it will bring you near New Ark [Newark] and Elizabeth Town."[20]

Washington pushed the march farther south, and on July 27, at two o'clock in the afternoon, he sent John Hancock a complete and comprehensive report regarding the locations and movements of the army's various divisions, along with his immediate intentions:

> Gen. Green's Division, consisting of Muhlenburg [VA.] & Weedons [PA.] Brigades, is now here. It will proceed Six or seven Miles farther this Evening. Genls Sullivan & Stirlings Divisions have repassed Hudson's River. The former will proceed by this Rout – The Latter by way of Pyramus [modern-day Paramus, New Jersey] and Bound Brook or Brunswick. Genl Stephen with his own & Lincoln's Division (Genl Lincoln being ordered to join Genl Schuyler) is marching on a back Road from Chester through Sussex to Howel's Ferry on Delaware. Moylans & Blands Regiments of Horse, which were pasturing about Bound Brook & on the communication towards Woodbridge, were ordered to march too on

the first intelligence, I received, of the Fleets sailing.
Morgan's Corps of Light Troops is also on the march
through Brunswic with directions to halt at Trenton
'till further Orders, or till he gets certain information
of the appearance of the Fleet in Delaware. I intend,
in like manner, that Ld Stirling's Division shall halt &
remain there or at Bristol, till we have further information of the Enemy. From either of these places,
they will be sufficiently near Philadelphia, and may
proceed in time on any emergency.[21]

The next day, Washington arrived along the banks of the Delaware River at Lambertville with General Greene's division, from where
he wrote Hancock again on July 30: "Genl Stephen with his own and
Lincoln's Division also arrived, a little time after [Greene's arrival], at
Howel's Ferry – four Miles above this. I have thought proper to halt the
whole Army at these Two places & at Trentown, 'till our knowledge
of the Enemy's destination becomes more certain. If the Delaware is
their Objective, we are now within Two day's easy March of Philadelphia, and can be in time, I trust, to make every necessary disposition
for opposing them."[22] The forced march from the Hudson to the Delaware had put Washington in position to defend the American capital
at Philadelphia—no small achievement.

On the 30th—as General Washington was explaining the unit
dispositions he had taken to John Hancock—Archibald Robertson,
sailing down the coast aboard the *Fanny*, was cruising off Henlopen
Bay, not far from the mouth of the Delaware River. He tells us that
"about 7 in the morning made Cape Henlopen at the Mouth of the
Delaware, went up near to Cape James. The *Roebuck* who was Station'd
there Spoke [communicated] with the Admiral at 3 in the Afternoon
the wind fair up the River. The Admiral made a Signal for the Fleet to
come under his Stern and stood out of the River. The General Officers
Went on board the Admiral. Said the Rebels had a great many fire rafts
etc., etc., in the Delaware."

For the British, this was disconcerting news. Because any excursion
up the Delaware River, due to the defensive precautions the Americans
now had in place (fire rafts were designed to float amongst the fleet
and spread fires vessel to vessel), now appeared extremely dangerous.
So it was decided to bypass the Delaware and sail farther south toward

the Chesapeake Bay. British officer James Murray wrote home, saying, "The wind came right ahead next morning and so remained with little variation. We were by this means so long in getting to the mouth of the river that the Rebels judging our destination, had had time to make certain preparations for our entertainment; which not being taken in good part we stood off next morning for Chesapeake Bay."[23]

Gaining the Bay, then sailing north, the troops could be disembarked in Maryland, it was thought, possibly unopposed, while avoiding any undue danger to the fleet. "The Admiral stood toward the Chesapeake,"[24] Robertson tells us, as the British fleet slipped past Delaware Bay, continuing a southward course toward the mouth of the James River at Hampton Roads. Johann Ewald, aboard one of the transports sailing behind the warships, also recalled the moment: "On the 31st we were at 39° north latitude and discovered the two promontories, Capes Henlopen and St. James which bordered on the mouth of the Delaware Bay. We found here the man-of-war *Phoenix*, 64 guns, which cruised before the mouth of the Delaware and delivered its report to Admiral Howe."[25]

But the British warships cruising near the mouth of the Delaware had been immediately spotted, and a message was instantly relayed to General Washington, still encamped at Coryell's Ferry on the Delaware. The message arrived early on the morning of July 31 in an express from John Hancock. Hancock's letter included a note from Caesar Rodney, then in command of the Delaware militia, which read: "Just now by Express from Lewis [modern-day Lewes, Delaware] I am Informed that two hundred and Twenty Eight of the Enemy's ships have appeared in the offing – I have Sent a fresh man and Horse that this Intelligence may be the sooner with you."[26] So, at that moment, it appeared clear to George Washington that the battle for the American capital was about to begin, the British fleet soon to enter the Delaware River. This intelligence set off a rapid chain of events.

Responding immediately, Washington wrote to General Sullivan, advising him that "I am this moment advised by Express that the Enemy's Fleet is arrived at Delaware; I request that you will proceed immediately to Philadelphia with the Division under your command, in the most expeditious manner you can, observing a good order of March & conducting it so as not to injure the Troops."[27] One half-hour later—at ten o'clock in the morning—he responded to John Hancock: "I am this Moment Honor'd with yours of 5 OClock this morning, &

have accordingly sett the Army in Motion One Division had Cross'd the Deleware the day before Yesterday, & I am in hopes the whole of the Troops now here will be able to reach Philada tomorrow Evening Lord stirlings Division lies just in my rear & will move on with us I propose setting off for your City [Philadelphia] as soon as I can get the Chief part of the Army over."[28]

The fight Washington had been anticipating for the entire year had finally arrived, and all he could do now was to concentrate the entire army at Philadelphia or in those Delaware counties immediately south of the city. Subsequently, that same day, General Orders at Coryell's Ferry were both brief and compelling: "The army is to cross the Delaware with all possible dispatch, and proceed to Philadelphia."[29]

With the passage of the Continental army back across the Delaware River, the bitter fighting in New Jersey passed into history, just as a new campaign to defend the American capital rapidly emerged to take its place. Thus ended the New Jersey Campaign of 1777: one of the most violent, bloody, and consequential periods of the entire American Revolutionary saga.

POSTSCRIPT

Philadelphia

On August 5, General Washington entered Philadelphia to a hero's welcome, riding at the head of the Continental army. Standing in the crowd that day was a young man who had recently arrived from France, twenty-year-old Marie-Joseph Paul Yves Roch Gilbert du Motier, Marquis de Lafayette, soon to be known in the United States as simply Lafayette. Starstruck, the young Frenchman later recalled his first glimpse of General George Washington: "Although he was surrounded by officers and citizens," he wrote, "it was impossible to mistake for a moment his majestic figure and deportment; nor was he less distinguished by the noble affability of his manor."[1] After his victories at Trenton and Princeton and his staring down of British forces during the recent seven months of fighting in New Jersey, George Washington had risen substantially in the eyes of many of his countrymen. And in early August 1777—with the British thought to be closing rapidly by sea—he was greeted that day as the capital's savior. While Washington and Lafayette would develop a lifelong friendship, the general's elevated status would, on the other hand, soon lose some of that luster in his attempt to defend the capital.

As the commander in chief was making his way south toward Philadelphia, the Hessian Ewald—perhaps enjoying the salty breezes of the open sea—noticed on August 1 that "the wind was good; the fleet ran to sea again and erred southward. We perceived that under this turning toward the Delaware lay a hidden stratagem of the admiral to make the enemy army uncertain of our landing."[2] Whether that southward turning had been wily stratagem or simple miscalculation is unclear. But Washington would remain unsure of the location of the British landing point until late August. It was then when he finally received hurried reports that the Redcoats had disembarked near where the Elk River empties into the Chesapeake Bay, in the vicinity of modern-day Elkton, Maryland.

As this was playing out, in northern New York, all the early reports had proven correct: General Burgoyne had laid siege to Fort Ticonderoga, and on July 6, the fort had fallen without a shot being fired. Unfortunately for Burgoyne, his expedition was woefully unprepared for campaigning in the North American wilderness, and from that point forward, his fatigue parties were forced to hack a new road through the woods where no road existed. Short on wagons and horses—while simultaneously trying to muscle one hundred and thirty pieces of artillery, along with an immense train of supplies through the dense, almost impenetrable forest—his column crawled forward at a glacial pace toward Fort Edward at the southern end of Lake George. It was there that, on August 3, a weary courier from Howe finally got through to Burgoyne, advising "Gentleman Johnny" that Howe would not be moving north up the Hudson to cooperate. Utterly stunned by the news, Burgoyne kept the information from his staff, fearing the bewilderment it might cause throughout his army.

Now desperate for horses, supplies, and wagons to continue his march, Burgoyne dispatched roughly eight hundred Brunswickers on an expedition to impress supplies from nearby farms. On August 16, while approaching an American depot at Bennington, Vermont, they ran headfirst into a substantial force of New Hampshire state troops and militia under the command of Brigadier General John Stark, who had returned to New England after, it can be recalled, leading Sullivan's column into Trenton the preceding December. The Brunswickers were all but wiped out—the majority taken as prisoners of war—a defeat that significantly depleted Burgoyne's manpower while greatly boosting American fighting confidence. Nevertheless, responding to fearful pleas from New York legislators, on August 17, Washington ordered Daniel Morgan and his corps north to help defend against Burgoyne, temporarily relinquishing one of his most effective detachments.

Back in Pennsylvania, in late August, Washington led his army south to Brandywine Creek, thirty-five miles below Philadelphia, where he deployed in a defensive posture not far from the Delaware state line. Howe's point of disembarkation—not far away in Maryland—had accomplished the one thing the Englishman had been unable to do in New Jersey: force Washington to face him on the field of battle. While the Continentals had surely gained in confidence and know-how during the New Jersey Campaign, those gains had come, by and large, during small unit actions, rarely over division size. As a result, Washington's army—now swelled to over twenty thousand effective troops—remained woefully undertrained and ineffective when it came to large-scale combat. On September 11, the Americans finally met the British army along Brandywine Creek, and the result was sadly predictable: while the Americans fought hard and bravely, the engagement proved a lopsided British victory. Congress fled to York, Pennsylvania, while the Continentals tumbled back through Philadelphia. The British, following up their triumph, happily occupied the American capital.

On September 19, Burgoyne advanced against the Americans at Bemis Heights, New York, a dominating position along the banks of the Hudson River. Gates had ordered Morgan forward to act as a covering force, and he was attacked by the British. Morgan was reinforced by a wing under the command of General Benedict Arnold, but Arnold was forced into retreat. While General Horatio Gates had taken command of the Continental forces at Bemis Heights, it was Benedict Arnold and Daniel Morgan who supplied most of the tactical ingenuity and battlefield initiative. Burgoyne recoiled and dug in, then suffered terribly at the hands of Morgan's rifle corps during a brief interlude. Then, on October 7, Burgoyne advanced a reconnaissance in force toward the American lines. The British were repulsed, and the Americans swarmed after the Redcoats as they retreated. Burgoyne's army was soon surrounded and pinned against the banks of the Hudson River, where, on October 17, with few options available, Burgoyne surrendered his army—then about six thousand, six hundred effective troops—to Gates at the village of Saratoga. It was, for the American cause, an extraordinary victory that—in combination with Washington's attack at Germantown, just northwest of Philadelphia—contributed to the decision that would bring the French into the Revolution on the side of the Americans.

Thus, for the rebels, the American Revolution took one enormous leap forward and another one backward at essentially the same time in two battles that shook not only the country but the world. Rather naturally, recollections of the seven-month period of constant skirmishing and small unit engagements in New Jersey became instantly overshadowed by these far more tumultuous events and soon forgotten as the war shifted into an entirely new phase. Nevertheless, the importance of the New Jersey Campaign cannot be overlooked.

Taken in its entirety, the New Jersey Campaign of 1777 was one of the most uniquely violent and impactful phases of the American Revolution and should be recognized as such. What began as a desperate attempt by Washington to reignite the Revolution soon turned into a ferocious struggle over forage, then later into something even more intense. Washington, taking advantage of interior lines and a clearer sense of the strategic picture, was able to fight the British to a standstill. British foraging operations continued into the spring, when warming weather finally altered the nature of conflict but not the conflict itself. Both armies continued fighting in the same positions they had occupied in March, violence growing in scale. General Washington's strategic objectives had barely changed since he stood at McConkey's Ferry that cold December 25, anticipating the attack on Trenton—to keep his army intact, the cause alive, and, lastly, to drive the British from New Jersey, if at all possible. In that sense, the battles at Trenton and Princeton were of a piece with those at Quibbletown, Piscataway, Bound Brook, Short Hills, and Westfield. Nothing had changed, and nothing would change, until General Howe sailed off with his army, altering the strategic picture dramatically. Thus would the New Jersey Campaign continue until word reached Washington that the British fleet was nearing Delaware Bay, forcing him to cross the river again, ending one campaign while beginning another.

Given the nature of combat during the New Jersey Campaign, it is nearly impossible to accurately catalog the number of engagements fought or casualties sustained by either side. Fighting went on for so long and at such varying levels of intensity that many small encounters were probably never cataloged to begin with. Nevertheless, even rough numbers can be revealing when comparing campaigns or significant engagements during the American Revolution, and those rough numbers are fortunately available. Historian David Hackett Fischer lists fifty-eight separate engagements having been fought during the months of January, February, and March,[3] and Norman Desmarais adds an additional seventy-one in central New Jersey from April through July.[4] Adding the first three engagements of the campaign—two at Trenton and one at Princeton—to that list, a rough total of 132 engagements can be established for the entire New Jersey Campaign. But, of course, that ignores many of the small, daily skirmishes described by Ewald and others from Quibbletown to Woodbridge; brief encounters that, in all probability, will never be accurately tabulated. While 132 engagements surely substantiate the extreme level of combat that took place during the New Jersey Campaign, it is the number of casualties suffered—wounded, killed, taken prisoner, and missing—that reduces an army's fighting capacity and, therefore, serves as a far more objective gauge of overall lethality than the number of engagements fought.

During the New York Campaign of 1776 (July–November 1776), Fischer lists a total of one thousand, five hundred and ten[5] British casualties sustained during a campaign that passed through a series of significant engagements—Long Island, Kip's Bay, Harlem Heights, Throgs Neck, White Plains, and Fort Washington, to name a few. By comparison, during the first three months alone of the New Jersey Campaign, Fischer lists 2,687 British casualties—both battles of Trenton: 1,283; Princeton: four hundred and fifty, and forage war: 954—and yet that figure includes only twenty-three out of the fifty-eight engagements fought during the forage war period (January–March). "This is a lower-bound estimate for 23 engagements," Fischer explains. "Many others left no record of casualties."[6] In other words, casualty counts for a significant number of engagements during the forage war simply don't exist. Complicating the picture even further, Robert Mayers writes that, for the same period, "Generals Washington and Greene maintained that the enemy losses were much higher, perhaps between 2,000 and 3,000."[7] So was it 954 British casualties suffered during the forage war, or three thousand? No records have been uncovered to set the record straight. This uncertainty perfectly illustrates the lack of solid figures historians must contend with when analyzing the Revolutionary era. Fortunately, this uncertainty does not limit our ability to make reasonable evaluations. By simply accepting the "lower-bound" figure, sensible comparisons can still be made.

Even when we accept the lower-bound figure of 2,687 casualties, however, that number remains incomplete because it does not include British casualties suffered during those seventy-one engagements from April through July, when the fighting across New Jersey intensified. To correct for this, I have suggested approximately five hundred additional casualties could be added to the total (also a low figure), providing a final count of 3,187 British casualties suffered during the entire New Jersey Campaign. Now, conceding that 3,187 is a "lower-bound" figure, it nevertheless dwarfs the British count for the entire New York Campaign of one thousand, five hundred and ten. The point being that the unheralded New Jersey Campaign was, at a minimum, more than twice as costly for British manpower as the far better-known New York Campaign.

Casualties are surely a grim yardstick, yet they reveal something of importance. At the battles of Long Island and Brandywine, the British suffered 388 and 587 casualties, respectively, during intense, one-day engagements. The New Jersey Campaign, on the other hand, represented something entirely different for the British: a slow bloodletting more akin to Chinese lingchi, "death from a thousand cuts." While fighting no major battles, the British nonetheless suffered (by means of our calculations listed above) a minimum of 3,187 casualties—and a count that was increasing daily. No wonder General Howe decided to forego a march across New Jersey for a seaborne junket to Maryland. His army was being bled to death for no discernable good and with no end in sight. Over seven months, and through countless small actions, the New Jersey militias, the people of New Jersey, and the Continental army had inflicted a serious setback on British arms, forcing General Howe to flee the state or watch his army slowly disintegrate before his eyes. He sensibly chose flight. And yet over the years, few have stopped to recognize the New Jersey Campaign for the decided American success it was.

In early January 1777, British Generals Howe and Cornwallis had the opportunities to inflict serious harm on Washington's depleted army: first at Trenton, then on the march to Pluckemin, and lastly in the mountains at Morristown. The Continental army was then no better off than it had been on December 25 at McConkey's Ferry and was bleeding enlistments daily. General Howe's army, despite the setbacks at Trenton and Princeton, still vastly outmanned Washington's fatigued troops. Yet over seven months of fighting in New Jersey, Howe was unable to lay a glove on the American leader. Instead—and despite constant protests from General Washington—Howe allowed his troops to plunder, rob, and abuse the people, sending them flying into the ranks of his opponent. This was surely one of the most bizarre, passive-aggressive military strategies in history, offering the citizenry platitudes of care and magnanimity while routinely abusing them. How had that happened?

Both William Howe and Charles Cornwallis—along with all their senior officers—were members of the British aristocracy and used to a culture of aristocratic superiority. In Europe, farmers knew their place and rarely had the good fortune to rise above it. They followed orders unquestioningly, thus making obedient soldiers. In the United States, however, farmers were free men and women who had enjoyed the autonomy of local self-governance for almost one hundred and fifty years. The average farmer in the United States enjoyed a lifestyle well beyond that of European peasants, and the colonies under British rule had prospered as a result. Americans were successful people who thought for themselves and routinely acted in their own best interest. The British view of all this was that those people still loyal to the crown had to be protected from the revolutionaries; thus, harsh measures were called for. Over time, many in New Jersey became enraged by these measures and countered the violence they had been forced to endure with violence of their own. Rather than pacify the population, the British inflamed it.

In that manner, Washington's fragile army survived another critical chapter, when it may well have dissolved or been defeated. In weeks only, many people in New Jersey had risen in anger and determination to oppose the British. No greater evidence of this can be found than in the words of a grateful-yet-astonished George Washington, who advised John Hancock in June that "the people were in & flying to Arms in every Quarter to oppose him." This was no minor inversion of loyalties. Not only had the British managed to turn the people violently against the crown, but they had also—as we have seen from the comments of British officers themselves—provided the Americans with an extended period of training in which they gained confidence and experience in the art of war, a fact that would come back to haunt the British in the years to come. Likewise, this botched stratagem would have cascading negative effects for the British, not the least of which was General Howe's determination to flee New Jersey by sea. As we have seen, this decision ultimately left General Burgoyne alone in the wilderness to suffer the worst British defeat of the war (prior to Cornwallis's surrender at Yorktown), which, in turn, helped to bring the French into the conflict on the American side, a fact that altered the strategic picture.

The New Jersey Campaign of 1777 was a campaign in which the British suffered significant psychological, strategic, and manpower reversals. On the American side, Washington's army not only survived but, by late July, had grown significantly. American officers—Maxwell,

Sullivan, Alexander, Morgan, and Washington—gained valuable combat experience. So too did scores of junior officers, along with the men in the ranks who routinely went toe-to-toe with the cream of the British army in villages like Spanktown, Quibbletown, Connecticut Farms, and Samptown. Today, those names may be long forgotten, but what occurred there had lasting effects. Success breeds confidence, and by July 1777, the Americans were a far more confident lot than they had been in the early days of the war. The people had risen in defiance of British rule and abuse, fighting for their freedom and independence; yet a freedom and independence that at the time remained far from defined. The Articles of Confederation and the Constitution were yet to be written, and a distinct American identity was something only then beginning to emerge.

Americans were most certainly fighting for their freedom, but what form that freedom would ultimately take remained unclear for the rebels of 1777, just as it would continue to be debated, redefined, and improved upon for the next two hundred and fifty years. Nevertheless, if we glance back through the first pages of the New Jersey Campaign, it is possible to catch a brief glimpse of that emerging American character amongst the hard rocks and freezing conditions at Pluckemin. It was there, it can be recalled, where Captain Thomas Rodney noticed something memorable as he watched his exhausted men bed down at night in the snowy mountains without food to eat or even a blanket for cover. "Most of the army were militia and they bore all this with a spirit becoming Free-men and Americans," he wrote, marking the moment, as well he should have.

Formed in the freezing snows and desperate conditions of places like Pluckemin, Jockey Hollow, and Valley Forge, a uniquely American identity was being forged in the crucible of war: a national character based upon freedom, individual rights, and self-government. It was a character that intuitively understood that in a world dominated by tyrants, freedom would never be free and that, once gained, would require eternal vigilance. While the birth of that American freedom—of the *American Dream*—was surely limited by our standards of inclusion today, the conditions had been created that would foster a period of unprecedented growth. Given time, that evolving American Dream—living, working, aspiring, worshipping, and speaking *freely*—would one day produce the most free, most prosperous, and most generous people in the history of the world, along with an optimal template for self-governance, wherever on earth that impulse might arise. The Revolution, and the Constitution it spawned, have thus served as beacons of hope for the oppressed and guiding lights no propaganda or prevarication can obscure. In that sense, the American Revolution might best be understood as one of the most significant watershed moments in the history of humankind and the New Jersey Campaign of 1777 as a foundational building block in that unprecedented American achievement.

APPENDIX
Biographical Vignettes

The British

General William Howe: Born in August 1729, Howe served with the
British army in America during the French and Indian War,
where he earned a solid reputation as an up-and-coming young
commander. In 1775, he returned to the colonies, where he assist-
ed General Thomas Gage during the siege of Boston and, more
prominently, at the Battle of Bunker Hill. He took over as commander in chief in the second half of 1775. Landing his army near
New York in 1776, he conducted a successful campaign, driving
American forces across the Hudson River, then ultimately across
New Jersey into Pennsylvania. In late August 1777, Howe shifted his
forces south to the Chesapeake Bay, from where he marched on
Philadelphia, the American capital. Defeating the Americans at
Brandywine Creek and later Germantown, he settled into winter
quarters in Philadelphia but, by the following spring, had come
under increasing criticism for not having destroyed Washington's
army when he had the chance. He resigned his command in 1778,
returning to England, where he remained in the army. William
Howe died on July 12, 1814, at Twickenham, near London.

General Charles Cornwallis: Cornwallis was born on December 31,
1738, in London into a family of high nobility. His father, Charles
Cornwallis, was Fifth Baron Cornwallis, and his mother the daugh-
ter of Charles Townshend. He was educated at Eton and Clare
College, Cambridge, and was commissioned as an ensign in the
British army in 1757. Cornwallis served with distinction in Europe
during the Seven Years' War (the French and Indian War in North
America) and became Earl Cornwallis upon his father's passing.

He entered the House of Lords in 1762. He saw considerable action during the American Revolution, serving under William Howe and Henry Clinton. Cornwallis oversaw the British Southern Campaign, soundly defeating Horatio Gates at the Battle of Camden but eventually surrendering his army to Washington at Yorktown. Returning to England, he retained the king's confidence and served in numerous governmental positions. Most prominently, in 1786, he was appointed governor general of India, where he served successfully for many years. He died in India in 1805.

General William Erskine: Erskine was born in Scotland to Colonel William Erskine of Torrie in 1728. Erskine fought in the Seven Years' War with distinction and was knighted for his valor. He was later posted to the United States in 1776 as a staff officer for General Henry Clinton. He fought in the New York Campaign, at Trenton and Princeton, and during Howe's Philadelphia Campaign. Promoted to brigadier general in 1777, he served with Clinton at the Battle of Monmouth and was eventually promoted to major general in 1779. Erskine particularly raised the ire of General George Washington, who believed Erskine's detachments were especially barbarous during the American Revolution. Returning to England in 1779, he later served with distinction in the French Revolutionary Wars. Erskine died in 1795 and was buried at Torryburn, Scotland.

Lt. Colonel Stephen Kemble: Kemble was born in 1740 in New Brunswick, New Jersey, into a prominent and politically connected New Jersey family. He went to college in Philadelphia and later was commissioned as an ensign in the British army. He was promoted to adjutant general of British forces in North America in 1772, and his family remained loyal to the crown during the American Revolution. He served with William Howe in New Jersey, then with both Howe and Clinton during the Philadelphia Campaign. In 1778, he was promoted to lt. colonel of the First Battalion, Sixtieth Foot, and fought with Clinton at Monmouth Courthouse. He resigned his post as deputy adjutant general but went on to fight against the Spanish in the Caribbean from Nicaragua to Grenada. He retired from the army in 1786 and lived in England until 1805, when he returned to New Brunswick. There, he resided in his family's old home until his death in 1822. He was buried at Christ Episcopal Church in New Brunswick.

Captain-Lieutenant Archibald Robertson: Robertson was believed
to have been born around 1745 in Scotland; a grandson to William
Robertson of Gledney, Fifeshire, an old Scottish family. Little if
anything is known of Archibald's youth, and he first appears in
the historic record on March 17, 1759, when he was commissioned
as an ensign in the royal engineers, with the position of practi-
tioner engineer and ensign. He remained active in the army for
twenty-seven years, finally resigning his commission in 1786. He
then married and retired to an estate named Lawers in Perthshire,
Scotland. Robertson is today famous not for his engineering service but for the many drawings he made while serving in the king's
army, titled *Archibald Robertson: his diaries and sketches in America,
1762–1786*. He died in 1813.

Captain Johann Ewald: Born March 20, 1744, in Hesse-Cassel (modern-day Germany); son of a bookmaker. When both of his parents died, Ewald was raised by his grandmother. He enlisted in
the army in 1760 and soon saw action in the Seven Years' War.
He was promoted to ensign for bravery, wounded, and later
promoted to second lieutenant in 1766. After the war, Ewald remained in the army, studied at the Collegium Carolinum, and
was promoted to captain in 1774. In 1776, Ewald arrived in New
York as head of a company of Jägers. Ewald saw extensive action during the American Revolution, including the New York
Campaign, the New Jersey Campaign of 1777, the Philadelphia
Campaign; the siege of Charleston, South Carolina, and later
actions along the James River in Virginia. At war's end, Ewald's
Jägers unit was one of the last to depart New York in 1784. He
returned to Germany, but when only officers of noble birth
received advancement in the peacetime army, he resigned his
commission and accepted a commission in the Danish Army as
lt. colonel. He remained in the Danish army and was awarded
the Order of the Dannebrog, ultimately rising to the ranking of
lt. general. Today, in the United States, Ewald is best known for
his journal titled *Diary of the American War: A Hessian Journal*,
considered by many a classic of the period. Johann Ewald died
on June 25, 1813, surrounded by his wife, son, and five daughters. He was buried in Kiel, Germany.

The Americans

Captain Thomas Rodney: Born on June 4, 1744, near Dover, Delaware, Thomas Rodney was the younger brother of Caesar Rodney. Before the Revolution, he served as judge probate of wills and clerk of the Orphans' Court in Dover. He was appointed to the Delaware General Assembly, then later as a delegate to the Continental Congress. During the war, Rodney was appointed captain of a militia company known as the Dover Light Infantry and later colonel of the Eighth Regiment of the Delaware Militia. After the war, he served in numerous legal positions and, in 1783, was appointed chief justice of the Mississippi Territory, where the town of Rodney was later named in his honor. He died in Natchez, Mississippi, in 1811.

Captain Charles Willson Peale: Charles Willson Peale was born on April 15, 1741, near Centreville on Maryland's Eastern Shore. Early in life, he worked as a saddle maker but soon found his calling as an artist; in particular for portraits. In 1767, he moved to Annapolis, where he opened a shop. Drawn to Revolutionary politics, he moved to Philadelphia in 1776 and rose to the rank of captain in the militia. While in the service, he honed his skills as an artist, and today, he is best known for his portraits of American Revolutionary luminaries such as John Hancock, Thomas Jefferson, Benjamin Franklin, Alexander Hamilton, and George Washington. After the war, he continued his painting while also delving into such varied fields as shoemaking, optometry, dentistry, and carpentry. He died on February 22, 1827, and was buried in Philadelphia.

General John Sullivan: Sullivan was born on February 17, 1740, in Somersworth, New Hampshire, into a family of recent Irish immigrants. Early in life, he practiced law and, in 1772, was appointed captain in the militia by the royal governor. As enmity grew between the crown and the citizens of New England, Sullivan increasingly sided with the rebel cause and, in 1775, journeyed to Philadelphia to argue for war. He was appointed brigadier general by Congress when George Washington was appointed commander in chief. He served throughout the war with mixed results and returned to New Hampshire, where he was elected to the Continental Congress. He served in the New Hampshire Assembly, then later as governor. Sullivan died on January 23, 1795, and was buried in Durham, New Hampshire.

General William Maxwell: Maxwell was born in 1733 in County Tyrone, Ireland. His family moved to New Jersey around 1747, and Maxwell enlisted in the militia in 1754, serving in the ill-fated Braddock expedition into the Ohio country. Gaining the rank of lieutenant, he remained in the militia until tensions between the colonies and Great Britain began to peak, at which time he resigned his commission. He joined the New Jersey militia in 1775 as colonel and rose to the rank of brigadier general by 1776. Maxwell served throughout the Revolutionary War with distinction, but feeling his efforts underappreciated, resigned his commission in 1780. He died on November 4, 1796, and was buried in Warren Country, New Jersey.

General Benjamin Lincoln: Lincoln was born on January 24, 1733, in Hingham, Massachusetts, into one of the founding families of the Massachusetts Bay Colony. In 1755, Lincoln joined the Third Regiment of the Suffolk County militia and, in 1757, was elected town clerk for Hingham. He continued in the militia and, by 1763, had risen to the rank of major. After fighting broke out at Lexington and Concord, he was promoted to major general in the Massachusetts Militia. He handled a brigade under Washington during the New York Campaign and was promoted to major general in the Continental army in February 1777. Lincoln served during the New Jersey Campaign and the Saratoga Campaign and was eventually placed in command of the Southern Army at Charleston, South Carolina, which fell to the British in 1780. He served as secretary of war from 1781 through 1783. Lincoln died on May 9, 1810, and was buried in Hingham, Massachusetts.

General William Alexander (Lord Stirling): William was born on December 4, 1726, in New York City. His father was both a lawyer and a merchant, and William was well educated. Upon the death of his father, he inherited a substantial fortune and built a manor near Basking Ridge, New Jersey, while pursuing the title of the earldom of Stirling in his family's native Scotland. As war approached, he joined the New Jersey militia and, because he was willing to outfit the unit himself, attained the rank of colonel. He was commissioned a brigadier general in the Continental army in March 1776. Stirling fought with skill at the Battle of Long Island and with distinction during the New Jersey Campaign, the Philadelphia Campaign, and at the Battle of Monmouth Courthouse.

Always a heavy drinker, and suffering from poor health, Stirling died on January 15, 1783, near Albany, New York.

John Hancock: John Hancock was born on January 23, 1737, in Braintree, Massachusetts, to Colonel John and Mary Hancock. In 1744, after his father's death, he went to live with his uncle, Thomas Hancock, a wealthy businessman in Boston. He graduated from Harvard in 1754 and went to work for his uncle, learning the import-export business. When his uncle died in 1764, John inherited the business, instantly becoming one of the most wealthy and influential men in the colonies. As relations between Great Britain and the colonies began to decline, Hancock took the side of the Whigs in part because his business ventures were suffering under heavy British taxation. In 1775, he traveled to Philadelphia to attend the First Continental Congress and was unanimously elected president. He remained in Congress until 1778, when he returned to Massachusetts. He was elected governor in 1780 and served in that capacity until 1785. Today, John Hancock is remembered as one of the stalwarts of the Revolutionary era. He died on October 8, 1793, and was buried in Boston.

General Nathanael Greene: Greene was born on August 7, 1742, in Warwick, Rhode Island, into a Quaker family of means. Schooling himself due to the Quakers' disdain for advanced education, Greene familiarized himself while growing up with mathematics, law, and Enlightenment thought. Like many Americans, he became disillusioned with British rule due to the imposition of harsh taxes and the repression of Boston merchants. He helped form a militia unit known as the Kentish Guards and marched as their leader to Boston after the fighting at Lexington and Concord. Greene soon fell under General Washington's eye and was noticed as a man of ability. He was promoted to major general in 1776 during the New York Campaign and soon became Washington's most trusted lieutenant. Greene served during the New Jersey Campaign, Philadelphia Campaign; at Monmouth Courthouse, and was appointed commander of the Southern Army in 1781 after serving with distinction as commissary general. He fought numerous battles throughout the south; never winning but always surviving. After the war, he moved to Mulberry Hill, a plantation he was awarded for his wartime efforts by Congress near Savannah, Georgia. On June 11, 1786, Greene fell ill with heatstroke and died at Mulberry Hill on June 19. He is buried in Savannah, Georgia.

Major James Wilkinson: Wilkinson was born on March 24, 1757, on a farm in Calvert County, Maryland. While his father fell into financial difficulties during Wilkinson's youth, James was nevertheless educated by tutors, and he enrolled at the University of Pennsylvania in Philadelphia. After serving briefly with Washington during the New Jersey Campaign, Wilkinson became an aide to General Horatio Gates but later became known primarily for his intrigues. Twice forced to resign his commissions, Wilkinson quickly started down a path of endless self-aggrandizement and chicanery, earning this stunning denunciation from Theodore Roosevelt: "In all our history, there is no more despicable character." The intrigues Wilkinson became involved in are too numerous to detail here, but the major ones were his attempt to have Kentucky—then a part of Virginia—recognized as a separate state, which he might then govern. When these efforts failed, he traveled to New Orleans and renounced his American citizenship, proposing that, in exchange for Spain's recognition of Kentucky and Wilkinson's exclusive right of navigation on the Mississippi River, he would rule the region on their behalf. When all this failed, he returned to the United States and reentered the army, at which time a bitter rivalry developed between Wilkinson and General Anthony Wayne. Eventually promoted to brigadier, Wilkinson continued passing intelligence to the Spanish. Wayne discovered the treason but died before Wilkinson could be brought to trial. By means of several retirements, Wilkinson rose to senior commander of the American Army, and after the Louisiana Purchase, he renewed his correspondence with the Spanish, passing intelligence to them for payments. Then—while the details remain murky—it appears Wilkinson fell in with Aaron Burr in his plot to create a Western Republic of his own. Burr was subsequently tried for treason, and Wilkinson turned on him as a witness for the prosecution. Burr was eventually acquitted, and Wilkinson's involvement was never disclosed. Wilkinson was appointed US envoy to Mexico after his military career ended, where he secretly asked the Mexican government for a land grant in Texas. He died in Mexico in 1825, his request still pending, and was buried in Mexico City. American historian Frederick Jackson Turner suggested that Wilkinson was "the most consummate artist in treason that the nation ever possessed."

Lt. Colonel Daniel Morgan: Morgan was born in 1735, most probably in eastern New Jersey, into a family of Welsh immigrants. According to rumor, in his later teens, Morgan left home after an argument with his father, finally settling near Winchester, Virginia. There, he did manual labor, ultimately hiring on as a teamster, then buying a wagon and team of his own to haul goods over the Blue Ridge. Tough and athletic, he developed a reputation as a fighter, drinker, and carouser early in life but matured beyond that lifestyle in midlife. He married, purchased a farm, and became experienced as an army ranger during the French and Indian War and later as an officer fighting Native Americans in the Ohio Territory. In 1775, he was elected to lead a regiment of riflemen north to Boston. During the Revolution, Morgan served at Boston, on the Canadian Invasion, the New Jersey Campaign, Saratoga; the Monmouth Campaign, and later commanded in the south at the Battle of Cowpens. Morgan rose to the rank of brigadier general and, at Cowpens, overwhelmed a British detachment under Banastre Tarleton in one of the most lopsided victories in American military history. After the war, he returned to the Shenandoah Valley, where he farmed, joined the Presbyterian Church, and built an estate named Saratoga along the Blue Ridge. He was later elected to Congress. Today, Daniel Morgan is considered one of the finest battle leaders ever to serve in the American military. He died on July 6, 1802, and was buried in Mt. Hebron Cemetery in Winchester, Virginia.

General George Washington: Washington was born on February 22, 1732, in Westmoreland County, Virginia. Schooled in mathematics and surveying, he began his career as a surveyor in western Virginia before entering the military, where he had both positive and negative experiences. He inherited Mount Vernon when his brother passed away, and he married Martha Dandridge Custis, a wealthy widow, in 1759. He was appointed to the First Continental Congress and later given command of the American Army in 1775. He served in that capacity until the end of the war; no doubt the single most important individual in earning that victory. He was later appointed president general of the Constitutional Convention and elected the first president of the United States, serving two terms in that capacity. While Washington can certainly be criticized for his lagging views regarding slavery, he was nonetheless—as historian Thomas Flexner styled him—*The Indispensable Man*, the one individual without whom the Revolution, the early government, and the nation would never have come into being or long survived. George Washington died on December 14, 1799, and was buried at Mount Vernon.

BIBLIOGRAPHY

Andre, John, *Major John Andre's Journal: Operations of the British Army Under Lieutenant Generals Sir William Howe and Sir Henry Clinton June 1777 to November 1778*. New York: *The New York Times* & Amo Press, 1968.

Archives of the State of New Jersey, 1st Series, Vol. 10, 1758.

Atwood, Rodney, *The Hessians*. Cambridge: Cambridge University Press, 2002.

Baker, William S. *The Itinerary of General Washington, from June 15, 1775, to December 23, 1783*. Philadelphia: J.B. Lippincott Company, 1892.

Billias, George, *George Washington's Opponents*. New York: Morrow, 1969.

Black, Jeremy, *War for America: The Fight for Independence, 1775–1783*. New York: St. Martin's Press, 1991.

Boatner, Mark M. III, *Encyclopedia of the American Revolution*. Mechanicsburg, PA: Stackpole Books, 1994.

Boom, A.A., *A report of the Middlebrook Encampment by the Continental Army in the Middle of 1777 and in the Winter of 1778–1779*. Sponsored by the Somerset Historical Society, typewritten manuscript, Collections of the Warren Township Library.

Buchanan, John, *The Road to Guilford Courthouse*. New York: John Wiley & Sons, Inc., 1997.

--- *The Road to Valley Forge*. New York: John Wiley & Sons, 2004.

Burr, William Hanford, Atwell, George C., Arms, H. Phelps, Miller, Francis Trevelyan, "Invasion of Connecticut by the British Army in the War for American Independence." *The Connecticut Magazine*, Vol. 10, The Connecticut Magazine Company, 1906.

Burrows, Edwin G., *Forgotten Patriots*. New York: Basic Books, 2008.

Calhoon, Robert M., *The Loyalists in Revolutionary America, 1760–1781*. New York: Harcourt Brace Jovanovich, 1965.

Carrington, Henry B., *Battles of the American Revolution, 1775–1781*. New York: Barnes, 1876.

Chernow, Ron, *Washington; A Life*. New York: Penguin Books, 2010.

Clarke, Alured, *Lieutenant Colonel Clarke's Orderly Book*. British Seventh Regiment of Foot. June 21, 1778.

Clayton, Woodford W., *History of Union And Middlesex Counties with Biographical Sketches of Many of The Pioneers and Prominent Men*. Philadelphia: Everts & Pack, 1882.

Clinton, Henry. Gilder Lehrman Collection # GIC04283

Coggins, Jack, *Boys in the Revolution; Young Americans Tell Their Stories in the War for Independence*. Harrisburg, PA: Stackpole Books, 1967.

Cohen, Lester H., *The Revolutionary Histories; Contemporary Narratives of the American Revolution*. Ithaca, NY: Cornell University Press, 1980.

Collections of the New Jersey Historical Society Vols. V & VI.

Collins, James, *Autobiography of a Revolutionary Soldier, Sixty Years in the Nueces Valley: 1870–1930*. San Antonio: Naylor Printing Co., 1930.

Collins, Varnum Lansing, ed., *A Brief Narrative of the Ravages of the British and Hessians at Princeton in 1776–1777. A Contemporary Account of the Battles of Trenton and Princeton*. Princeton: Princeton University Library, 1906.

Constable, George, *The Winds of Revolution*. Alexandria, VA: Time-Life Books, 1989.

Cummings, William P., and Hugh Rankin, eds., *The Fate of a Nation: The American Revolution Through Contemporary Eyes*. London: Phaidon Press, 1975.

Dann, John C., *The Revolution Remembered*. Chicago: University of Chicago Press, 1980.

Davie, William Richardson, *The Revolutionary War Sketches of William R. Davie*. Blackwell P. Robinson ed. Raleigh: North Carolina Division of Archives & History, 1976.

Davis, T.E., *The Battle of Bound Brook*. Bound Brook, N.J: The Chronicle Printery, 1896.

Dawson, Henry, *Battles of the United States; Sea and Land*, New York: Fry & Company, 1858.

Dearborn, Henry, *Revolutionary War Journals of Henry Dearborn*. Howard H. Peckham ed. Chicago: The Caxton Club, 1939.

Denman, Jeffrey, "In New Jersey, Ominous Lessons for the British Emerge from a Little-Known Campaign in the Bitter Winter of 1777," *Military History Quarterly*, April 2014.

Desmarais, Norman, *The Guide to the American Revolutionary War in New Jersey; Battles, Raids, and Skirmishes.* Ithaca: Busca, Inc., 2011.

Dimmock, Martha McHutchinson, *A Chronicle of the Revolutionary War.* New York: Perennial Library, 1976.

Dupuy, Trevor N., *The Evolution of Weapons and Warfare.* New York: Da Capo Press, 1984.

Ellis, Joseph, *His Excellency, George Washington.* New York: Vintage Books, 2004.

Ewald, Johann, *Diary of the American War: A Hessian Journal.* ed. Joseph P. Tustin. New Haven: Yale University Press, 1979.

Ferling, John, *Almost a Miracle: The American Victory in the War of Independence.* New York: Oxford University Press, 2007.

Fischer, David Hackett, *Washington's Crossing.* New York: Oxford University Press, 2004.

Fisher, Elijah, *Elijah Fisher's Journal While in the War for Independence, and Continued Two Years After He Came to Maine, 1775–1784.* Augusta, ME: Press of Badger and Manley, 1880.

Flexner, James Thomas, *Washington: The Indispensable Man.* New York: Little Brown, 1979.

Flood, Charles Bracelen, *Rise, and Fight Again: Perilous Times Along the Road to Independence.* New York: Dodd Mead & Company, 1976.

Force, Peter, *American Archives: consisting of a collection of authentic records, state papers, debates, and letters, and other notices of publick affairs, the whole forming a documentary history of the origin and progress of the North American colonies; of the causes and accomplishment of the American Revolution; and of the Constitution of government for the United States, to the final ratification thereof. In Six series.* Washington: 1837–1853.

Fox, Ebenezer, *The Adventures of Ebenezer Fox in the Revolutionary War.* Boston: Fox, 1848.

Freeman, Douglas Southall, *Biography of George Washington.* New York: Charles Scribner and Sons, 1952.

Gaines, James R., *For Liberty and Glory; Washington, Lafayette, and Their Revolutions.* New York: W.W. Norton & Company, 2007.

Gavin, John R., *The Minute Men: The first Fight: Myths and Realities of the American Revolution.* Washington, D.C: Brassey's, 1996.

Gerlach, Larry ed., "Journal of a Militia man (William Churchill Houston). *Princeton Standard*, May 1863, *New Jersey in the Revolution, A Documentary History.* New Jersey Historical Commission, 1975.

Graham, James, *The Life of General Daniel Morgan of the Virginia Line of the Army of the United States.* New York: Derby & Jackson, 1856.

Green, Charles E., *The Story of Delaware in the Revolution*. Wilmington: Press of William N. Cann, 1975.

Green, Peter, *Alexander of Macedon*. Berkeley: University of California Press, 1989.

Greene, Francis Vinton, *General Greene*. New York: D. Appleton & Company, 1893.

Greene, Nathanael, *Nathanael Greene Collection*. Rhode Island Historical Society, Military Official, Rhode Island, Papers 1768–1786. Processed by Elizabeth Delmage, September 2005, Box I, Folder II.

Greenwood, John, *The Revolutionary Services of John Greenwood of Boston, and New York, 1775–1783*. New York: Mrs. Joseph Rudd Greenwood, 1922.

--- *The Revolutionary Services of John Greenwood of Boston and New York, 1775–1783*. New York: Mrs. Joseph Rudd Greenwood, 1922.

Hamilton, Alexander, *The Papers of Alexander Hamilton, Vol. I, 1768–1778*. Harold C. Syrett ed. New York: Columbia University Press, 1961.

Hammond, Samuel, Pension Application S21807, 1832: transcribed by Will Graves.

Heath William, *Memoirs Major General William Heath, by Himself*. William Abbatt, ed., New Edition with Illustrations and Notes. New York: William Abbatt, 1901.

Heitman, Francis B., *Historical Register of Officers of the Continental Army During the War of Revolution, April 1775, to December 1783*. Washington: The Rare Book Shop Publishing Company, 1914.

Hibbert, Christopher, *Redcoats and Rebels; The American Revolution Through British Eyes*. New York: Avon Books, 1991.

Higginbotham, Don, *Daniel Morgan; Revolutionary Rifleman*. Chapel Hill: University of North Carolina Press, 1961.

--- *The War of Independence: Military Attitudes, Policies, and Practice, 1763–1789*. New York: Macmillan, 1971.

Ives, J. Moss, Atwell, George C., Arms, H. Phelps, Miller, Francis Trevelyan, "A Connecticut Battlefield in the American Revolution." *The Connecticut Magazine, Volume 7*, The Connecticut Magazine Company, 1906.

Jacques, Tony, *Dictionary of Battles & Sieges*. Santa Barbara, CA: Greenwood, 2007.

Johnson, William, *Sketches of the Life and Correspondence of Nathanael Greene, Major General of the Armies of the United States, in the War of the Revolution*. Charleston, S.C: A.E. Miller, 1822.

Jones, W.T., *Masters of Political Thought*. Boston: Houghton Mifflin, 1969.

Keegan, John, *A History of Warfare*. New York: Vintage, 1993.

Kemble, Stephan, *The Kemble Papers*. New York: The New York Historical Society, 1883.

Ketcham, Richard, M. *The Winter Soldiers*. New York; Henry Holt and Company, 1973.

Kidder, William L., *Revolutionary Princeton, 1774–1783. The Biography of A Town In The Heart of A Civil War*. Knox Press, 2020.

Kirkwood, Robert, *The Journal and Order Book of Captain Robert Kirkwood of the Delaware Regiment of the Continental Line*. Dover: Press of the Delawarean, 1910.

Kraft, John Charles Philip von, *Journal of Lieutenant John Charles Philip von Kraft*. New York: New York Historical Society, 1883.

Kwasny, Mark V., *Washington's Partisan War, 1775–1783*. Kent, OH: Kent State University Press, 1996.

Lafayette, *Memoirs and Manuscripts of General Lafayette, Vol. 1*. New York: Saunders & Otley, MDCCCXXXVii.

Lagemann, Robert, and Manucy, Albert C., *The Long Rifle*. New York: Eastern Acorn Press, 1993.

Lamb, Roger, *An Original and Authentic Journal of the Occurrences During the late American War, From its Commencement to the Year 1783*. Dublin: Wilkinson and Courtney, 1809.

Lee, Henry, *The Revolutionary War Memoirs of General Henry Lee*. Robert E. Lee ed., New York: Da Capo Press, 1998.

Leiby, Adrian Coulter, *The Revolutionary War in the Hackensack Valley; The Jersey Dutch and the Neutral Ground*. New Brunswick: Rutgers University Press, 1962.

Lender, Mark Edward, and Gary Wheeler Stone, *Fatal Sunday: George Washington, the Monmouth Campaign, and the Politics of Battle*. Norman: University of Oklahoma Press, 2016.

Lord Cornwallis to Lord Germain, January 8,1777. The Historical Manuscripts commission Great Britain. Boston: Gregg Press, 1972.

Mackesy, Piers, *The War For America, 1775–1783*. Lincoln: University of Nebraska Press, 1993.

Martin, Joseph Plumb, *A Narrative of Some of the Adventures, Dangers and Sufferings of a Revolutionary Soldier*. George Scheer ed. New York: Eastern National, 1962.

Mattern, David, *Benjamin Lincoln and the American Revolution*. Columbia, SC: University of South Carolina Press, 1998.

May, Robin, *The British Army in North America, 1775–1783*. London: Osprey, 1997.

Mayers, Robert A., *Revolutionary New Jersey; Forgotten Towns and Cross-roads of the American Revolution*. Staunton, VA: American History Press, 2018.

McCullough, David, *1776*. New York: Simon & Schuster, 2005.

McGuire, Thomas J., *The Philadelphia Campaign; Germantown and the Roads to Valley Forge*. Mechanicsburg, PA: Stackpole Books, 2007.

Mirante, Rand, "From Savior to Accused in Just One Day." *Journal of the American Revolution*, 2018.

Morgan, Curtis Jr., *General Horatio Gates; A Biography*. Baton Rouge: LSU Press, 1976.

Munn, David C., *Battles and Skirmishes of the American Revolution in New Jersey*. New Jersey Geological Survey, 1976.

Murray, James, Eric Robson ed., *Letters From America, 1773–1780*. New York: Barnes & Noble, Inc., 2011.

Nash, Solomon, and Bushnell, Charles I., eds., *Journal of Solomon Nash, Soldier of the Revolution, 1776–1777*. New York: 1861.

Nelson, William, *History of the City of Patterson and the County of Passaic*. Patterson: Press Print and Publishing Co., 1901.

O'Connell, Robert I., *Of Arms and Men: A history of War, Weapons, and Aggression*. New York: Oxford University Press, 1989.

Orlando, Anthony, "What George Washington Taught Us in His Darkest Hour. *South Florida Sun Sentinel*, February 22, 2013.

Palmer, Dave A., *George Washington, Military Genius*. Washington, D.C: Regency History, 2012.

Papers of the Continental Congress, No. 72 folio 353.

Peale, Charles Willison, *Charles Willison Peale; Artist and Soldier*. The Pennsylvania Magazine of History and Biography, Vol. XXXVIII, No. 3, 1914.

Pebbles, John, *John Pebbles' American War; The Diary of a Scottish Grena-dier, 1776–1782*. Ira D. Gruber, ed., Publications of the Army Records Society. Book 13. Mechanicsburg, PA: Stackpole Books, 1998.

Peckham, Howard H., *The War for Independence: A Military History*. Chicago: University of Chicago Press, 1958.

--- *The Toll of Independence*. Chicago: University of Chicago Press, 1974.

--- ed., *Sources of American Independence*. Vol. II. Chicago: University of Chicago Press, 1978.

Peden, Henry C., *Revolutionary War Patriots of Baltimore Town and Balti-more County, 1775–1783*. Silver Spring, MD: Family Line Publica-tions, 1988.

Philhower, Charles A., *History of Town of Westfield, Union County, New*

Jersey. New York: Lewis Historical Publishing Company, 1923.

Piecuch, Jim, and John Beakes, *John Eager Howard in the American Revolution*. Charleston, SC: The Nautical and Aviation Publishing Co., 2009.

Powell, William S., "A Connecticut Soldier Under Washington: Elisha Bostwick's Memoirs of the First Years of the Revolution." Williamsburg: *The William and Mary Quarterly*, Jan. 1949.

Raphael, Ray, *A People's History of the American Revolution*. New York: The New Press, 2001.

Ricord, Frederick W., *History of Union County*. Newark: East Jersey History Company, 1897.

Robertson, Archibald, *His Diaries and Sketches in America, 1762– 1780*. New York: The New York Public Library and Arno Press, 1971.

Rodney, Thomas, *The Diary of Captain Thomas Rodney, 1776– 1777*. Newark, Delaware: The Historical Society of Delaware, 1888.

Rossie, Jonathan Gregory, *The Politics of Command in the American Revolution*. Syracuse: Syracuse University Press, 1975.

Royster, Charles, *Light Horse Harry Lee and the Legacy of the American Revolution*. Baton Rouge: LSU Press, 1981.

--- *A Revolutionary People at War: The Continental Army and American Character*. New York: W.W. Norton, 1979.

Sabine, George H., *A History of Political Thought*. New York: Holt, Rinehart, and Winston, 1961.

Schaun, George, and Virginia Schaun, *Everyday life in Colonial Maryland*. Lanham: Maryland Historical Press, 1996.

Scheer, George F., and Hugh F. Rankin, *Rebels and Redcoats*. New York: The World Publishing Company, 1957.

Schleicher, William and Susan Winter, *Somerset County; Crossroads of the American Revolution*. Charleston, SC: Arcadia Publishing, 1999.

Schoeph, David Johann, *Travels in the Confederation*. Alfred Morrison, ed. Philadelphia: William H. Campbell, 1911.

Serle, Ambrose, *The American Journal of Ambrose Serle Secretary to Lord Howe 1776–1778*. Edward H. Tatum, Jr. ed. San Marion, CA: The Huntington Library, 1940.

Shreve, John, "Personal Narrative of the Services of Lieut. John Shreve of the New Jersey Line of the Continental Army." *The Magazine of American History with Notes and Queries*, Vol. III, 1879.

Skull, G.D., *The Montressor Journals*. Collections of the New York Historical Society, 1881.

"Somerset County 1688–1938," *Somerset Messenger*. Somerville, NJ:

Somerset Press, 1976.

Steadman, Charles, *The History of the Origin, Progress, and Termination of the American War.* Two Volumes, London: N.p., 1794.

Stempel, Jim, *American Hannibal; The Extraordinary Account of Revolutionary War Hero Daniel Morgan at the Battle of Cowpens.* Tucson: Penmore Press, 2017

--- "Cowpens, A Miracle in the Wilderness", *Drumbeat, Publication of the General Society, Sons of the Revolution, Vol. 35, number 2–3,* Fall 2018.

--- *The Nature of War; Origins and Evolution of Violent Conflict.* Jefferson, N.C: McFarland Publishing Company, 2012.

--- *Valley Forge to Monmouth; Six Transformative Months of the American Revolution.* Jefferson, N.C: McFarland Publishing Company, 2021.

Stephen, Leslie ed. *Dictionary of National Biography.* London: Smith, Elder & Company, 1885.

Stephenson, Michael, *Patriot Battles; How the War of Independence Was Fought.* New York: HarperCollins, 2007.

Steuart, Rieman, *A History of the Maryland Line in the Revolutionary War, 1775–1783.* Baltimore: Society of the Cincinnati of Maryland, 1972.

Steuben, Frederick William, Baron von, *Baron von Steuben's Revolutionary War Drill Manual.* New York: Dover Publications, Inc., 1985.

Stryker, William, S. *Documents Relating to the Revolutionary History, State of New Jersey, Vol. 1.* Trenton: The John L. Murphy Publishing Co., 1901.

Swartout, Bernardus, *Bernardus Swartout Diary.* New York: New York Historical Society, n.d.

Swearinger, Richard, Pension Application S31402, Transcribed by Will Graves.

Thatcher, James, M.D., *A Military Journal During the American Revolutionary War from 1775 to 1783.* New York: Arno Pres, 1969.

Thorbahn, Clifton, "Colonel Kelly Saved Troops of Washington By Wrecking Bridge. *The Sunday News.* Lancaster, Pennsylvania: 1932.

Vermeule, Cornelius C. *The Revolutionary Camp Ground at Plainfield.* New York: The Evening Post Job Printing Office, Inc., 1923.

Volo, Dorothy Denneen, and James M. Volo, *Daily Life During the American Revolution.* Westport CT: Greenwood Press, 2003.

Waller, George M. *The American Revolution in the West.* Chicago: Nelson Hall, 1976.

Ward, Christopher, Alden, John Richard, ed., *The War of the Revolution.*

New York: MacMillan Company, 1952.

Ward, Harry M., *General George Weedon and the American Revolution*. Philadelphia: The American Philosophical Society, 1979.

--- *Charles Scott and the Spirit of '76*. Charlottesville: University of Virginia Press, 1988.

--- *General William Maxwell and the New Jersey Continentals*. Westport, CT: Greenwood Press, 1977.

Washington, George. *The Papers of George Washington*, Revolutionary War Series, Vol. 7, 21 October 1776–January 1777. Ed. Philander D. Chase. Charlottesville: University of Virginia Press, 1997.

--- *The Papers of George Washington*. Revolutionary War Series, Vol. 14, March 1776–30 April 1778. Ed. David R. Hoth, Charlottesville: University of Virginia Press, 2004.

--- *The Papers of George Washington*. Revolutionary War Series. W. w. Abbott, Dorothy Twohig, Philander D. Chase, Edward G. Langel, Theodore J. Crackel, And David R. Hoth, eds. Charlottesville: University of Virginia Press, 1998–1999.

--- *The Writings of George Washington*, Vol. VI, 1777–1778, Worthington Chauncey Ford, editor, New York: G.P. Putnam's Sons, 1890.

--- *The Papers of George Washington*. Revolutionary War Series, Vol. 15, May–June 1778. Ed. Edward Lengel, Charlottesville: University of Virginia Press, 2006.

Weeden, George, *Valley Forge Orderly Book of General George Weeden of the Continental Army Under Command of Genl. George Washington: In the Campaign of 1777–1778, Describing the Events of the Battles of Brandywine, Warren Tavern, Germantown, and Whitemarsh, and of the Camps at Neshaminy, Wilmington, Penypacker's Mill, Skippack, Whitemarsh, & Valley Forge*. New York: Dodd, Mead and Company, 1902.

Whitehead, William, *Contributions to The Early History of Perth Amboy and Adjoining Country*. New York: D. Appleton & Company, 1856.

Wickersty, Jason R, "A Shocking Havoc: The Plundering of Westfield, New Jersey, June 26, 1777. *Journal of the American Revolution*, July 21, 2015.

Wickshire, Franklin, and Mary Wickshire, *Cornwallis: The American Adventure*. New York: Houghton Mifflin, 1970.

Wilkinson, James, *Memoirs of My Own Times, Vol. 1*. Philadelphia: Abraham Small, 1816.

Williams Seymour, *Historic American Buildings Survey*. Rahway: State of New Jersey, 1937.

Young, Thomas, *Memoirs of Major Thomas Young: A Revolutionary Patriot of South Carolina. Orion Magazine*, October 1834.

Zielinski, Adam E., "A Phantom at Middlebrook—Washington in the New Jersey Short Hills. *Journal of the American Revolution*, April 11, 2018.

CHAPTER NOTES

Prologue

1 "From George Washington to Samuel Washington, 18 December 1776," Founders Online, National Archives, https://founders.archives.gov/documents/Washington/03-07-02-0299. [Original source: *The Papers of George Washington, Revolutionary War Series, vol. 7, 21 October 1776–5 January 1777*, ed. Philander D. Chase. Charlottesville: University Press of Virginia, 1997, pp. 369–372.] https://bit.ly/3EgnWrH

2 Wilkinson, James, *Memoirs of My Own Times, Vol. I* (Philadelphia, Abraham Small, 1816) 148.

3 Greenwood, John, *The Revolutionary Services of John Greenwood of Boston and New York, 1775–1783.* (New York: Mrs. Joseph Rudd Greenwood, 1922).

4 Rodney, Thomas, *The Diary of Captain Thomas Rodney, 1776–1777* (Newark, Delaware, The Historical Society of Delaware, 1888) 22.

5 Ketcham, Richard M., *The Winter Soldiers* (New York, Henry Holt and Company, 1973) 253.

6 Wilkinson, 129.

7 Fischer, David Hackett, *Washington's Crossing* (New York, Oxford University Press, 2004) 237.

8 Wilkinson, 129.

9 Extract from an officer of distinction, dated December 27, 1776, *Pennsylvania Evening Post*, December 28, 1776, Stryker, William S. ed, Documents Relating to the Revolutionary History, State of New Jersey, Vol I (Trenton, The John L. Murphy Publishing Co., 1901) 248–249.

10 Wilkinson, 131.

11 Fischer, 254.

12 McCullough, David, *1776* (New York, Simon & Schuster, 2005) 292.

13 Wilkinson, 132.

14 "From George Washington to John Hancock, 29 December 1776," Founders Online, National Archives, https://founders.archives.gov/documents/Washington/03-07-02-0371. [Original source: *The Papers of George Washington, Revolutionary War Series, vol. 7, 21 October 1776–5 January 1777*, ed. Philander D. Chase. Charlottesville: University Press of Virginia, 1997, pp. 477–478.]

15   "To George Washington from John Hancock, 27 December 1776," Founders
     Online, National Archives, https://founders.archives.gov/documents/Wash-
     ington/03-07-02-0356. [Original source: *The Papers of George Washington, Rev-
     olutionary War Series, vol. 7, 21 October 1776–5 January 1777*, ed. Philander D.
     Chase. Charlottesville: University Press of Virginia, 1997, pp. 461–463.]
16   Fischer, 272–273.
17   Ewald, Johann, *Diary of the American War: A Hessian Journal*, ed. Joseph P.
     Tustin (New Haven, Yale University Press, 1979) 44.
18   Wilkinson, 136–137.
19   Robertson, Archibald, *His Diaries and Sketches in America, 1762–1780* [New
     York]: (New York Public Library and Arno Press, 1971), 119.
20   Fischer, 304.
21   Wilkinson, 138.
22   Ibid., 139.
23   Robertson, 120.
24   Rodney, 32.
25   Wilkinson, 141.
26   Rodney, 33.
27   Ibid., 34.
28   Wilkinson, 143.
29   Fischer, 334.
30   Wilkinson, 145.

Chapter One - The Bridge at Stony Brook

1   Fischer, David, Hackett, 400–401, Appendix K, weather recordings of Phin-
     eas Pemberton.
2   Collins, Varnum Lansing ed., *A Brief Narrative of the British and Hessians At
     Princeton in 1776–77* (Princeton, N.J. The University Library, 1936) 35.
3   Thorbahn, Clifton, "Colonel Kelly Saved Troops of Washington By Wreck-
     ing Bridge," *The Sunday News*, Lancaster, Pennsylvania: April 17, 1932. 1, 14.
4   Ketcham, 314.
5   Robertson, 120.
6   "From George Washington to John Hancock, 5 January 1777," Founders On-
     line, National Archives, https://founders.archives.gov/documents/Wash-
     ington/03-07-02-0411. [Original source: *The Papers of George Washington,
     Revolutionary War Series, vol. 7, 21 October 1776–5 January 1777*, ed. Philander
     D. Chase. Charlottesville: University Press of Virginia, 1997, pp. 519–530.]
7   Kemble, Stephen, *The Kemble Papers* (New York, New York Historical Soci-
     ety, 1883) 105.
8   Ewald, 45–49.
9   Kidder, William L., *Revolutionary Princeton 1774-1783: The Biography Of A
     Town In The Heart of A Civil War* (Knox Press, 2020) 149.
10   Collins, 35.

11 Rodney, 36.
12 Kidder, 21.
13 Rodney, 36–37.
14 Wilkinson, 148.
15 Collins, 36.
16 Ibid., 36–37.
17 Ibid., 38.
18 Rodney, 37.
19 Ewald, 50.
20 Ketchum, 313.
21 Robertson, 120.
22 Ewald, 50.
23 Mirante, Rand, "From Savior to Accused In Just One Day," *Journal of the American Revolution*, January 9, 2018.
24 Ketcham, 316.
25 Wilkinson, 148.

Chapter Two - Pluckemin

1   Kidder, 11.
2   Rodney, 37.
3   Ibid., 37.
4   Ibid., 37–38.
5   Ketcham, 31.
6   Rodney, 38.
7   Wilkinson, 148.
8   Robertson, 120–121.
9   Ewald, 50–51.
10 Rodney, 38.
11 Peale, Charles Willison, "Charles Willison Peale; Artist and Soldier" (*The Pennsylvania Magazine of History and Biography*, Vol. XXXVIII, No. 3, 1914) 282–283.
12 Williams, Seymour, *Historic American Buildings Survey* (Rahway: State of New Jersey, 1937) 2.
13 Rodney, 39.
14 "From George Washington to John Hancock, 5 January 1777," Founders Online, National Archives, https://founders.archives.gov/documents/Washington/03-07-02-0411. [Original source: *The Papers of George Washington, Revolutionary War Series, vol. 7, 21 October 1776–5 January 1777*, ed. Philander D. Chase. Charlottesville: University Press of Virginia, 1997, pp. 519–530.]
15 "From George Washington to Major General William Heath, 5 January 1777," Founders Online, National Archives, https://founders.archives.gov/documents/Washington/03-07-02-0412. [Original source: *The Papers of*

George Washington, Revolutionary War Series, vol. 7, 21 October 1776–5 January 1777, ed. Philander D. Chase. Charlottesville: University Press of Virginia, 1997, p. 531.]

16 "From George Washington to Major General Israel Putnam, 5 January 1777," Founders Online, National Archives, https://founders.archives.gov/documents/Washington/03-07-02-0416. [Original source: *The Papers of George Washington, Revolutionary War Series, vol. 7, 21 October 1776–5 January 1777*, ed. Philander D. Chase. Charlottesville: University Press of Virginia, 1997, pp. 535–536.]

17 Peale, 283.

18 Rodney, 39.

19 Williams, 2.

20 Wilkinson, 119.

Chapter Three - Morristown

1 Ewald, 51.

2 Ibid., xix.

3 Ibid., xix–xx.

4 Ibid., 51.

5 Rodney, 41.

6 Peale, 284.

7 Wilkinson, 149–150.

8 Rodney, 41.

9 Peale, 284.

10 "From George Washington to John Hancock, 7 January 1777," Founders Online, National Archives, https://founders.archives.gov/documents/Washington/03-08-02-0008. [Original source: *The Papers of George Washington, Revolutionary War Series, vol. 8, 6 January 1777–27 March 1777*, ed. Frank E. Grizzard, Jr. Charlottesville: University Press of Virginia, 1998, pp. 9–10.]

11 Ellis, Joseph, *His Excellency, George Washington* (New York: Vintage Books, 2004) 11–12.

12 Numerous texts and sources have been used to produce the biographical information regarding George Washington in this book, but the most prominent were two highly recommended modern biographies. The first is Joseph J. Ellis' *His Excellency, George Washington* (New York: Vintage Books, 2004), and the second is Ron Chernow's *Washington: A Life* (New York: Penguin Books, 2010)

13 "From George Washington to Major General William Heath, 7 January 1777," Founders Online, National Archives, https://founders.archives.gov/documents/Washington/03-08-02-0009. [Original source: *The Papers of George Washington, Revolutionary War Series, vol. 8, 6 January 1777–27 March 1777*, ed. Frank E. Grizzard, Jr. Charlottesville: University Press of Virginia, 1998, pp. 10–11.]

14 Kemble, 105–106.
15 Lord Cornwallis to Lord Germain, January 8, 1777, *The Historical Manuscripts Commission Great Britain* (Boston: Gregg Press, 1972) 55–56.

Chapter Four - Spanktown

1 Kemble, 98.
2 McCullough, David, 1776 (New York, Simon & Schuster, 2005) 260–261.
3 Kemble, 102.
4 Ewald, 22.
5 Ketcham, 152–153.
6 *The Historical Manuscripts Commission Great Britain* (Boston: Gregg Press, 1972) 51.
7 Whitehead, William A., *Contributions to The Early History of Perth Amboy And Adjoining Country* (New York: D. Appleton & Company, 1856) 338–339.
8 Rodney, 41.
9 Peale, 284.
10 Orlando, Anthony, "What George Washington Taught us in His Darkest Hour," *South Florida Sun Sentinel*, as quoted, February 22, 2013.
11 "From George Washington to John Hancock, 19 January 1777," Founders Online, National Archives, https://founders.archives.gov/documents/Washington/03-08-02-0110. [Original source: *The Papers of George Washington, Revolutionary War Series, vol. 8, 6 January 1777–27 March 1777*, ed. Frank E. Grizzard, Jr. Charlottesville: University Press of Virginia, 1998, pp. 102–104.]
12 Desmarais, Norman, *The Guide to the American Revolutionary War In New Jersey; Battles, Raids, and Skirmishes*, (Ithaca, New York: Busca, Inc., 2011) 113.
13 "From George Washington to Major General William Heath, 12 January 1777," Founders Online, National Archives, https://founders.archives.gov/documents/Washington/03-08-02-0052. [Original source: *The Papers of George Washington, Revolutionary War Series, vol. 8, 6 January 1777–27 March 1777*, ed. Frank E. Grizzard, Jr. Charlottesville: University Press of Virginia, 1998, pp. 48–49.]
14 Whitehead, 339.
15 Ibid., 339.
16 Desmarais, 98–99.
17 Whitehead, 339.
18 Kemble, 106.
19 Stryker, William S. ed, *Documents Relating to the Revolutionary History, State of New Jersey, Vol. I* (Trenton, The John L. Murphy Publishing Co., 1901) 277–278.
20 Kemble, 107.

Chapter Five - Quibbletown

1   "From George Washington to John Hancock, 26 January 1777," Founders On-
    line, National Archives, https://founders.archives.gov/documents/Washing-
    ton/03-08-02-0167. [Original source: *The Papers of George Washington, Revolu-
    tionary War Series, vol. 8, 6 January 1777–27 March 1777*, ed. Frank E. Grizzard,
    Jr. Charlottesville: University Press of Virginia, 1998, pp. 160–163.]

2   Rodney, 44.

3   Peale, 286.

4   "From George Washington to John Hancock, 26 January 1777," Founders On-
    line, National Archives, https://founders.archives.gov/documents/Washing-
    ton/03-08-02-0167. [Original source: *The Papers of George Washington, Revolu-
    tionary War Series, vol. 8, 6 January 1777–27 March 1777*, ed. Frank E. Grizzard,
    Jr. Charlottesville: University Press of Virginia, 1998, pp. 160–163.]

5   Kemble, 107–108

6   Robertson, 122.

7   Journal of a Militia man (William Churchill Houston), *The Princeton Stan-
    dard*, May 1–15, 1863, *New Jersey in the Revolution, a documentary History*, ed.
    Larry Gerlach (New Jersey Historical Commission, 1975) 334–336.

8   Stryker, 276.

9   The account of Samuel Sutphen, slave and militia man, *New Jersey in the
    Revolution, a documentary History*, ed. Larry Gerlach (New Jersey Historical
    Commission, 1975) 354–360.

10 Journal of a Militia man (William Churchill Houston), 334–336.

11 Stryker, 276.

12 "From George Washington to John Hancock, 22 January 1777," Founders On-
    line, National Archives, https://founders.archives.gov/documents/Washing-
    ton/03-08-02-0135. [Original source: *The Papers of George Washington, Revolu-
    tionary War Series, vol. 8, 6 January 1777–27 March 1777*, ed. Frank E. Grizzard,
    Jr. Charlottesville: University Press of Virginia, 1998, pp. 125–129.]

13 Robertson, 122.

14 Desmarais, 52–53.

15 Ibid., 58, 68, 89.

16 The Reverend Alexander MacWhorter on British Brutality, *Pennsylvania
    Evening Post*, April 26, 1777, *New Jersey in the Revolution, a documentary His-
    tory*, ed. Larry Gerlach (New Jersey Historical Commission, 1975) 296 – 297

17 "In the most melancholy Situation of Poverty and Distress," *New York Ga-
    zette and Weekly Mercury*, February 5, 1777, Stryker, 278–279.

18 "From George Washington to William Livingston, 24 January 1777," Found-
    ers Online, National Archives, https://founders.archives.gov/documents/
    Washington/03-08-02-0153. [Original source: *The Papers of George Washing-
    ton, Revolutionary War Series, vol. 8, 6 January 1777–27 March 1777*, ed. Frank E.
    Grizzard, Jr. Charlottesville: University Press of Virginia, 1998, pp. 147–148.]

19 Ewald, 52.

20 Whitehead, William A., 340–341.

21 "From George Washington to John Hancock, 26 January 1777," Founders Online, National Archives, https://founders.archives.gov/documents/ Washington/03-08-02-0167. [Original source: *The Papers of George Washington, Revolutionary War Series, vol. 8, 6 January 1777–27 March 1777*, ed. Frank E. Grizzard, Jr. Charlottesville: University Press of Virginia, 1998, pp. 160–163.]

22 "Proclamation concerning Persons Swearing British Allegiance, 25 January 1777," Founders Online, National Archives, https://founders.archives.gov/documents/Washington/03-08-02-0160. [Original source: *The Papers of George Washington, Revolutionary War Series, vol. 8, 6 January 1777–27 March 1777*, ed. Frank E. Grizzard, Jr. Charlottesville: University Press of Virginia, 1998, pp. 152–153.]

23 Kemble, 109.

24 Ewald, 52.

Chapter Six - Drake's Farm

1   Whitehead, William A., 340–341.

2   Desmarais, 61.

3   Robertson, 122–123.

4   Desmarais, 61.

5   Powell, William S., "A Connecticut Soldier Under Washington: Elisha Bostwick's Memoirs of the First Years of the Revolution," Williamsburg: *The William and Mary Quarterly*, Jan. 1949, Vol 6, No. 1, 105–106.

6   Denman, Jeffrey, "In New Jersey, Ominous Lessons for the British Emerge From a Little-known Campaign in the Bitter Winter of 1777," *Military History Quarterly*, April, 2014

7   "From George Washington to William Livingston, 3 February 1777," Founders Online, National Archives, https://founders.archives.gov/documents/ Washington/03-08-02-0249. [Original source: *The Papers of George Washington, Revolutionary War Series, vol. 8, 6 January 1777–27 March 1777*, ed. Frank E. Grizzard, Jr. Charlottesville: University Press of Virginia, 1998, pp. 234–236.], note 2.

8   "From George Washington to Samuel Chase, 5 February 1777," Founders Online, National Archives, https://founders.archives.gov/documents/ Washington/03-08-02-0265. [Original source: *The Papers of George Washington, Revolutionary War Series, vol. 8, 6 January 1777–27 March 1777*, ed. Frank E. Grizzard, Jr. Charlottesville: University Press of Virginia, 1998, pp. 247–248.]

9   "From George Washington to John Hancock, 5 February 1777," Founders Online, National Archives, https://founders.archives.gov/documents/Washing-

ton/03-08-02-0268. [Original source: *The Papers of George Washington, Revolutionary War Series, vol. 8, 6 January 1777–27 March 1777*, ed. Frank E. Grizzard, Jr. Charlottesville: University Press of Virginia, 1998, pp. 249–253.]

10   Kemble, 109.

11   "From George Washington to Major General William Heath, 4 February 1777," Founders Online, National Archives, https://founders.archives.gov/documents/Washington/03-08-02-0256. [Original source: *The Papers of George Washington, Revolutionary War Series, vol. 8, 6 January 1777–27 March 1777*, ed. Frank E. Grizzard, Jr. Charlottesville: University Press of Virginia, 1998, pp. 240–241.]

12   "From George Washington to Major General John Sullivan, 3 February 1777," Founders Online, National Archives, https://founders.archives.gov/documents/Washington/03-08-02-0252. [Original source: *The Papers of George Washington, Revolutionary War Series, vol. 8, 6 January 1777–27 March 1777*, ed. Frank E. Grizzard, Jr. Charlottesville: University Press of Virginia, 1998, pp. 237–238.]

13   Ewald, 53.

14   Robertson, 124.

15   Ewald, 55.

16   "From George Washington to John Hancock, 14 February 1777," Founders Online, National Archives, https://founders.archives.gov/documents/Washington/03-08-02-0357. [Original source: *The Papers of George Washington, Revolutionary War Series, vol. 8, 6 January 1777–27 March 1777*, ed. Frank E. Grizzard, Jr. Charlottesville: University Press of Virginia, 1998, pp. 331–333.]

Chapter Seven - Ash Swamp

1   Ewald, 55.

2   "From George Washington to John Hancock, 14 February 1777," Founders Online, National Archives, https://founders.archives.gov/documents/Washington/03-08-02-0357. [Original source: *The Papers of George Washington, Revolutionary War Series, vol. 8, 6 January 1777–27 March 1777*, ed. Frank E. Grizzard, Jr. Charlottesville: University Press of Virginia, 1998, pp. 331–333.]

3   Powell, 106.

4   Desmarais, 64.

5   Ewald, 55.

6   "From George Washington to Major General Horatio Gates, 19 February 1777," Founders Online, National Archives, https://founders.archives.gov/documents/Washington/03-08-02-0403. [Original source: *The Papers of George Washington, Revolutionary War Series, vol. 8, 6 January 1777–27 March 1777*, ed. Frank E. Grizzard, Jr. Charlottesville: University Press of Virginia, 1998, pp. 370–371.]

7   "From George Washington to John Hancock, 20 February 1777," Founders Online, National Archives, https://founders.archives.gov/documents/Washington/03-08-02-0416. [Original source: *The Papers of George Washington, Revolutionary War Series, vol. 8, 6 January 1777–27 March 1777*, ed. Frank E. Grizzard, Jr. Charlottesville: University Press of Virginia, 1998, pp. 381–383.]

8   Lord Germain to Sir Guy Carleton, 1777, March 26, Whitehall, *The Historical Manuscripts Commission Great Britain* (Boston: Gregg Press, 1972) 60.

9   Robertson, 124.

10 Peebles, John, *The Diary of a Scottish Grenadier, 1776–1782,* Ira D. Gruber, ed. (Mechanicsburg, PA: Stackpole Books, 1998) 96.

11 Murray, James, *Letters From America, 1773–1780* (New York: Barnes & Noble, Inc.) 40.

12 Peebles, 97–98.

13 Desmarais, 68–70.

14 Peebles, 98.

15 Robertson, 124–125.

16 Desmarais, 70.

17 Peebles, 98.

18 "From George Washington to John Hancock, 28 February 1777," Founders Online, National Archives, https://founders.archives.gov/documents/Washington/03-08-02-0490. [Original source: *The Papers of George Washington, Revolutionary War Series, vol. 8, 6 January 1777–27 March 1777*, ed. Frank E. Grizzard, Jr. Charlottesville: University Press of Virginia, 1998, pp. 463–465.]

19 "From George Washington to John Augustine Washington, 24 February 1777," Founders Online, National Archives, https://founders.archives.gov/documents/Washington/03-08-02-0467. [Original source: *The Papers of George Washington, Revolutionary War Series, vol. 8, 6 January 1777–27 March 1777*, ed. Frank E. Grizzard, Jr. Charlottesville: University Press of Virginia, 1998, pp. 439–440.]

20 Ewald, 55.

21 Clayton, 341.

22 Kemble, 110–111.

Chapter Eight - Punk Hill

1   Stryker, 321.

2   Ibid., 319.

3   Clayton, 341.

4   Stryker, 319–320.

5   Kemble, 111.

6   Stryker, 321.

7   "To George Washington from Robert Morris, 27 February 1777," Founders Online, National Archives, https://founders.archives.gov/documents/Wash-

ington/03-08-02-0486. [Original source: *The Papers of George Washington, Revolutionary War Series, vol. 8, 6 January 1777–27 March 1777*, ed. Frank E. Grizzard, Jr. Charlottesville: University Press of Virginia, 1998, pp. 456–458.]

8 "From George Washington to Robert Morris, 2 March 1777," Founders Online, National Archives, https://founders.archives.gov/documents/Washington/03-08-02-0510. [Original source: *The Papers of George Washington, Revolutionary War Series, vol. 8, 6 January 1777–27 March 1777*, ed. Frank E. Grizzard, Jr. Charlottesville: University Press of Virginia, 1998, pp. 486–489.]

9 Desmarais, 53–54.

10 Stryker, 322.

11 Ibid., 324.

12 Ibid., 322–323.

13 "From George Washington to John Hancock, 14 March 1777," Founders Online, National Archives, https://founders.archives.gov/documents/Washington/03-08-02-0607. [Original source: *The Papers of George Washington, Revolutionary War Series, vol. 8, 6 January 1777–27 March 1777*, ed. Frank E. Grizzard, Jr. Charlottesville: University Press of Virginia, 1998, pp. 570–572.]

14 Stryker, 326.

15 Ibid., 328.

Chapter Nine Hudson's River

1 "Return of the American Forces in New Jersey, 15 March 1777," Founders Online, National Archives, https://founders.archives.gov/documents/Washington/03-08-02-0615. [Original source: *The Papers of George Washington, Revolutionary War Series, vol. 8, 6 January 1777–27 March 1777*, ed. Frank E. Grizzard, Jr. Charlottesville: University Press of Virginia, 1998, pp. 576–577.]

2 Desmarais, 54.

3 Stryker, 329.

4 "From George Washington to Samuel Washington, 15 March 1777," Founders Online, National Archives, https://founders.archives.gov/documents/Washington/03-08-02-0622. [Original source: *The Papers of George Washington, Revolutionary War Series, vol. 8, 6 January 1777–27 March 1777*, ed. Frank E. Grizzard, Jr. Charlottesville: University Press of Virginia, 1998, pp. 584–585.]

5 "From George Washington to Brigadier General Alexander McDougall, 20 March 1777," Founders Online, National Archives, https://founders.archives.gov/documents/Washington/03-08-02-0648. [Original source: *The Papers of George Washington, Revolutionary War Series, vol. 8, 6 January 1777–27 March 1777*, ed. Frank E. Grizzard, Jr. Charlottesville: University Press of Virginia, 1998, p. 603.]

6 "From George Washington to John Hancock, 26 March 1777," Founders Online, National Archives, https://founders.archives.gov/documents/Washington/03-08-02-0689. [Original source: *The Papers of George Washington,*

Revolutionary War Series, vol. 8, 6 January 1777–27 March 1777, ed. Frank E. Grizzard, Jr. Charlottesville: University Press of Virginia, 1998, pp. 635–636.]

7   Sir William Howe to Lord George Germain 1777, April 2, New York, *The Historical Manuscripts Commission Great Britain* (Boston: Gregg Press, 1972) 64.

8   Stryker, 336.

9   Ibid., 338.

10 Kemble, 112.

11 "From George Washington to Major General William Heath, 29 March 1777," Founders Online, National Archives, https://founders.archives.gov/documents/Washington/03-09-02-0015. [Original source: *The Papers of George Washington, Revolutionary War Series, vol. 9, 28 March 1777–10 June 1777*, ed. Philander D. Chase. Charlottesville: University Press of Virginia, 1999, pp. 11–12.]

12 "From George Washington to Brigadier General Alexander McDougall, 31 March 1777," Founders Online, National Archives, https://founders.archives.gov/documents/Washington/03-09-02-0030. [Original source: *The Papers of George Washington, Revolutionary War Series, vol. 9, 28 March 1777–10 June 1777*, ed. Philander D. Chase. Charlottesville: University Press of Virginia, 1999, p. 29.]

13 Sir William Howe to Lord George Germain 1777, April 2, New York, *The Historical Manuscripts Commission Great Britain* (Boston: Gregg Press, 1972) 64–65.

14 Sir William Howe to Sir Guy Carleton, 1777, April 5, New York, *The Historical Manuscripts Commission Great Britain* (Boston: Gregg Press, 1972) 65–66.

15 Lord George Germain to Sir William Howe. 1777, May 18, Whitehall, *The Historical Manuscripts Commission Great Britain* (Boston: Gregg Press, 1972) 67.

16 Desmarais, 65.

17 Ewald, 55.

18 Ibid., 55.

Chapter Ten Bound Brook

1   Ewald, 55.

2   Davis, T.E., *The Battle of Bound Brook* (Bound Brook, NJ: The Chronicle Steam Printery, 1896) 4.

3   Mattern, David, *Benjamin Lincoln and the American Revolution* (Columbia, SC: University of South Carolina Press, 1998) 37.

4   Davis 7.

5   Ewald, 56.

6   Ibid., 56.

7   Davis, 7.

8   Ewald, 56–57.

9   Davis, 8.

10 Ewald, 56.

11   Davis, 8.
12   Ibid., 8.
13   Ewald, 57.
14   Ibid., 57
15   Davis, 10.
16   Ewald, 57.
17   Robertson, 126.
18   Kemble, 113.
19   Stryker, 341.
20   Ewald, 57.
21   Fischer, 196–197.
22   McCullough, 6.
23   Davis, 18.

Chapter Eleven Danbury

1   "From George Washington to Brigadier General Alexander McDougall,
     17–18 April 1777," Founders Online, National Archives, https://founders.
     archives.gov/documents/Washington/03-09-02-0172. [Original source: *The
     Papers of George Washington, Revolutionary War Series, vol. 9, 28 March
     1777–10 June 1777*, ed. Philander D. Chase. Charlottesville: University Press
     of Virginia, 1999, pp. 186–189.]
2   "From George Washington to Brigadier General William Maxwell, 17 April
     1777," Founders Online, National Archives, https://founders.archives.gov/
     documents/Washington/03-09-02-0175. [Original source: *The Papers of
     George Washington, Revolutionary War Series, vol. 9, 28 March 1777–10 June
     1777*, ed. Philander D. Chase. Charlottesville: University Press of Virginia,
     1999, pp. 193–194.]
3   "From George Washington to John Hancock, 12–13 April 1777," Found-
     ers Online, National Archives, https://founders.archives.gov/documents/
     Washington/03-09-02-0129. [Original source: *The Papers of George Washing-
     ton, Revolutionary War Series, vol. 9, 28 March 1777–10 June 1777*, ed. Philander
     D. Chase. Charlottesville: University Press of Virginia, 1999, pp. 128–130.]
4   "Orders to Major General Arthur St. Clair, 9 April 1777," Founders On-
     line, National Archives, https://founders.archives.gov/documents/Wash-
     ington/03-09-02-0106. [Original source: *The Papers of George Washington,
     Revolutionary War Series, vol. 9, 28 March 1777–10 June 1777*, ed. Philander D.
     Chase. Charlottesville: University Press of Virginia, 1999, pp. 107–109.]
5   "From George Washington to Brigadier General Alexander McDougall,
     17–18 April 1777," Founders Online, National Archives, https://founders.
     archives.gov/documents/Washington/03-09-02-0172. [Original source: *The
     Papers of George Washington, Revolutionary War Series, vol. 9, 28 March
     1777–10 June 1777*, ed. Philander D. Chase. Charlottesville: University Press
     of Virginia, 1999, pp. 186–189.]

6   Ives, J. Moss, Atwell, George C., Arms, H. Phelps, Miller, Francis Trevelyan, "A Connecticut Battlefield in the American Revolution," *The Connecticut Magazine, Volume 7*, The Connecticut Magazine Company, 1900, 141.

7   Burr, William Hanford, Atwell, George C., Arms, H. Phelps, Miller, Francis Trevelyan, "Invasion of Connecticut by the British Army in the War for American Independence," *The Connecticut Magazine, Volume 10*, The Connecticut Magazine Company, 1906, 141.

8   Robertson, 126.

9   Ives, Atwell, Arms, Miller, Trevelyan, 429.

10 Robertson, 126–127.

11 Kemble, 116.

12 Robertson, 127.

13 Ives, Atwell, Arms, Miller, Trevelyan, 431.

14 Robertson, 127.

15 Ives, Atwell, Arms, Miller, Trevelyan, 433.

16 Burr, Atwell, Arms, Miller, Trevelyan, 147.

17 Ives, Atwell, Arms, Miller, Trevelyan, 435.

18 Robertson, 127.

19 Kemble, 116.

20 Burr, Atwell, Arms, Miller, Trevelyan, 147.

21 Robertson, 127–128.

22 Burr, Atwell, Arms, Miller, Trevelyan, 147.

23 Robertson, 128.

24 Ibid., 128.

25 Burr, Atwell, Arms, Miller, Trevelyan, 149.

26 Kemble, 116–117.

27 Robertson, 129.

28 Burr, Atwell, Arms, Miller, Trevelyan, 149.

29 Kemble, 117.

30 Robertson, 129.

31 Burr, Atwell, Arms, Miller, Trevelyan, 149.

32 Robertson, 129–131.

33 Ward, Christopher, Alden, John Richard, ed., *The War of the Revolution* (New York: MacMillan Company, 1952) 492.

34 Robertson, 129–130.

Chapter Twelve Bonamtown

1   Robertson, 131.

2   "To George Washington from Brigadier General Alexander McDougall, 27 April 1777," Founders Online, National Archives, https://founders.archives.gov/documents/Washington/03-09-02-0273. [Original source: *The Papers of George Washington, Revolutionary War Series, vol. 9, 28 March 1777–10 June*

1777, ed. Philander D. Chase. Charlottesville: University Press of Virginia, 1999, pp. 287–288.]

3   "To George Washington from Brigadier General Alexander McDougall, 27 April 1777," Founders Online, National Archives, https://founders.archives. gov/documents/Washington/03-09-02-0273. [Original source: *The Papers of George Washington, Revolutionary War Series, vol. 9, 28 March 1777–10 June 1777*, ed. Philander D. Chase. Charlottesville: University Press of Virginia, 1999, pp. 287–288.] note 2.

4   "From George Washington to John Hancock, 28 April 1777," Founders Online, National Archives, https://founders.archives.gov/documents/Washington/03-09-02-0278. [Original source: *The Papers of George Washington, Revolutionary War Series, vol. 9, 28 March 1777–10 June 1777*, ed. Philander D. Chase. Charlottesville: University Press of Virginia, 1999, pp. 293–294.]

5   "From George Washington to Brigadier Generals George Clinton and Alexander McDougall, 2 May 1777," Founders Online, National Archives, https://founders.archives.gov/documents/Washington/03-09-02-0310. [Original source: *The Papers of George Washington, Revolutionary War Series, vol. 9, 28 March 1777–10 June 1777*, ed. Philander D. Chase. Charlottesville: University Press of Virginia, 1999, pp. 325–326.]

6   "From George Washington to Brigadier General John Glover, 26 April 1777," Founders Online, National Archives, https://founders.archives.gov/documents/Washington/03-09-02-0257. [Original source: *The Papers of George Washington, Revolutionary War Series, vol. 9, 28 March 1777–10 June 1777*, ed. Philander D. Chase. Charlottesville: University Press of Virginia, 1999, p. 274.]

7   "From George Washington to Major General Benjamin Lincoln and Brigadier Generals William Maxwell and John Peter Gabriel Muhlenberg, 27 April 1777," Founders Online, National Archives, https://founders.archives. gov/documents/Washington/03-09-02-0271. [Original source: *The Papers of George Washington, Revolutionary War Series, vol. 9, 28 March 1777–10 June 1777*, ed. Philander D. Chase. Charlottesville: University Press of Virginia, 1999, pp. 285–286.]

8   Desmarais, 59.

9   Stryker, 354.

10   Desmarais, 59.

11   Ewald, 57.

12   Ibid., 57.

13   Lagemann, Robert, and Manucy, Albert C., *The Long Rifle* (New York: Eastern Acorn Press, 1993) 8.

14   Ibid., 26.

15   Ibid., 6.

16   Ewald, 57.

17   "From George Washington to John Hancock, 3 May 1777," Founders Online, National Archives, https://founders.archives.gov/documents/Wash-

ington/03-09-02-0320. [Original source: *The Papers of George Washington, Revolutionary War Series, vol. 9, 28 March 1777–10 June 1777*, ed. Philander D. Chase. Charlottesville: University Press of Virginia, 1999, pp. 333–335.]

18 Ewald, 57, 62.

Chapter Thirteen Piscataway

1 "To George Washington from James Mease, 12 April 1777," Founders Online, National Archives, https://founders.archives.gov/documents/Washington/03-09-02-0133. [Original source: *The Papers of George Washington, Revolutionary War Series, vol. 9, 28 March 1777–10 June 1777*, ed. Philander D. Chase. Charlottesville: University Press of Virginia, 1999, pp. 139–140.]

2 "From George Washington to James Mease, 12 May 1777," Founders Online, National Archives, https://founders.archives.gov/documents/Washington/03-09-02-0394. [Original source: *The Papers of George Washington, Revolutionary War Series, vol. 9, 28 March 1777–10 June 1777*, ed. Philander D. Chase. Charlottesville: University Press of Virginia, 1999, p. 399.]

3 "From George Washington to Major General Stirling, 6 May 1777," Founders Online, National Archives, https://founders.archives.gov/documents/Washington/03-09-02-0345. [Original source: *The Papers of George Washington, Revolutionary War Series, vol. 9, 28 March 1777–10 June 1777*, ed. Philander D. Chase. Charlottesville: University Press of Virginia, 1999, pp. 358–359.]

4 "To George Washington from Major General Stirling, 6 May 1777," Founders Online, National Archives, https://founders.archives.gov/documents/Washington/03-09-02-0346. [Original source: *The Papers of George Washington, Revolutionary War Series, vol. 9, 28 March 1777–10 June 1777*, ed. Philander D. Chase. Charlottesville: University Press of Virginia, 1999, pp. 359–360.]

5 Desmarais, 65.

6 *The Pennsylvania Evening Post*, May 20, 1777, Stryker, 385.

7 Peebles, 111.

8 Desmarais, 66.

9 *The Pennsylvania Evening Post*, May 24, 1777, Stryker, 386.

10 "From George Washington to John Hancock, 12 May 1777," Founders Online, National Archives, https://founders.archives.gov/documents/Washington/03-09-02-0391. [Original source: *The Papers of George Washington, Revolutionary War Series, vol. 9, 28 March 1777–10 June 1777*, ed. Philander D. Chase. Charlottesville: University Press of Virginia, 1999, pp. 394–396.]

11 "General Orders, 8 May 1777," Founders Online, National Archives, https://founders.archives.gov/documents/Washington/03-09-02-0356. [Original source: *The Papers of George Washington, Revolutionary War Series, vol. 9, 28 March 1777–10 June 1777*, ed. Philander D. Chase. Charlottesville: University Press of Virginia, 1999, p. 368.]

12 "General Orders, 10 May 1777," Founders Online, National Archives, https://
    founders.archives.gov/documents/Washington/03-09-02-0366.   [Original
    source: *The Papers of George Washington, Revolutionary War Series, vol. 9, 28
    March 1777–10 June 1777*, ed. Philander D. Chase. Charlottesville: University
    Press of Virginia, 1999, pp. 372–373.]
13 "To George Washington from Benjamin Rush, 13 May 1777," Founders On-
    line, National Archives, https://founders.archives.gov/documents/Wash-
    ington/03-09-02-0410. [Original source: *The Papers of George Washington,
    Revolutionary War Series, vol. 9, 28 March 1777–10 June 1777*, ed. Philander D.
    Chase. Charlottesville: University Press of Virginia, 1999, p. 415.]
14 "From George Washington to Benjamin Rush, 16 May 1777," Founders On-
    line, National Archives, https://founders.archives.gov/documents/Wash-
    ington/03-09-02-0441. [Original source: *The Papers of George Washington,
    Revolutionary War Series, vol. 9, 28 March 1777–10 June 1777*, ed. Philander D.
    Chase. Charlottesville: University Press of Virginia, 1999, pp. 447–448.]
15 Ewald, 62.

Chapter Fourteen Middlebrook

1   "Circular to the Brigade Commanders, 20 May 1777," Founders On-
    line, National Archives, https://founders.archives.gov/documents/Wash-
    ington/03-09-02-0475. [Original source: *The Papers of George Washington,
    Revolutionary War Series, vol. 9, 28 March 1777–10 June 1777*, ed. Philander D.
    Chase. Charlottesville: University Press of Virginia, 1999, pp. 483–484.]
2   "To George Washington from Major General Nathanael Greene, 24 May
    1777," Founders Online, National Archives, https://founders.archives.gov/
    documents/Washington/03-09-02-0511. [Original source: *The Papers of
    George Washington, Revolutionary War Series, vol. 9, 28 March 1777–10 June
    1777*, ed. Philander D. Chase. Charlottesville: University Press of Virginia,
    1999, pp. 516–517.]
3   "To George Washington from Major General Nathanael Greene, 25 May
    1777," Founders Online, National Archives, https://founders.archives.gov/
    documents/Washington/03-09-02-0520. [Original source: *The Papers of
    George Washington, Revolutionary War Series, vol. 9, 28 March 1777–10 June
    1777*, ed. Philander D. Chase. Charlottesville: University Press of Virginia,
    1999, pp. 524–525.]
4   Ewald, 63
5   "From George Washington to John Hancock, 28 May 1777," Founders On-
    line, National Archives, https://founders.archives.gov/documents/Wash-
    ington/03-09-02-0541. [Original source: *The Papers of George Washington,
    Revolutionary War Series, vol. 9, 28 March 1777–10 June 1777*, ed. Philander D.
    Chase. Charlottesville: University Press of Virginia, 1999, pp. 546–548.]
6   Extract from a letter from a place called Mount Pleasant, near Bound
    Brook, *The Pennsylvania Evening Post*, June 5, 1777, Stryker, 389–90.

7   Ewald, 63.

8   *The Pennsylvania Evening Post*, Stryker, 390.

9   "Enclosure, 20 May 1777," Founders Online, National Archives, https://
    founders.archives.gov/documents/Washington/03-09-02-0486-0002.
    [Original source: *The Papers of George Washington, Revolutionary War Series,
    vol. 9, 28 March 1777–10 June 1777*, ed. Philander D. Chase. Charlottesville:
    University Press of Virginia, 1999, pp. 492–493.]

10 Ward, Harry M., *General George Weedon and the American Revolution* (Phila-
    delphia: The American Philosophical Society, 1979) 31.

11 "General Orders, 29 May 1777," Founders Online, National Archives, https://
    founders.archives.gov/documents/Washington/03-09-02-0547.   [Original
    source: *The Papers of George Washington, Revolutionary War Series, vol. 9, 28
    March 1777–10 June 1777*, ed. Philander D. Chase. Charlottesville: University
    Press of Virginia, 1999, pp. 551–552.]

12 Zielinski, Adam E., "A Phantom at Middlebrook—Washington in the New
    Jersey Short Hills," *Journal of the American Revolution*, April 11, 2018.

13 "General Orders, 4 June 1777," Founders Online, National Archives, https://
    founders.archives.gov/documents/Washington/03-09-02-0600.   [Original
    source: *The Papers of George Washington, Revolutionary War Series, vol. 9, 28
    March 1777–10 June 1777*, ed. Philander D. Chase. Charlottesville: University
    Press of Virginia, 1999, pp. 602–603.]

14 "From George Washington to John Hancock, 6 June 1777," Founders On-
    line, National Archives, https://founders.archives.gov/documents/Wash-
    ington/03-09-02-0619. [Original source: *The Papers of George Washington,
    Revolutionary War Series, vol. 9, 28 March 1777–10 June 1777*, ed. Philander D.
    Chase. Charlottesville: University Press of Virginia, 1999, pp. 618–621.]

15 "From George Washington to Major General John Sullivan, 7 June
    1777," Founders Online, National Archives, https://founders.archives.gov/
    documents/Washington/03-09-02-0635. [Original source: *The Papers of
    George Washington, Revolutionary War Series, vol. 9, 28 March 1777–10 June
    1777*, ed. Philander D. Chase. Charlottesville: University Press of Virginia,
    1999, pp. 639–641.]

16 Kemble, 118.

17 Ewald, 63–64.

18 Ibid., 63.

19 "General Orders, 8 June 1777," Founders Online, National Archives, https://
    founders.archives.gov/documents/Washington/03-09-02-0637.   [Original
    source: *The Papers of George Washington, Revolutionary War Series, vol. 9, 28
    March 1777–10 June 1777*, ed. Philander D. Chase. Charlottesville: University
    Press of Virginia, 1999, pp. 642–643.]

20 Mayers, Robert A, *Revolutionary New Jersey; Forgotten Towns and Crossroads
    of the American Revolution* (Staunton, VA: American History Press, 2018) 47.

21 Robertson, 135–136.

22   Ibid., 135–136.
23   Ewald, 64.

Chapter Fifteen Howe Tries to Ensnare the Fox

1   "From George Washington to Major General John Sullivan, 12 June
     1777," Founders Online, National Archives, https://founders.archives.gov/
     documents/Washington/03-10-02-0016. [Original source: *The Papers of
     George Washington, Revolutionary War Series, vol. 10, 11 June 1777–18 August
     1777*, ed. Frank E. Grizzard, Jr. Charlottesville: University Press of Virginia,
     2000, pp. 17–18.]

2   "General Orders, 12 June 1777," Founders Online, National Archives, https://
     founders.archives.gov/documents/Washington/03-10-02-0007.   [Original
     source: *The Papers of George Washington, Revolutionary War Series, vol. 10, 11
     June 1777–18 August 1777*, ed. Frank E. Grizzard, Jr. Charlottesville: University
     ty Press of Virginia, 2000, pp. 6–9.]

3   Buchanan, John, The Road to Guilford Court House (New York, John Wi-
     ley & Sons, Inc. 1997) 284

4   Higginbotham, Don, *Daniel Morgan; Revolutionary Rifleman* (Chapel Hill:
     University of North Carolina Press, 1961) 1–43.

5   "Orders to Colonel Daniel Morgan, 13 June 1777," Founders Online, Na-
     tional Archives, https://founders.archives.gov/documents/Washington/
     03-10-02-0026. [Original source: *The Papers of George Washington, Revolu-
     tionary War Series, vol. 10, 11 June 1777–18 August 1777*, ed. Frank E. Grizzard,
     Jr. Charlottesville: University Press of Virginia, 2000, p. 31.]

6   Higginbotham, 57.
7   Robertson, 136.
8   Mayers, 47.
9   Ewald, 64.
10   Higginbotham, 58.
11   "From George Washington to John Hancock, 14 June 1777," Founders On-
     line, National Archives, https://founders.archives.gov/documents/Wash-
     ington/03-10-02-0032. [Original source: *The Papers of George Washington,
     Revolutionary War Series, vol. 10, 11 June 1777–18 August 1777*, ed. Frank E.
     Grizzard, Jr. Charlottesville: University Press of Virginia, 2000, pp. 36–37.]

12   Higginbotham, 58.
13   Ibid., 58.
14   Kemble, 120.
15   "Order of March, 14 June 1777," Founders Online, National Archives, https://
     founders.archives.gov/documents/Washington/03-10-02-0030.   [Original
     source: *The Papers of George Washington, Revolutionary War Series, vol. 10, 11
     June 1777–18 August 1777*, ed. Frank E. Grizzard, Jr. Charlottesville: University
     ty Press of Virginia, 2000, pp. 34–36.]

16 "From George Washington to Major General John Sullivan, 14 June 1777," Founders Online, National Archives, https://founders.archives.gov/documents/Washington/03-10-02-0037. [Original source: *The Papers of George Washington, Revolutionary War Series, vol. 10, 11 June 1777–18 August 1777*, ed. Frank E. Grizzard, Jr. Charlottesville: University Press of Virginia, 2000, pp. 40–41.]

17 "From George Washington to Major General John Sullivan, 14 June 1777," Founders Online, National Archives, https://founders.archives.gov/documents/Washington/03-10-02-0039. [Original source: *The Papers of George Washington, Revolutionary War Series, vol. 10, 11 June 1777–18 August 1777*, ed. Frank E. Grizzard, Jr. Charlottesville: University Press of Virginia, 2000, p. 41.]

18 Zielinski, Adam E., "A Phantom at Middlebrook—Washington in the New Jersey Short Hills." *Journal of the American Revolution,* April 11, 2018.

19 "From George Washington to Major General Philip Schuyler, 16 June 1777," Founders Online, National Archives, https://founders.archives.gov/documents/Washington/03-10-02-0055. [Original source: *The Papers of George Washington, Revolutionary War Series, vol. 10, 11 June 1777–18 August 1777*, ed. Frank E. Grizzard, Jr. Charlottesville: University Press of Virginia, 2000, pp. 53–54.]

20 "From George Washington to Major General Benjamin Lincoln and Brigadier General Anthony Wayne, 16 June 1777," Founders Online, National Archives, https://founders.archives.gov/documents/Washington/03-10-02-0052. [Original source: *The Papers of George Washington, Revolutionary War Series, vol. 10, 11 June 1777–18 August 1777*, ed. Frank E. Grizzard, Jr. Charlottesville: University Press of Virginia, 2000, p. 52.]

21 Zielinski, Adam E., "A Phantom at Middlebrook—Washington in the New Jersey Short Hills." *Journal of the American Revolution,* April 11, 2018.

22 Ewald, 64–65.

23 Robertson, 136.

24 "From George Washington to Major General John Sullivan, 17 June 1777," Founders Online, National Archives, https://founders.archives.gov/documents/Washington/03-10-02-0063. [Original source: *The Papers of George Washington, Revolutionary War Series, vol. 10, 11 June 1777–18 August 1777*, ed. Frank E. Grizzard, Jr. Charlottesville: University Press of Virginia, 2000, pp. 64–65.]

25 Robertson, 137.

26 Ewald, 65.

27 "From George Washington to John Hancock, 20 June 1777," Founders Online, National Archives, https://founders.archives.gov/documents/Washington/03-10-02-0084. [Original source: *The Papers of George Washington, Revolutionary War Series, vol. 10, 11 June 1777–18 August 1777*, ed. Frank E. Grizzard, Jr. Charlottesville: University Press of Virginia, 2000, pp. 84–86.]

28   "From George Washington to John Augustine Washington, 29 June
     1777," Founders Online, National Archives, https://founders.archives.gov/
     documents/Washington/03-10-02-0149. [Original source: *The Papers of
     George Washington, Revolutionary War Series, vol. 10, 11 June 1777–18 August
     1777*, ed. Frank E. Grizzard, Jr. Charlottesville: University Press of Virginia,
     2000, pp. 149–151.]
29   Mayers, 46.

Chapter Sixteen Samptown

1   "From George Washington to John Hancock, 20 June 1777," Founders On-
     line, National Archives, https://founders.archives.gov/documents/Wash-
     ington/03-10-02-0084. [Original source: *The Papers of George Washington,
     Revolutionary War Series, vol. 10, 11 June 1777–18 August 1777*, ed. Frank E.
     Grizzard, Jr. Charlottesville: University Press of Virginia, 2000, pp. 84–86.]
2   Mayer, 92.
3   Robertson, 137–138.
4   Kemble, 121.
5   "General Orders, 21 June 1777," Founders Online, National Archives, https://
     founders.archives.gov/documents/Washington/03-10-02-0091.   [Original
     source: *The Papers of George Washington, Revolutionary War Series, vol. 10, 11
     June 1777–18 August 1777*, ed. Frank E. Grizzard, Jr. Charlottesville: Universi-
     ty Press of Virginia, 2000, p. 93.]
6   Ewald, 65.
7   Ibid., 65.
8   "From George Washington to John Hancock, 22 June 1777," Founders On-
     line, National Archives, https://founders.archives.gov/documents/Washing-
     ton/03-10-02-0105. [Original source: *The Papers of George Washington, Revolu-
     tionary War Series, vol. 10, 11 June 1777–18 August 1777*, ed. Frank E. Grizzard, Jr.
     Charlottesville: University Press of Virginia, 2000, pp. 104–106.]
9   Peebles, 117.
10   Higginbotham, 59.
11   "From George Washington to Joseph Reed, 23 June 1777," Founders On-
     line, National Archives, https://founders.archives.gov/documents/Wash-
     ington/03-10-02-0114. [Original source: *The Papers of George Washington,
     Revolutionary War Series, vol. 10, 11 June 1777–18 August 1777*, ed. Frank E.
     Grizzard, Jr. Charlottesville: University Press of Virginia, 2000, pp. 113–115.]
12   Robertson, 138.
13   Ewald, 65.
14   Peale, 237.
15   "From George Washington to Joseph Reed, 23 June 1777," Founders On-
     line, National Archives, https://founders.archives.gov/documents/Wash-
     ington/03-10-02-0114. [Original source: *The Papers of George Washington,*

Revolutionary War Series, vol. 10, 11 June 1777–18 August 1777, ed. Frank E. Grizzard, Jr. Charlottesville: University Press of Virginia, 2000, pp. 113–115.]

16   Ewald, 65–68.

17   "General Orders, 23 June 1777," Founders Online, National Archives, https://founders.archives.gov/documents/Washington/03-10-02-0107.   [Original source: *The Papers of George Washington, Revolutionary War Series, vol. 10, 11 June 1777–18 August 1777*, ed. Frank E. Grizzard, Jr. Charlottesville: University Press of Virginia, 2000, pp. 108–109.]

18   "From George Washington to John Hancock, 25 June 1777," Founders Online, National Archives, https://founders.archives.gov/documents/Washington/03-10-02-0124. [Original source: *The Papers of George Washington, Revolutionary War Series, vol. 10, 11 June 1777–18 August 1777*, ed. Frank E. Grizzard, Jr. Charlottesville: University Press of Virginia, 2000, pp. 123–125.]

19   Desmarais, 55.

20   The Pennsylvania Gazette, June 25, 1777, Stryker 405–406.

21   "From George Washington to John Hancock, 25 June 1777," Founders Online, National Archives, https://founders.archives.gov/documents/Washington/03-10-02-0124. [Original source: *The Papers of George Washington, Revolutionary War Series, vol. 10, 11 June 1777–18 August 1777*, ed. Frank E. Grizzard, Jr. Charlottesville: University Press of Virginia, 2000, pp. 123–125.]

22   Desmarais, 55.

23   Kemble, 122.

24   Robertson, 138.

25   "From George Washington to John Hancock, 25 June 1777," Founders Online, National Archives, https://founders.archives.gov/documents/Washington/03-10-02-0124. [Original source: *The Papers of George Washington, Revolutionary War Series, vol. 10, 11 June 1777–18 August 1777*, ed. Frank E. Grizzard, Jr. Charlottesville: University Press of Virginia, 2000, pp. 123–125.]

26   Stryker, 407.

27   Ewald, 68.

Chapter Seventeen The Short Hills & Westfield

1   Philhower, Charles A., *History of Town of Westfield, Union Country, New Jersey* (New York: Lewis Historical Publishing Company, 1923) 27.

2   Robertson, 138.

3   Peale, 236.

4   Ewald, 69.

5   Mayers, 57.

6   Zielinski, Adam E., "A Phantom at Middlebrook—Washington in the New Jersey Short Hills." *Journal of the American Revolution*, April 11, 2018.

7   "General Orders, 26 June 1777," Founders Online, National Archives, https://founders.archives.gov/documents/Washington/03-10-02-0128.   [Original

source: *The Papers of George Washington, Revolutionary War Series, vol. 10, 11 June 1777–18 August 1777*, ed. Frank E. Grizzard, Jr. Charlottesville: University Press of Virginia, 2000, p. 128.]

8   Ewald, 69.
9   Zielinski, Adam E., "A Phantom at Middlebrook—Washington in the New Jersey Short Hills." *Journal of the American Revolution*, April 11, 2018.
10 Kemble, 122.
11 Ewald, 69.
12 Robertson, 139.
13 Desmarais, 131.
14 Ibid., 131.
15 Philhower, 25.
16 Ewald, 69.
17 Robertson, 139.
18 Philhower, 24.
19 Ibid., 22.
20 Mayers, 59.
21 Philhower, 25.
22 Ibid., 27.
23 Mayers, 61.
24 Ibid., 62.
25 Philhower, 26.
26 Wickersty, Jason R., "A Shocking Havoc: The Plundering of Westfield, New Jersey, June 26, 1777," *Journal of The American Revolution*, July 21, 2015.

Chapter Eighteen Amboy

1   Kemble, 122–123.
2   Philhower, 25.
3   Ewald, 69.
4   Andre, John, *Major John Andre's Journal: Operations of the British army Under Lieutenant Generals Sir William Howe and Sir Henry Clinton June, 1777 to November, 1778* (The New York Times & Amo Press, 1968) 42.
5   Robertson, 139.
6   "General Orders, 27 June 1777," Founders Online, National Archives, https://founders.archives.gov/documents/Washington/03-10-02-0131.   [Original source: *The Papers of George Washington, Revolutionary War Series, vol. 10, 11 June 1777–18 August 1777*, ed. Frank E. Grizzard, Jr. Charlottesville: University Press of Virginia, 2000, pp. 130–131.]
7   Ewald, 69.
8   Kemble, 123.
9   Robertson, 139.
10 "From Alexander Hamilton to Robert R. Livingston, 28 June 1777," Founders Online, National Archives, https://founders.archives.gov/documents/

Hamilton/01-01-02-0201. [Original source: *The Papers of Alexander Hamilton, vol. 1, 1768–1778*, ed. Harold C. Syrett. New York: Columbia University Press, 1961, pp. 274–277.]

11 Philhower, 27.

12 "From George Washington to John Hancock, 29–30 June 1777," Founders Online, National Archives, https://founders.archives.gov/documents/Washington/03-10-02-0145. [Original source: *The Papers of George Washington, Revolutionary War Series, vol. 10, 11 June 1777–18 August 1777*, ed. Frank E. Grizzard, Jr. Charlottesville: University Press of Virginia, 2000, pp. 145–147.]

13 Ewald, 69–70.

14 *Papers of the Continental Congress*, No. 72, folio 353, p. 464.

15 "From George Washington to John Hancock, 1 July 1777," Founders Online, National Archives, https://founders.archives.gov/documents/Washington/03-10-02-0163. [Original source: *The Papers of George Washington, Revolutionary War Series, vol. 10, 11 June 1777–18 August 1777*, ed. Frank E. Grizzard, Jr. Charlottesville: University Press of Virginia, 2000, pp. 164–165.]

16 "General Orders, 2 July 1777," Founders Online, National Archives, https://founders.archives.gov/documents/Washington/03-10-02-0166. [Original source: *The Papers of George Washington, Revolutionary War Series, vol. 10, 11 June 1777–18 August 1777*, ed. Frank E. Grizzard, Jr. Charlottesville: University Press of Virginia, 2000, pp. 166–167.]

17 "From George Washington to John Hancock, 2 July 1777," Founders Online, National Archives, https://founders.archives.gov/documents/Washington/03-10-02-0169. [Original source: *The Papers of George Washington, Revolutionary War Series, vol. 10, 11 June 1777–18 August 1777*, ed. Frank E. Grizzard, Jr. Charlottesville: University Press of Virginia, 2000, pp. 168–170.]

18 Stryker, 418.

19 Kemble, 123.

20 Ewald, 71.

Chapter Nineteen Sandy Hook

1   "From George Washington to John Hancock, 5 July 1777," Founders Online, National Archives, https://founders.archives.gov/documents/Washington/03-10-02-0190. [Original source: *The Papers of George Washington, Revolutionary War Series, vol. 10, 11 June 1777–18 August 1777*, ed. Frank E. Grizzard, Jr. Charlottesville: University Press of Virginia, 2000, pp. 195–196.]

2   "From George Washington to Major General John Sullivan, 8 July 1777," Founders Online, National Archives, https://founders.archives.gov/documents/Washington/03-10-02-0220. [Original source: *The Papers of George Washington, Revolutionary War Series, vol. 10, 11 June 1777–18 August 1777*, ed. Frank E. Grizzard, Jr. Charlottesville: University Press of Virginia, 2000, pp. 230–231.]

3 "General Orders, 10 July 1777," Founders Online, National Archives, https:// founders.archives.gov/documents/Washington/03-10-02-0230. [Original source: *The Papers of George Washington, Revolutionary War Series, vol. 10, 11 June 1777–18 August 1777*, ed. Frank E. Grizzard, Jr. Charlottesville: University Press of Virginia, 2000, pp. 236–238.]

4 "From George Washington to John Hancock, 10 July 1777," Founders Online, National Archives, https://founders.archives.gov/documents/Washington/03-10-02-0233. [Original source: *The Papers of George Washington, Revolutionary War Series, vol. 10, 11 June 1777–18 August 1777*, ed. Frank E. Grizzard, Jr. Charlottesville: University Press of Virginia, 2000, pp. 240–241.]

5 "From George Washington to Major General John Sullivan, 12 July 1777," Founders Online, National Archives, https://founders.archives.gov/ documents/Washington/03-10-02-0258. [Original source: *The Papers of George Washington, Revolutionary War Series, vol. 10, 11 June 1777–18 August 1777*, ed. Frank E. Grizzard, Jr. Charlottesville: University Press of Virginia, 2000, p. 262.]

6 "From George Washington to John Hancock, 14 July 1777," Founders Online, National Archives, https://founders.archives.gov/documents/Washington/03-10-02-0270. [Original source: *The Papers of George Washington, Revolutionary War Series, vol. 10, 11 June 1777–18 August 1777*, ed. Frank E. Grizzard, Jr. Charlottesville: University Press of Virginia, 2000, pp. 277–278.]

7 "General Orders, 15 July 1777," Founders Online, National Archives, https:// founders.archives.gov/documents/Washington/03-10-02-0276. [Original source: *The Papers of George Washington, Revolutionary War Series, vol. 10, 11 June 1777–18 August 1777*, ed. Frank E. Grizzard, Jr. Charlottesville: University Press of Virginia, 2000, pp. 284–286.]

8 Robertson, 140.

9 Ewald, 70–71.

10 "From George Washington to John Hancock, 22 July 1777," Founders Online, National Archives, https://founders.archives.gov/documents/Washington/03-10-02-0347. [Original source: *The Papers of George Washington, Revolutionary War Series, vol. 10, 11 June 1777–18 August 1777*, ed. Frank E. Grizzard, Jr. Charlottesville: University Press of Virginia, 2000, pp. 356–357.]

11 Ewald, 72.

12 Robertson, 140.

13 "From George Washington to Major General John Sullivan, 22 July 1777," Founders Online, National Archives, https://founders.archives.gov/ documents/Washington/03-10-02-0359. [Original source: *The Papers of George Washington, Revolutionary War Series, vol. 10, 11 June 1777–18 August 1777*, ed. Frank E. Grizzard, Jr. Charlottesville: University Press of Virginia, 2000, p. 367.]

14 "From George Washington to Major General Benjamin Lincoln, 24 July 1777," Founders Online, National Archives, https://founders.archives.gov/

documents/Washington/03-10-02-0378. [Original source: *The Papers of George Washington, Revolutionary War Series, vol. 10, 11 June 1777–18 August 1777*, ed. Frank E. Grizzard, Jr. Charlottesville: University Press of Virginia, 2000, p. 385.]

15 "From George Washington to Colonel Daniel Morgan, 24 July 1777," Founders Online, National Archives, https://founders.archives.gov/documents/Washington/03-10-02-0380. [Original source: *The Papers of George Washington, Revolutionary War Series, vol. 10, 11 June 1777–18 August 1777*, ed. Frank E. Grizzard, Jr. Charlottesville: University Press of Virginia, 2000, p. 390.]

16 "From George Washington to William Livingston, 25 July 1777," Founders Online, National Archives, https://founders.archives.gov/documents/Washington/03-10-02-0403. [Original source: *The Papers of George Washington, Revolutionary War Series, vol. 10, 11 June 1777–18 August 1777*, ed. Frank E. Grizzard, Jr. Charlottesville: University Press of Virginia, 2000, pp. 412–413.]

17 "From George Washington to Major General John Sullivan, 25 July 1777," Founders Online, National Archives, https://founders.archives.gov/documents/Washington/03-10-02-0410. [Original source: *The Papers of George Washington, Revolutionary War Series, vol. 10, 11 June 1777–18 August 1777*, ed. Frank E. Grizzard, Jr. Charlottesville: University Press of Virginia, 2000, p. 420.]

18 "General Orders, 25 July 1777," Founders Online, National Archives, https://founders.archives.gov/documents/Washington/03-10-02-0393. [Original source: *The Papers of George Washington, Revolutionary War Series, vol. 10, 11 June 1777–18 August 1777*, ed. Frank E. Grizzard, Jr. Charlottesville: University Press of Virginia, 2000, pp. 402–403.]

19 "From George Washington to Major General Adam Stephen, 26 July 1777," Founders Online, National Archives, https://founders.archives.gov/documents/Washington/03-10-02-0423. [Original source: *The Papers of George Washington, Revolutionary War Series, vol. 10, 11 June 1777–18 August 1777*, ed. Frank E. Grizzard, Jr. Charlottesville: University Press of Virginia, 2000, p. 432.]

20 "From George Washington to Major General Stirling, 26 July 1777," Founders Online, National Archives, https://founders.archives.gov/documents/Washington/03-10-02-0424. [Original source: *The Papers of George Washington, Revolutionary War Series, vol. 10, 11 June 1777–18 August 1777*, ed. Frank E. Grizzard, Jr. Charlottesville: University Press of Virginia, 2000, pp. 432–433.]

21 "From George Washington to John Hancock, 27 July 1777," Founders Online, National Archives, https://founders.archives.gov/documents/Washington/03-10-02-0429. [Original source: *The Papers of George Washington, Revolutionary War Series, vol. 10, 11 June 1777–18 August 1777*, ed. Frank E. Grizzard, Jr. Charlottesville: University Press of Virginia, 2000, pp. 435–437.]

22 "From George Washington to John Hancock, 30 July 1777," Founders Online, National Archives, https://founders.archives.gov/documents/Washing-

ton/03-10-02-0458. [Original source: *The Papers of George Washington, Revolutionary War Series, vol. 10, 11 June 1777–18 August 1777*, ed. Frank E. Grizzard, Jr. Charlottesville: University Press of Virginia, 2000, pp. 459–460.]

23 Murray, 47.

24 Robertson, 141.

25 Ewald, 73.

26 "To George Washington from John Hancock, 31 July 1777," Founders Online, National Archives, https://founders.archives.gov/documents/Washington/03-10-02-0469. [Original source: *The Papers of George Washington, Revolutionary War Series, vol. 10, 11 June 1777–18 August 1777*, ed. Frank E. Grizzard, Jr. Charlottesville: University Press of Virginia, 2000, pp. 467–468.], note 1.

27 "From George Washington to Major General John Sullivan, 31 July 1777," Founders Online, National Archives, https://founders.archives.gov/documents/Washington/03-10-02-0473. [Original source: *The Papers of George Washington, Revolutionary War Series, vol. 10, 11 June 1777–18 August 1777*, ed. Frank E. Grizzard, Jr. Charlottesville: University Press of Virginia, 2000, p. 471.]

28 "From George Washington to John Hancock, 31 July 1777," Founders Online, National Archives, https://founders.archives.gov/documents/Washington/03-10-02-0470. [Original source: *The Papers of George Washington, Revolutionary War Series, vol. 10, 11 June 1777–18 August 1777*, ed. Frank E. Grizzard, Jr. Charlottesville: University Press of Virginia, 2000, p. 468.]

29 "General Orders, 31 July 1777," Founders Online, National Archives, https://founders.archives.gov/documents/Washington/03-10-02-0465. [Original source: *The Papers of George Washington, Revolutionary War Series, vol. 10, 11 June 1777–18 August 1777*, ed. Frank E. Grizzard, Jr. Charlottesville: University Press of Virginia, 2000, pp. 465–466.]

Postscript

1 Lafayette, *Memoirs and Manuscripts of General Lafayette, Vol. 1* (New York: Saunders & Otley, MDCCCXXXVII) 20.

2 Ewald, 73.

3 Fischer, Appendix T and U, 415–419.

4 Desmarais, 46–163.

5 Fischer, Appendix U, 419.

6 Ibid., 418.

7 Mayers, 49.

ACKNOWLEDGMENTS

*E*very book is a collective effort, and *The Enemy Harassed; Washington's New Jersey Campaign of 1777* was no different. First I would like to thank Roger Williams of Knox Press for his inspiration, editing, continued patience, and steady guidance, without which this project would never have been completed. As a George Washington Fellow, President of the New Jersey Society of the Sons of the American Revolution, Princeton-Cranbury Chapter, member of the National Council on Public History, and executive producer of *The Crossing and the Ten Crucial Days,* Roger's detailed knowledge of the American Revolution proved invaluable throughout the entirety of the project. Secondly, I would like to thank Don Hagist, Editor of the *Journal of the American Revolution*—and one of the most well-informed scholars in the country regarding the American War of Independence—for his willingness to read and edit the manuscript, in the process offering any number of detailed improvements which enhanced the book considerably. I would also like to recognize historian and author, Dr. Glenn F. Williams for his expert advice and editing, drawn from an extensive knowledge of the American Revolution. As a former U.S. Army officer, current historian of the American Battlefield Protection Program of the National Park Service, and recently retired Senior Historian at the U.S. Army Center of Military History, Dr. Williams is uniquely qualified as a scholar, author, and editor regarding all aspects of American military history. Thanks, as well to Bill Welsch, president of the

American Revolution Roundtable of Richmond, and author David Price for their editing and valuable suggestions. Great credit goes to Mayor Bob Fazen of the Borough of Bound Brook New Jersey for his assistance, and his permission to use Herb Patullo's striking depiction of the Battle of Bound Brook for the book's cover. I would also like to thank Director Catherine DeBerry and Ashley Soulier of the Somerset County Library System, Bound Brook Archive, for collecting a trove of material regarding the Battle of Bound Brook for our use. Many thanks as well to Aleigha Kely, Managing Editor at Post Hill Press along with all the professionals there who worked tirelessly to turn a rough manuscript into a fabulous book. Lastly—and as always—thanks to my wife, Sandie—mother, grandmother, physics professor, troubleshooter, and general jack-of-all-trades—for all her efforts, too numerous to describe.

Rarely does an author have the opportunity to work with a team of such knowledgeable and talented individuals. Their collective efforts have had a significant, positive impact on the book and are much appreciated.

ABOUT THE AUTHOR

*J*im Stempel is a speaker and author of ten books and numerous articles regarding American history, warfare, and spirituality. He resides in rural Maryland with his wife and family.

INDEX

A

Abercromby, Colonel, 67, 171–172
Alexander, William, *160*
    in battle of Short Hills and Westfield, 209–212
    biographical sketch of, 248–249
    Howe on, 207
    letter to Lincoln from, 131
    march of, toward Short Hills, 203
    march south of, 231, 232
    at Quibbletown, 60
    reinforcement of Maxwell by, 197
    troops under, 174
    Washington to, on march back from New York, 231
    Washington's involvement in personal affairs of, 159–162
    Washington's updates to Hancock on, 203, 204
Amboy
    as British resupply location, 40, 97–98
    British troops on ships at, 105, 106
    British withdrawal to, 199, 200–201, 220
    Howe's trip to, 100–102
    Kemble on Vaughan's march to, 63
    movement of British to Staten Island from, 221–225
    Robertson, on arriving at, 177
    Washington, on British troop numbers at, 90
    See also foraging skirmishes
American identity, formation of, 242–243
American supply depot at Danbury, 139–142
Amwell Road, 189
Andre, John, 219

animal fodder, British hunt for. *See* foraging skirmishes
Arnold, Benedict, 140–146, 182, 237
Arnold's tavern, 43–44
Ash Swamp, 94–97, 209–210

B

Basking Ridge, 60, 129, 159, 166
Bemis Heights, New York, 237
biographical sketches
    of American generals, 247–252
    of British generals, 244–246
Bloomfield, Joseph, 112
Bonhamtown, 70, 99, 102, 151–152, 196, 200
Bostwick, Elisha, 77, 78, 88–89
Bound Brook
    Abercromby's skirmish with Lincoln at, 171–173
    ambushes of British troops near, 72–73
    American troop strength in, 110
    battle of, 123–127, *126,* 129, 130
    Ewald-Ottendorf skirmish at, 119–120
    Ewald's reconnaissance mission to, 169–171
    lessons learned by Washington from, 135–137, 166
    Lincoln's defenses at, 122
    return of American troops to, 131
    selection of, as post, 121
    shortcomings of British plan of attack on, 132–134
Braddock, Edward, 48, 181
Bridge Town. *See* Spanktown
British cavalry
    foiling of, at Millstone River, 30–31

and need for fodder, 61
in picket line from Brunswick to
   Millstone, 185
Scott's attack on, 77
Washington on status of, 103
British Forty-Sixth Regiment, 62
British posts in New Jersey, 19–20
British strategy and communication delays,
   92–93
British supply line, 66, 97–98, 189
British troops
   consolidation of, 9–10, 40–41
   quartering of, 53
   treatment of prisoners of war by, 79–80
   troop strength of, 66, 90–91, 124
Brunswick
   arrival of Hessian troops near, 176
   British as virtual prisoners in, 107
   complete evacuation of, 199
   consolidation of British troops in, 40–41
   Howe's withdrawal to, 191
   movement of British troops to, 177–178
   Washington, on troop numbers at, 90
   Washington's decision to forego march to,
      27–28
   Washington's plan to advance to, 19
   See also foraging skirmishes
Brunswickers, 236
Buckner, Mordecai, 73–74
Burgoyne, John
   at Bemis Heights, 237
   British plans concerning, 91–93, 117
   and Fort Ticonderoga, 224, 226, 228, 236
   Howe's abandonment of, 118, 241
burning of towns. See plundering
Buster, Richard, 183

C

Cadwalader, John, 3, 14–15
Campbell, Mungo, 94–95, 189
Carleton, Guy, 92–93, 117
casualties
   in Ash Swamp skirmish, 96
   at Bound Brook, 129–130
   at Danbury and Ridgefield, 147
   at Drake's Farm, 78–79
   in early March skirmishes, 106
   near Piscataway, 163
   in the New Jersey campaign, 237–240
   at Princeton, 24
   at Punk Hill, 102
   at Ridgefield, 144

at Trenton, 6–7
Chase, Samuel, 79
Chatham, American troop strength in, 111
Chesapeake Bay, 116, 233, 244
Christie, William, 55
Civil War weapons, 154
civilians
   and battle of Princeton, 23–24
   British troops' treatment of, 53
   effect of British plundering and violence
      on, 240–241
   reports on Continental Army's abuse of,
      230–231
Clark, William, 14
Clinton, Henry, 117, 139, 150, 245
Clove, New York, 227–228
College of New Jersey, 107
comical issues faced by Washington, 157–162
communication delays, British, 92–93
Compo Hill, 145
Congress
   Continental Army, establishment of the,
      45
   Danbury raid response of, 150
   Flag Resolution of 1777, 223
   powers granted to Washington by, 8
   Washington, as delegate to, 48–49
   Washington to, on the Van Nest's Mill
      skirmish, 69
   Washington to, on troop numbers, 112–
      113
   Washington's commission from, 49
Connecticut Farms skirmish, 70
The Connecticut Magazine, 144
consolidation, troop
   Americans, 138–139, 165–166
   British, 9–10, 40–41
Continental Army
   enlistment period extension, 8–9
   recruitment figures for, 137–138
   reports to Washington, on abuses of,
      230–231
   troop strength of, 44–45, 110–111, 173–
      174
   uniform colors for the, 157–159
Continental Congress. See Congress
Conway, Thomas, 207, 209, 222
Cook, Edward, 151
Cornwallis, Charles, 20
   assumptions of, concerning Washington,
      51–52
   and battle of Short Hills, 207, 208–209,

211–212
biographical sketch of, 244–245
Bound Brook attack plan, 123–126, *126*
and Bound Brook reconnaissance
    mission, 170
decision to delay attack by, 11–12, 19
and division of troops at Kingston, 30
embarkation of, to Staten Island, 222
encounter with Frazee, 213–214
Ewald on plans of, 21
foraging plan of, 82–83
leave granted to, 2
march of, to Princeton, 8, 17–18
march of, to Trenton, 10–11
march towards Brunswick, 32
plundering by troops under, 240–241
pursuit of Washington outside of
    Princeton, 27
shortcomings in strategic thinking of, 137
at Stony Brook bridge, 21–22
strategic shortcomings of, 132–134
Washington's letter to, 49
worry concerning attack on New
    Brunswick, 19–20
Coryell's Ferry, 43, 233, 234
Cresswell, Nicholas, 203

D

Danbury, British raid on, 139–142, 147, 148–
    150, 155–156
Deane, Silas, 23
Declaration of Independence, 49
Delaware River
    first offensive crossing of, 1–7
    second offensive crossing of, 8
    Washington's positioning of troops at,
        231–232
deserters, 74, 107, 112, 150, 151, 155, 188
Dibble, Nehemiah, 141
Dickinson, Philemon, 60, 67–68, 69
Dinwiddie, Robert, 46, 47, 48
discipline, military, 164–165
Donop, Carl von, 124, 125, 127–128, 185–
    186, 208–209
Drake's Farm, 76–80
Dunmore's War, 181
Durham boats, 4

E

Edison Township. *See* Bonhamtown
Eighth Pennsylvania Regiment, 110

Elizabethtown, 50–51, 58, 182, 214
Elk River, 236
Elkton, Maryland. *See* Elk River; Head of Elk
Enlightenment thought, 48
enlistment period, 8–9, 45, 59
Erskine, William
    biographical sketch of, 245
    departure from New York of, 177
    in Drake's Farm skirmish, 76, 78, 79–80
    foraging expedition of, 69
    objection of, to Cornwallis's plan, 12
    at Ridgefield, 144, 145, 146
    Stephen's complaints to, 79
Ewald, Johann
    on Abercromby-Lincoln skirmish, 172
    ambush of, at Bound Brook and
        Quibbletown, 72–73
    on Americans' intent to attack Brunswick,
        26
    on arrival of new Hessian troops, 176
    background of, 41–42
    on being able to keep horse, 223
    biographical sketch of, 246
    from on board transport ship, 233
    and Bound Brook attack, 121, 125, 129,
        130
    Brunswick, withdrawal to, 191
    on Brunswick's defensive posture, 40–41
    and change in Bound Brook attack plan,
        130
    on consolidation of American troops, 166
    on Cornwallis's foraging plan, 82
    on Cornwallis's plans for Trenton, 21
    on daily skirmishes, 87
    on defeat at Princeton, 25
    defensive measures taken by, 156
    on entering New Jersey, 54
    on fleet's southward turn, 235
    on march to Brunswick, 32–33
    on march to Westfield, 208–209
    march towards Amboy by, 200–201, 220
    on Millstone deployment, 185–186
    on need to forage, 74–75
    Ottendorf's engagement with, 119–120
    on patrolling British defenses, 205
    on plan to lure Washington out of
        Middlebrook, 178
    on provisions for British troops, 98
    quartering of troops of, 53
    and Quibbletown skirmish, 82–86
    in Raritan River skirmishes, 152–153,
        154–155

relief of light infantry at Samptown by, 196–197

removal to Brunswick, for recovery, 173

Samptown, withdrawal from, 199

on setting, 228

on setting sail, 229

on Short Hills and Westfield battle, 211, 212, 213

on snow, 89

on Staten Island embarkation, 225

on troop movement from Amboy to Staten Island, 222

on underestimating Washington, 10

on Washington's holding position, 189

Westfield, withdrawal from, 219

wounding of, 169–171

Ewing, James, 3

F

Fairfax Independent Militia, 48–49

Fanny (ship), 228, 229, 232

Fenner House, 34

Fifth Virginia Regiment, 77–80

Fifty-Seventh British Regiment of Food, 94–95

First Establishment regiments, 45, 64–65

First Pennsylvania Rifle Company, 111

Fitzgerald, John, 38–39

Flag Resolution of 1777, 223

Flemington, 188, 190

fodder. *See* foraging skirmishes

foraging skirmishes

at Ash Swamp, 93–97

at Drake's Farm, 76–79

Ewald on, 75

in March, 112

near Springfield, 70

at Quibbletown, 83–86

at Spanktown, 61–62

at Van Nest's Mill, 67–69

on Woodbridge Road, 106

Forbes expedition, 48

Forrest, Thomas, 5, 11, 18–19, 22, 24

Fort Independence, 80–81, 82, 115

Fort Necessity, 47–48

Fort Ticonderoga, 93, 224, 226, 228, 236

Forty-Second (Royal Highland) Regiment, 76–77, 94, 99–100, 162

Forty-Sixth British Regiment, 62

Fourteenth Continental Regiment, 4

Frazee, Barbara, 213–214

French and Indian War, 41, 46–48, 100, 174

French troops in Ohio country, 46–47

funding of the American cause, by Morris, 103

G

gambling, Washington's order on, 164

Gates, Horatio, 89, 237

George III, 41

Germain, George

communication delays of, 92–93

Cornwallis's letter to, 51

Howe to, expressing diminished hopes, 113

Howe to, on abandoning Hudson River operation, 117

Howe to, on battle of Bound Brook, 129

Howe to, on battle of Short Hills, 215

Howe to, on moving troops to Staten Island, 222

Howe to, on surprise attack on Washington, 206

reply to Howe's letter on the Hudson River campaign, 118

German troops. *See* Hessian troops; Jägers

Glover, John, 4, 150

Grant, James, 2, 124, 125, 126, 130–131, 135

Greene, Nathanael, *198*

at Basking Ridge, 60

and battle of Princeton, 13–14

biographical sketch of, 249

and the British withdrawal from Brunswick, 197

on enemy losses, 239

failure of, to strike British rearguard, 201–202

march to the Delaware, 231, 232

and plan for battle of Trenton, 3, 4, 5

at Pluckemin, 34

and pursuit of British towards Amboy, 199

reoccupation of Bound Brook by, 131, 133

response to Bound Brook attack by, 129

troops under, 174

to Washington, on consolidation efforts, 168–169

Washington's orders for, at Middlebrook, 175

Greenwood, John, 4

Gregory, John, 78

H

Hamilton, Alexander, 98, 221–222
Hancock, John
  biographical sketch of, 249
  letter to Washington, on movement of
    British fleet, 233
  Washington's letters to
    on Ash Swamp skirmish, 96–97
    on battles of Trenton and Princeton, 35
    on Bound Brook skirmish, 172, 173
    on British barbarity, 79–80
    on British troop movements, 176
    on British vs. American troops
      strength, 90–91
    on change in British operations, 191
    on choosing not to strike Brunswick,
      28
    on Danbury raid, 149–150, 155–156
    on desire to cross the Delaware, 7–8
    on failure of Greene and Maxwell to
      strike British rearguard, 202
    on foraging skirmishes, 86
    on Heath, 65
    on Howe's move from Staten Island,
      224–225
    on march towards the Hudson River,
      227
    on militia harassment of British
      troops, 192
    on Morgan's intelligence, 186
    on movement of British to Staten
      Island, 222–223, 224
    on movement south towards Delaware,
      231–232
    on post at Quibbletown, 203
    on pressing the British, 197
    on public opinion, 241
    on recruitment, 64, 137–138
    on the situation on June 25th, 204
    on skirmish near Piscataway, 163–164
    on troop strength, 44, 59–60
Hand, Edward, 10–11
Harcourt, William, 124–125, 127, 128
Haslet, John, 14
Head of Elk, 116
health and medical issues, 165–166
Heath, William
  at Fort Independence, 80–81
  Washington to, after British plundering,
    115–116
  Washington to, on denying forage for the

    British, 61
  Washington to, on drawing the British to
    New York, 36
  Washington to, on intelligence gathering,
    37
  Washington to, on movement to New
    York City, 49–50
  Washington to Hancock on, 65
Heister, Lieopold Philip de, 178
Henry, Captain, 13
Hessian troops
  ambush of at Bound Brook and
    Quibbletown, 72–73
  arrival of new troops of, near Brunswick,
    176
  attack on picket post of, 106
  British use of, in North America, 41
  defeat of, in Trenton, 1–7
  at Fort Independence, 80
  quartering of, 53
  at Van Nest's Mill, 67–68
  Woodbridge Road skirmish, 106
  See also Jägers
Hillsborough, 67, 185–186, 187
Hopkinson, Francis, 223
horses, officers' use of, 165
Howe, Richard, 118
Howe, William, 59
  abandonment of Hudson River operation,
    117
  American intelligence on location of, 188
  biographical sketch of, 244
  bounty for American deserters, 155
  British effort to ensure safe travel of,
    99–102
  cancellation of Cornwallis's leave, 8
  to Germain, on battle of Bound Brook,
    130
  to Germain, on battle of Short Hills, 213
  to Germain, on diminished hopes, 113
  to Germain, on moving troops from
    Amboy to Staten Island, 222
  headquarters of, at Millstone, 185
  Kemble on movements of, 176
  march towards Metuchen, 208
  plan of, to lure Washington out of
    Middlebrook, 178, 179
  plan to abandon New Jersey for
    Philadelphia, 118
  and plan to sever New England, 91
  plundering by troops under, 240–241
  Proclamation of November 1776, 55–56, 74

Robertson on movements of, 177
setting sail for sea, 228
Short Hills and Westfield battle planning by, 207
Washington-Morris correspondence on situation of, 103–106
Washington to Hancock on, 35
Washington to Schuyler on intentions of, 188–189
Washington's assumptions on plans of, 12
Washington's complaints to, on British barbarity, 79
Washington's intelligence on plans of, 89–91
winter quartering of troops of, 1–2
and withdrawal from Millstone to Amboy, 206
withdrawal of, to Brunswick, 191, 195
Howland, John, 11
Hudson River operation, 92–93, 116, 117
Humphries, Capt., 38
Huntington, Jedediah, 144, 148–149

J

Jägers
  at Bound Brook, 127–128, 169–171
  as elite company, 42
  march to Amboy by, 201
  Ottendorf's engagement with, 119–120
  at Quibbletown, 83–86
  at Raritan River, 152–153, 154–155
  at Samptown, 197–198
  See also Hessian troops
Jumonville, Joseph Coulon de, 47

K

Kelly, John, 17–19, 21–22
Kelly, William, 78, 79–80
Kemble, Stephen
  biographical sketch of, 245
  on Bound Brook, 129–130
  on British and Hessian troops' behavior, 53–54
  on British posts in New Jersey, 20
  on British troop movements, 176
  on change in British outlook, 63
  on crossing the Saugatuck River, 145
  on Danbury raid, 140, 142
  on engagement near Elizabethtown, 50
  on Howe's trip to Amboy, 102
  on the impact of weather, 98

on information received, on June 28th, 220
on Morgan's attack near Hillsborough, 187
note of January 31st, 1777, 74
on officers' dissatisfaction with Howe's strategy, 225
on Ridgefield, 145
on scattered British posts, 36
on Short Hills, 211, 218–219
on splitting of the Army, 203–204
on troop numbers, 66, 111
on withdrawal to Brunswick, 195
Kingston, 25–26, 27, 30
Knox, Henry, 34

L

Lafayette, 235
Lamb, John, 145–146
Lambert, James, 215
Lancaster Sunday News, 18
Leslie, Alexander, 21, 38, 39, 178, 201
Leslie, William, 38–39
Lincoln, Benjamin
  background of, 121–122
  biographical sketch of, 248
  and Bound Brook, 128–129, 131, 136
  march to the Delaware, 229, 231, 232
  orders from Washington on intelligence gathering, 189
  skirmish with Abercromby, 171–173
  troops under, 174
  Washington to, on cooperation with Heath, 49
Lindsley, Eleazer, 95
Livingston, Susannah French, 159–162
Livingston, William, 57, 72, 159, 221–222, 230
Lodge, Lieutenant, 152
long rifles *vs.* muskets, 153–154
Lorey, Captain, 156
Loyalists
  in New Jersey, 55, 56–57
  newspapers friendly to the, 71, 114–115
  at Spanktown, 62

M

MacWhorter, Alexander, 70–71
Maitland, Thomas, 124, 125–126, 127, 128, 132
Manville. *See* Van Nest's Mill

maps, 65–66
Maryland, British landing in, 236–237
Mawhood, Charles, 13–14, 15, 107
Maxwell, William
    at Ash Swamp, 94, 95
    attack on British near Piscataway, 162–
        163
    attack on Forty-Second Highland
        Regiment by, 99–100
    background of, 100
    and battle of Short Hills and Westfield,
        209, 211, 212, 213
    biographical sketch of, 248
    failure of, to strike British rearguard,
        201–202
    Greene on, 168
    Howe on, 207
    march toward Westfield, 202
    at Metuchen, 60
    in Punk Hill skirmish, 101–102
    reinforcement of, by Alexander, 197
    Spanktown skirmish, 62
    Washington to, on consolidating his
        frontline posts, 137
    Washington to, on strategy, 136
McCabe, James, 151–152
McCay, Tomas, 78–79
McDougall, Alexander, 112, 135, 138–139,
    148–150
McKnatt, Sergeant, 34
Mease, James, 157–159
Mercer, Hugh, 14, 78
Metuchen, 60, 163, 204
Middle Bush, New Jersey, 185
Middlebrook
    American withdrawal to, 210, 213, 214–
        215
    Bound Brook troops' relocation to, 173
    claim that first U.S. flag flew over, 223–
        224
    Greene to Washington, on consolidation
        efforts at, 168–169
    Howe's plan to lure Washington from,
        185–186, 188–189, 194
    layout of encampment at, 175
    readiness of troops at, 180, 187
    strategic advantage of, 167–168
    Weeden on encampment at, 174
Mifflin, Thomas, 8, 13
military discipline, 164–165
militia
    British awareness of change in, 192–193

    at Danbury, 140, 148–149
    enlistment period of, 45
    harassment of British troops by, 191–192
    near Elizabethtown, 40–51
    at Ridgefield, 144, 146
    at Somerset Courthouse, 31
    troop strength of, 59, 111
    Washington as commander of, 48–49
    See also New Jersey militia
Millstone, 60, 185–186, 188, 189
Millstone River, 30–31, 67–68
Minnigerode, Colonel, 212
Mirante, Rand, 26–27
Moncrieff, James, 178
morale, 150–151
Morgan, Daniel, 184
    advance on British grenadiers by, 199
    assignment of, as commander of ranger
        corps, 182–184
    background of, 180–182
    and battle of Short Hills and Westfield,
        209–210
    at Bemis Heights, 237
    biographical sketch of, 251
    and the British withdrawal from
        Brunswick, 197–198
    engagement at Hillsborough, 186–187
    experience of, 81
    following of the British, retreating from
        Westfield, 219
    and orders to harass enemy, 189
    orders to help in New York, 236
    orders to march to Philadelphia, 229
    orders to remain at Trenton, 231
    pressing of the enemy near Brunswick,
        202
    report to Washington, on British
        maneuvering, 187–188
Morison, George, 182
Morris, Joseph, 95
Morris, Lewis, 43
Morris, Robert, 102–106
Morristown
    American troop strength in, 107, 110, 112
    arrival of troops in, 42–44
    Bound Brook's strategic importance to,
        120, 121
    Continental army's return to, 226, 231
    delay in pay at, 88
    Washington's fear of attack on, 97, 98,
        103
    Washington's letters from, 49

Moulder, Joseph, 26–27
Mount Vernon, 46, 48
Moylan, Colonel, 157, 158
Mulcaster, Captain, 220
Muller (bugler), 128, 171
Murray, James, 94–95, 233
music, camp, 175
muskets *vs.* long rifles, 153–154

N

New Brunswick. *See* Brunswick
New England
    British plan to cut off, 91–93, 116–117
    defeat of Brunswickers in, 236
New Jersey maps, *3, 90*
New Jersey militia
    attacks of, along Amwell Road, 189
    Connecticut Farms skirmish, 70
    plundering by, 71–72
    at Quibbletown, 89
    at Van Nest's Mill, 67–68
    Washington's release of, 201
    Wilkinson on, 57–58
New Market. *See* Quibbletown
New York Campaign, 1–2, 122, 239, 240
New York City, 49–50
New York Gazette and the Weekly Mercury, 71
newspapers, conflicting viewpoints of,
    114–115
Northumberland Associators, 17, 18, 22

O

officers
    American generals, biographical sketches
        of, 247–252
    British generals, biographical sketches of,
        244–246
    experience gained by, 241–242
    inexperience of, 81
    morale of, 150–151
    orders regarding horses used by, 165
Ogden, John, 71
Ohio country, 46–48, 181
Olden, Thomas, 24

P

Parker, Richard, 73–74
pay issues, 87–88, 151, 155
Peale, Charles Willson
    biographical sketch of, 247

    on enemy movements on June 26th, 208
    on march to Brunswick, 200
    on march to Morristown, 43
    on Morristown quarters, 44
    on Pluckemin, 33–34, 37–38
    on unit's departure, 64–65
Peebles, John, 94–95, 96, 162, 198–199
Peekskill, British plundering of, 115–116
Peekskill, plundering of, 139
Pennsylvania associators, 14–15, 17, 18, 22,
    33
Pennsylvania Evening Post
    on Bound Brook, 172–173
    on British at Brunswick, 107
    on British ravages, 71
    on enemy's evacuation of New Jersey,
        225
    on Maxwell's attack, 163
    on Middlebrook, 173
    on Stephen's attack, 162
    on troop strength, 108
Pennsylvania Gazette, 106–107, 108, 202
Pennsylvania Journal, 96, 114–115
Pennsylvania long rifles, 153–154
Pennsylvania Packet, 130
Perth Amboy. *See* Amboy
petite guerre, 152
Philadelphia
    orders for Morgan to march to, 229
    positioning of troops to defend, 231–232
    St. Clair's mission to rally troops to, 138
    Washington's arrival at, 235
    Washington's belief that Howe would
        move towards, 103, 106, 112
Philadelphia Brigade, 14–15
Philadelphia Light Infantry, 13
Piscataway, attack on British near, 162–164
Plainfield. *See* Samptown; Short Hills
Pluckemin encampment, 33–39
plundering
    by British troops, 53–54, 70–71, 115–116,
        202, 240–241
    by New Jersey militia, 71–72
Pompton, 226, 230
Post Road skirmish, 10–11
Potter, James, 17
Princeton
    after battle, 23–24
    American troop strength in, 110–111
    battle of, 12–15, 21, 34, 57
    consolidation of British forces in, 9–10
    orders for Sullivan to move from, 188

Putnam at, 60
prisoners of war, British treatment of, 79
Prueschenck, Captain, 176, 209
Punk Hill skirmish, 101–102
Putnam, Israel, 36–37, 60

Q

quartering of British troops, 53
Quebec attack, 182
Queen's Bridge, 122, 125, 127
Queen's Rangers, 200
Quibbletown
    Alexander at, 60
    ambushes of British troops near, 72–74
    attack on Forty-Second Regiment near,
        99–100
    late March attack on British at, 118–119
    militiamen strength at, 111
    skirmishes near, in February, 89
    as Washington's headquarters, 202

R

Rahway. See Spanktown
Rall, Johann, 5–6, 20
ranger corps. See Morgan, Daniel
Raritan Landing, 122, 122–123
Raritan River skirmishes, 152–153, 154–155
Rariton, troop strength in, 111
recruitment
    of American troops without muskets, 91
    for the Continental Army, 137–138
    effect of inflated troop numbers on, 59–60
    lack of money for, 87–88
    letter from Washington to Hancock on, 64
    Washington's frustration with, 107–108
Red Feather Company, 13
Reed, Joseph, 200
"Return of the American Forces in New
    Jersey," 110–111
Ridgebury Hill, 143
Ridgefield, battle of, 143–147
Robertson, Archibald, 142
    after Trenton, 19
    on American move towards Brunswick,
        25–26
    on American troop positions, 11
    on Ash Swamp skirmish, 93–94, 96
    biographical sketch of, 246
    on Bound Brook, 129
    on British foraging parties, 67, 69
    on British forces leaving Brunswick,

184–185
    on British maneuvers, 190
    on bypassing Delaware Bay, 233
    on Danbury raid, 139–140, 141, 142
    on Drake's Farm, 76–77, 78
    on embarkation to Staten Island, 204
    on the Fanny, 228, 229, 232
    on march to Brunswick, 32
    on movement from Amboy to Staten
        Island, 220–221
    and movement of troops to Brunswick,
        177, 178
    on Quibbletown, 85
    on Ridgefield, 143, 144, 145, 146, 147
    on Short Hills and Westfield, 207, 208,
        211, 213
    on sleeping on frozen ground, 12
    on snow of February 24, 97
    on withdrawal from Westfield, 219
    on withdrawal to Brunswick, 191, 195
Rodney, Caesar, 233
Rodney, Thomas
    on arrival at Morristown, 42–43
    on arrival at Somerset Courthouse, 32
    and battle of Princeton, 14
    biographical sketch of, 247
    on encampment at Pluckemin, 34
    on the end of soldiers' enlistments, 64
    on Leslie's death, 38
    on march to Princeton, 12–13
    on Pluckemin encampment, 33
    on possible collision with British, 30–31
    at Princeton, 22, 23, 25
    on spirit of the militiamen, 242
    on Trenton, 44
Romeyn, Dirck, 55
Ross, Betsy, 224
Royal Highland Regiment. See Forty-Second
    (Royal Highland) Regiment
Rush, Benjamin, 34, 38, 165–166, 167

S

Samptown, 196, 197, 199
Sandy Hook, 228–229
Saugatuck River, crossing of the, 145
Schuyler, Philip, 188–189
Scot's Plain, 60, 209
Scott, Charles, 77–78, 219, 222, 224
Second Establishment regiments, 45
Seven Years' War. See French and Indian War
Seventy-Fifth British Regiment of Foot, 151
Seventy-First British Regiment of Foot, 162

Short Hills and Westfield, battle of, 207–213, *208*
Shreve, Israel, 216–217
Silliman, Gold Selleck, 141, 143, 148, 149
Sixth Virginia Regiment, 73–74
Somerset Courthouse
    British withdrawal from, 202
    Dickinson's troops at, 60
    Howe at, 188
    ineffectiveness of militia at, 31
    Washington's decision to go to, 27–28
Somerville. *See* Somerset Courthouse
Spanktown, 62, 107, 111
Spencer, Oliver, 70
St. Clair, Arthur, 138
St. Leger, Barry, 91, 93, 117
Stark, John, 5, 81, 236
Staten Island, British at, 203–204, 220–223, 226
Steele's Gap, 190–191
Stephen, Adam
    and attack near Piscataway, 162, 163
    dispatch to Philadelphia, 230, 231
    at Metuchen, 60
    troops under, 174
Stirling, Lord. *See* Alexander, William
Stony Brook, crossing of, 13
Stony Brook bridge destruction, 17–19, 21–22
Stuart, Charles, 193
Sullivan, John
    animal removal plan of, 81–82
    biographical sketch of, 247
    at Flemington, 190
    march north of, 226, 227
    march to Brunswick, 197, 200
    order for withdrawal to Steele's Gap, 190–191
    at Pluckemin, 34
    and Princeton battle, 13
    at Scot's Plain, 60
    and Trenton battle, 2–3, 4, 5
    troops under, 174
    Washington to, on British movements, 176, 180, 187–188, 229, 233
    Washington to, on plundering by troops of, 230–231
    at Westfield, 214
supply depots, 139–142, 147, 150
supply line, British, 66, 97–98

T

tactical shift, British, 82–83

Tanaghrisson, 47
theater of operations, *3*
Third Establishment regiments, 45
thirteen-star American flag, 223–224
Thirty-Third British Regiment of Foot, 162
Thorbahn, Clifton, 18
Ticonderoga. *See* Fort Ticonderoga
Trautvetter, Lieutenant, 126, 153
Trenton
    battle of, 1–7, 57
    British march to, 13
    consolidation of troops south of, 9
    Morgan's orders to remain at, 231, 232
    Putnam at, 36–37
troop strength
    of American army, 44–45
    by brigade, 173–174
    of British forces, 41, 66, 124
    British *vs.* American, 90–91
    as reported in "Return of the American Forces in New Jersey," 110–111
    Washington to Congress on, 112–113
    Washington to Hancock on, 59–60, 64, 137–138
    Washington's frustration over, 107–108
Twelfth Pennsylvania Regiment, 151
Tyron, William, 139, 141, 142, 143

U

uniform colors, 157–159

V

Van Horne home, 122, *123*
Van Nest's Mill, 67–68, 196
Van Veghten's bridge, 122, 183, 189, 196
Vaughan, John, 70, 107, 207
Virginia Gazette, 79
Virginia House of Burgesses, 48
Virginia Regiment, 48
Von Heister, Leopold, 185
Von Ottendorf, Nicholas Dietrich, 119–120, 152–153, 154–155
Von Wangenheim, Lieutenant, 176

W

Waldeckers, 50, 70
Warner, Nathaniel, 60
Warren, Mercy Otis, 7
Washington, Augustine, 192
Washington, George, *47*

and abuse of Army towards civilians, 230–231
and advance to Brunswick, 19
and animal removal plan, 81–82
arrival at the Delaware, 232
background of, 45–49
at battle of Princeton, 15
biographical sketch of, 251–252
at Brandywine Creek, 236–237
on British barbarity, 79–80
on British fleet movements, 228–229
British underestimation of, 9–10
on British vs. American troop strength, 90–91
to brother Augustine, on British retreat, 192
to brother John, on Howe's intentions, 97
to brother Samuel, on Howe's intentions, 112
Buckner's arrest by, 73–74
on camp music, 175
comical issues faced by, 157–162
to Congress on the Van Nest's Mill skirmish, 69
to Congress on troop numbers, 112–113
Cornwallis's assumptions regarding, 51–52
crossing the Delaware and attack on Trenton, 1–7
and Danbury raid, 148–150
departure of, from Princeton, 24–25
on desertions and pay issues, 155
effort of, to obtain accurate maps, 65–66
on failure of Greene and Maxwell, 202
frustration of, over troop numbers, 107–108
to Gates, on enemy intelligence, 89
to Glover, on morale, 150–151
and Green's report on British attack at Bound Brook, 131
Hamilton's appointment as aide de camp to, 98
to Heath, after British plundering of Peekskill, 115–116
to Heath, asking for assistance, 36
to Heath, on denying forage to the British, 61
on Heath's performance, 80–81
and help for wounded British soldiers, 24
and Howe's intentions, 112
on lack of money, 87–88
to Leslie, on his son's death, 38–39
letters of, from Morristown, 49–50
to Livingston on behavior of militiamen, 72
Maxwell's appointment by, 100
to McDougall, on Bound Brook, 135
to McDougall, urging hastening of recruits, 112
Middlebrook encampment layout of, 175
and military discipline, 164–165
militia, opinion on the, 58
on militia's harassment of British troops, 191
Millstone River destruction orders of, 30–31
Morgan's appointment by, 182–184
to Morris, on British situation, 102–106
Morristown quarters of, 43–44
and movement of troops towards Philadelphia, 229–230, 233–234
New Jersey militia dismissal by, 201
news of triumphs of, 57
orders to destroy Stony Brook bridge, 17
at Pluckemin, 34
powers granted to, by Congress, 8
preparation for move north from Morristown, 226–227
Princeton attack plan of, 12
proclamation of January 25, 1777, 74
to Putnam, belief that British were in retreat, 36–37
to Reed, on major strike on the British, 200
retreat of, from Short Hills to Middlebrook, 213
Rush's letter to, on consolidation of troops, 165–166
to Schuyler on Howe's intentions, 188–189
selection of Middlebrook as encampment site, 167–168
sending of force to intercept British from Princeton, 10–11
and Somerset Courthouse decision, 27–28
Stony Brook bridge destruction orders of, 18
strategic objectives of, 238
to Sullivan, on British movements, 187–188, 229
and Sullivan's withdrawal to Steele's Gap, 190–191
and Trenton attack, 4–7
troop numbers available to, 111

See also Hancock, John, Washington's
  letters to
Washington, John Augustine, 97
Washington, Lawrence, 46
Washington, Martha, 48
Washington, Samuel, 2, 112
Washington Rock, 194–195
Watchung Mountains, 30, 33, 57, 60, 194–195.
  See also Short Hills and Westfield, battle
  of
Wayne, Anthony
  advance on British grenadiers by, 199
  and British withdrawal from Brunswick,
    197
  at Horne House, 128
  intelligence gathering orders for, 189
  at Middlebrook, 175
  orders to march to Chester, Pennsylvania,
    230
  pressing of the enemy near Brunswick,
    202
  Wilkinson's rivalry with, 250
weapons, 153–154
Weeden, George, 174
The Weekly Advertiser, 96
Westfield
  American troop strength in, 111
  British plundering of, 215–217
  residents' flight from, 214–215
  See also Short Hills and Westfield, battle
  of
Westmoreland County, Virginia, 45
Whippany, 111
Wilkinson, James
  on attack at Trenton, 5, 6
  biographical sketch of, 250
  on crossing of the Delaware, 4
  and desire to strike Brunswick, 27
  on facing Cornwallis's troops, 11
  on Fitzgerald's trip to notify Leslie of his
    son's death, 38–39
  on Mawhood-Mercer clash, 14
  on militia in open air, without blankets,
    32
  on morning of battle of Princeton, 13
  on Morristown's strategic benefit, 43
  on the New Jersey militia, 57–58
  on Post Road skirmish, 10–11
  on Princeton, 13
  on supplies found in Princeton, 23
  on Trenton, 7
Woodbridge, 62, 70, 96, 108–109, 208–209

Woodbridge Road skirmish, 106
Wooster, General, 140, 141, 143
Wreden, Captain, 119, 120, 176, 185–186, 200
Wurmb, Colonel, 176